Neoliberalism and Urban Development in Latin America

The Case of Santiago

Edited by Camillo Boano and Francisco Vergara Perucich

Routledge
Taylor & Francis Group

LONDON AND NEW YORK

First published 2018
by Routledge

2 Park Square, Milton Park, Abingdon, Oxfordshire OX14 4RN
52 Vanderbilt Avenue, New York, NY 10017

Routledge is an imprint of the Taylor & Francis Group, an informa business

First issued in paperback 2019

British Library Cataloguing-in-Publication Data
A catalogue record for this book is available from the British Library

Library of Congress Cataloging-in-Publication Data
A catalog record for this book has been requested

ISBN: 978-1-138-12369-4 (hbk)
ISBN: 978-0-367-87581-7 (pbk)

Typeset in Times New Roman
by Apex CoVantage, LLC

Contents

vi *Contents*

Figures

Contributors

AriztiaLAB is a multidisciplinary space that pursues the exchange of national and international knowledge, focused on learning, production and exhibition. AriztiaLAB is located in the mesh of inner galleries of Santiago's historic area. This location determines its objective: Producing through incorporating the urban dimension in the variables of practice, experience and discussion. AriztiaLAB members are the architects José Abásolo, Félix Reigada, and Nicolás Verdejo.

Camillo Boano, PhD, is Professor of Urban Design and Critical Theory at The Bartlett Development Planning Unit, UCL, and Co-director of the MSc in Building and Urban Design in Development and the UCL Urban Laboratory. He is the author of *The Ethics of a Potential Urbanism: Critical Encounters Between Giorgio Agamben and Architecture* (2017) and *Urban Geopolitics. Rethinking Planning in Contested Cities* (2017) with Jonathan Rokem.

Camila Cociña, PhD, is an Architect by Universidad Católica de Chile, Teaching Fellow at The Bartlett Development Planning Unit, UCL. Her current research focuses on housing policies and urban inequalities in the Chilean context.

Fundación Decide is a non-governmental organisation of professionals and university students, linked to different disciplines and interested in urban and environmental conflicts that occur throughout Chile. Its objective is to promote the social, political and ideological convergence of all social actors opposed to neoliberalism, with the conviction of transforming Chile based on principles of justice, democracy and solidarity. For this, the Foundation is organised in study groups, teams of territorial insertion and it´s online magazine, En Torno. The members of the Fundación Decide who wrote here were Patricia Kelly, Karen Pradenas, Valentina Saavedra and Pascal Volker.

Grupo TOMA is a collective of architects formed in Santiago de Chile at the end of 2012. It develops experimental projects of action and research inquiring in conflicts of community´s and the territory, in its link with the current context of neoliberal "progress". TOMA produces facilities, collages, activities, classes, articles, journals, interventions, collections, occupations, magazines, drawings, workshops, films, television programmes, plays, chats, sound pieces, files, web pages and other mechanisms of material and symbolic dispute. TOMA is composed by Leandro Cappetto, Eduardo Pérez, Ignacio Rivas, Mathías Klenner and Ignacio Saavedra.

Liliana De Simone is an Architect and Master in Urban Development by Universidad Católica de Chile. Currently, she is a lecturer at Communications School of Universidad Católica de Chile. She is the author of the book *Metamall: Los espacios del neoliberalismo en Chile 1973–2012*.

Francisco Díaz is an Architect by Universidad Católica de Chile and Master in Critical, Curatorial and Conceptual Practices at the Graduate School of Architecture, Planning and Preservation, Columbia University. He is the author of *Who Cares for Chilean Cities?* (New York and Santiago, 2014). Currently, he teaches at the School of Architecture at the Universidad Católica de Chile, and he is the Editor in Chief at Ediciones ARQ.

Matias Garreton is an Architect by Universidad Católica de Valparaiso, PhD in Urban Planning from Paris East University, an MSc in Urban Planning from the Institute of Urbanism of Paris. Currently, he is a researcher at the Centre of Territorial Intelligence, Universidad Adolfo Ibáñez and researcher at the Centre for Social Conflict and Cohesion Studies (COES). He studies the relationships between urban inequalities, residential and daily mobility, and governance in decentralised systems, focusing on political justice and the right to the city.

Miguel Lawner is an Architect by Universidad de Chile and former Director of the Corporation for Urban Improvement (CORMU) during the government of Salvador Allende. He has been author of several books, essays and articles denouncing the brutality of Pinochet's dictatorship and the effects in the Chilean society of its neoliberalisation. Currently he is advisor in the implementation of the National Policy of Urban Development.

Nicolás Valenzuela Levi is an Architect and Urbanist by Universidad Católica de Chile and PhD and former Secretary of Planning in Providencia Municipality, Santiago. He is currently a PhD Candidate at the University of Cambridge, where he is living and researching inequality and network technologies with special emphasis on public transport systems.

Ernesto Lopez-Morales is an Architect by Universidad de Chile and PhD by The Bartlett Development Planning Unit. Currently, he is Associate Professor in Universidad de Chile and Associate Researcher at the Centre for Social Conflict and Cohesion Studies (COES) where he focuses on land economics, gentrification, neoliberal urbanism and housing in Chile and Latin American cities.

Francisco Vergara Perucich is an Architect and Urbanist by Universidad Central de Chile and PhD Candidate by The Bartlett Development Planning Unit. Currently, he is a lecturer at Economics Department of Universidad Católica del Norte. He studies the contradictory condition of urban development under the neoliberal regime using a Marxist approach.

Fernando Portal is an architect, curator and publisher. He completed his MSc in Critical, Curatorial and Conceptual Practices of Architecture at Columbia GSAPP New York. His work stresses the relationship between architecture, design, and cultural policies, by linking cultural institutions and content with local spatial and economic development. Currently works as Content Director in Mil M2, developing curatorial projects and spatial strategies. He teaches as Adjunct Professor at the UC School of Architecture in Chile.

Acknowledgements

This volume has been a collective effort, which begun in a visit to Santiago de Chile in December 2014. We had the chance to meet a diverse range of urban thinkers making us recognise the fruitful disciplinary contradictions of urban development by a diverse rich and critical approach to an issue that concerned to us all: the neoliberalisation of Santiago.

We first and primarily want to thank all the authors for their contributions, patience and commitment to reflect on the neoliberal spatial presence and elaborating on the *Fabula* of Santiago, during the drafting process, without them this collective volume would not have come to life.

We also wish to thanks our families for their love and patience throughout the process of working on this book and in all our research endeavours. Francisco Vergara Perucich wishes to thank Nadja, Julian and León; and Camillo Boano Elena, Beatrice and Francesca. We would like to thank several colleagues who have supported us throughout our work on this book manuscript, not necessarily in any specific order: Julio Dávila Silva, Catalina Ortiz, Cristian Olmos, Cristian Silva, Martin Arias, Julia Wesely, Rodrigo Caimanque and Karinna Fernández, among several other colleagues for their fruitful conversations and discussions at different stages of the work on this book. We wish to offer a special thanks to Simon Zelestis for the precious help in proof reading the manuscript and to Miguel Lawner for agreeing to collaborate with us even if in a difficult moment. We also want to extend our thanks to thanks all colleagues in the Department of Economics, Universidad Católica del Norte, The Bartlett Development Planning Unit, UCL and the Becas Chile scholarship grant No. 1859/2013 for funding Francisco's research. Finally, we want to thank our Editors at Routledge; Elanor Best, Robert Langham and Lisa Thomson for all their support during the production process.

Introduction

A Fabula Santiago

Camillo Boano and Francisco Vergara Perucich

This book, as many or possibly all books, was born from a conversation. Actually, it emerged from a series of conversations among friends, colleagues and concerned citizen as well as 'rebel architects' to use some common labels. All these conversations happened in Santiago, in occupied factories, in universities as well as on the pages of magazines. All these conversations were concerned with the nature, material conditions and the pervasive dimensions of neoliberalism on all forms of urban life that we, the authors, were experimenting, suffering and, in diverse ways, attempting to resist. The different conversations were at times broken and not fully articulated due to the looseness and the fuzziness of the very nature of neoliberalism, as well as due to the distances and diverse approaches each of us were attempting to devise to 'attack' the subject. All these conversations were urban by nature as they matured, focused and were embodied within our kaleidoscopic and multiple identities as urbanists, architects, geographers, or simply by being interested in the urban form. Some of our conversations were lost either because some friends abandoned the projects, or simply because being all *homini economicus* made us forcefully redirect our attention elsewhere. At times there was simply too much to translate in English and the conversations lost the passion, the colour and the beauty of the Spanish language in which they originated. This book is the materialisation of our concerns, reflections, research and forms of resistance and rebellion to neoliberal discourses. It is both a reflection on Santiago's spatial order and the materialisation of the neoliberal experiment at large.

The book's main objective is to bring together a selected group of reflections engaging the urban development and the complex reality of the neoliberal urban production of Santiago de Chile. This book brings to the fore not only an analysis of the city in a transparent manner, but also it elaborates on risks and possible alternatives. The conversations, meetings, and discussions held since 2014 explored the complex existing totalising urbanisms of Santiago and the multiple visions around its neoliberal *delirium*, observing its opposition, reviewing the insurgent emergence of alternative and contested practices and urban narratives. Through the work of a young generation of urban scholars, architects, activists and artists the book assemble a cacophony of voices, visions and thoughts that illustrate and criticise at the same time the existing urbanism of Santiago and its different tensions, its competing and different qualities, and the irreducible tension between *polis* and *civitas* in the specific context of the unquestioned neoliberalism of Santiago. The reality of this Global South metropolis where to ground an investigation on the material conditions of neoliberalism is ideal to both discovering and experimenting alternatives, considering that Chile was one of the first places in the world in which neoliberal policies proposed by Milton Friedman were implemented. The dictatorship of Augusto Pinochet installed by force a system oriented to privilege free markets, reducing the power of the state to its minimum and keeping civil society unorganised. The effects of these changes are visible in the city of Santiago, whose delirium laissez-faire is visible everywhere in all aspect of the urban society. In a way, Santiago provides the perfect case study to see how neoliberalism works through urbanism.

In this regard, the book sits at the crossroads of a multiplicity of architectural and urban discourse debates on planning theory and neoliberalism in the Global South a conversation about the liberalisation of markets, insurgent planning and citizenship, the free-market city and collective action, political ideologies and the production of urban space, planning capacity and the dissemination of neoliberal practices, along with the recent development of a new radicalisms in Latin America cities. As such, it sits exactly in the space of the neoliberal *de-lirium* of Santiago and in a time of a complete expansion of an urbanisation model completely founded on the *oikos*. Conceived as a series of imperfect and unfinished conversations, the book explores the complex existing urbanisms of Santiago. It situates multiple visions around its neoliberal *delirium*, observing the antagonists, reviewing the insurgent emergence of alternative and contested practices and urban narratives and politely suggesting ways forward. Through the work of a young generation of urban scholars, architects, activists and artists the book assembles a cacophony of voices, visions and thoughts that illustrate – and criticise at the same time – the existing neoliberal urbanism of Santiago and its irreducible tension between *polis* and *civitas* in the specific context of the unquestioned neoliberalism of Santiago. The variegated, technocratic and post-authoritarian aspects of the neoliberal turn in the urban Chile serve as cultural and political *milieu*. This case study exhibits the different urban aspects of neoliberal urbanism emerging where free-market orthodoxies are colliding with endogenous, cultural and popular resistances and newly formed territories of contestation and antagonisms occur at different scales. Refusing an essentialist call, the book offers visions and reflections around the irreducible tension beyond the neoliberal and radical dichotomy and suggests an alternative understanding of the urban conditions, its compulsive repetition, fragmentation and seclusion, and its hallucinatory totalising managerial discourses in Santiago.

While some chapters focus on the diagnostic dimension, tracing and illustrating the contemporary neoliberal urbanism materiality and dynamics, others suggest radical experiment and alternative resistive approaches at different scale and along different disciplines.

Chapter 1, *Foucault and Agamben in Santiago: governmentality, dispositive and space* by Camillo Boano, draws from Michael Foucault and Giorgio Agamben reflections on governmentality and dispositif attempts to frame the perspective on neoliberalism as discursive practice that produce subjects as well as a series of 'conduct of conduct' and a form of existence or a form of life. Boano attempts to situate neoliberal urbanism as it emerged in the complex tension between *oikos* and *polis* where the *oikonomia* (economic) project took over the more social one, whereas Michel Foucault and Agamben have pointed out, the motor that triggers the apparatus of biopolitics is therefore no longer only the nexus connecting the juridical rule with the techniques of subjectivation, but the power of political economy at the centre.

Francisco Vergara Perucich, in his *The neoliberal urban utopia of Milton Friedman: Santiago de Chile as its realisation*, reconstructs the concrete utopia of Milton Friedman's vision of free markets as the key ontology to the achievement of happiness and how Santiago de Chile is an example that demonstrates the triumph of the private over the public. This chapter offer a vision around the indissoluble junction between Milton Friedman's ideology, the production of space and everyday life, sketching a possible palimpsest of a neoliberal city, which is presented as already materialising in the urban society of Santiago de Chile.

In Chapter 3 *Urban space production and social exclusion in Greater Santiago, under dictatorship and democracy*, Matias Garreton presents the exclusionary urban policies of Santiago in their historical progression since they were implemented by Pinochet's dictatorship and by democratic governments of the nineties showing how the public incentives for real estate development and the marginalisation of vulnerable populations in violent urban environments are deeply entangled processes. Grounding in Harvey's accumulation by dispossession, this chapter shows that the urban divide of Greater Santiago is not just an outcome of mechanical socioeconomic polarisation in an unregulated urban market, but mainly results from evolving forms of abuse of power that are intended for wealth hoarding, boosted by private profits, involving a deliberate imagination, (un)planning and praxis, orchestrated by oligopolistic economic agents.

Ernesto Lopez-Morales in Chapter 4, *The politico-economic sides of the high-rise new-build gentrification of Santiago, Chile*, continues the investigation on the specific spatialities of urban development in Santiago, reflecting on how different forms of gentrification are closely correlated with the ways in which contemporary capitalism and real estate speculation operate. This chapter deals with four politico-economic aspects that help understand what is essentially critical about the gentrification of Santiago, reflecting on the production of high-rise building and the privatisation of housing production and how the privately-led, high-rise urban renewal in Chilean cities is not an efficient solution for urban growth, rather it increases the problem through the displacement of the poorest social segments to the peripheries for reasons of ground rent accumulation. This chapter also offers some critical reflections on a more comprehensive public housing policy.

Camila Cociña in Chapter 5, *Urban universalism: the housing debt in the context of targeted policies* explores a very particular aspect of the neoliberal project, the logic of targeting public policies, its relation with the urban form and its consequences in terms of inequality. This chapter discusses the central paradox of housing and its particular consequences on the urban form of Santiago in terms of segregation and inequality. Finally, it offers a reflection on the challenges for urban and housing policies from a universalist perspective, introducing the idea of 'Urban Universalism', a specific way to understand universalism for housing policies, as a political and analytical frame that may help to reduce inequalities and segregation, particularly in the city of Santiago.

Nicolás Valenzuela Levi in Chapter 6, titled *The mobility regime in Santiago and possibilities of change* expands on reflections from housing related debates on the role of urban mobility discourses within the broader dispute about Chilean neoliberal social order from a political economy perspective. Discussing mobility and the city, this chapter seeks to provide an opportunity to produce an exploratory text on how power relations determine institutions that define the roles of the state, markets and civil society. The main idea behind this chapter is that Santiago's neoliberal mobility regime plays an increasingly important role in the general political settlement that defines Chile's neoliberal institutional arrangements.

In Chapter 7, *Retail urbanism: the neoliberalisation of urban society by consumption in Santiago de Chile*, Liliana De Simone opens up the debate in the uncharted territory of retail-lead urbanism. Liliana provides empirical reflections on the multiplication of spaces for mass consumption and their territorial organisation that emerged in the production of urban territories. Urban retailisation is understood as the infiltration of retail logics in the production of urban environments, in which collective consumption crystallises new social interaction patterns, as well as reflecting the relations between global capital and local urban configurations.

Francisco Díaz in Chapter 8 titled *Under the politics of deactivation: Culture's social function in neoliberal Santiago* speculates on Sergeant James, the protagonist of Kathryn Bigelow's movie *The Hurt Locker* to unfold and discover a new figure that is key to the recent history in Santiago: the 'deactivator', a character who took the role of the activist but, due to his/her anxiety for institutionalising everything, has ended up softening every potentially radical activity – an attitude that would have ultimately contributed to depoliticise the city. In a harmonious mix of architecture, critical theory and visual culture, Díaz is opening a series of reflections on the resistant side of neoliberalism discussing the discourse of activism finding support in a country which, after the 1973 coup, had become very afraid of anything that could disturb the status quo of the cultural urban scene.

The architectural collective AriztiaLAB (José Abásolo, Nicolás Verdejo, Félix Reigada) in Chapter 9 titled *Transparent processes of urban production in Chile: a case in Pedro Aguirre Cerda District*, offers a critical reading on a specific case study in Santiago: the ex-hospital of Ochagavia in the urban landscape of the Pedro Aguirre Cerda District in the south of Santiago. AriztiaLAB's socio-historical and design research analysis traces the historical evolution of this building, using the visualisation of data associated with the privatisation processes plus other data generated from participants' observations with the local community. AriztiaLAB's project aims to show the possibility of generating a tool of mediation and participation, through which the community is able to access information regarding the stakeholders, institutions and norms linked to the ex-hospital's recycling of territorial processes among the diverse organisations in the District, as well as encouraging citizens to oversee and supervise the external agents that seek to intervene in the *Comuna*, not forget its origins, built on solidarity and collaboration.

Fernando Portal, in Chapter 10 offers a reflection on *Artists self-organisation on the context of unregulated transformations in territories and communities* critically reflects on a self-organised cultural project emerged in Barrio Italia in January 2013 that sought the collective effort of a numerous group of neighbours and artists, which has allowed for the practical exploration of a new approach towards neighbourhood transformations, cultivating citizen participation and creative labour to resist gentrification. Fernando reviews the experience of this project illustrating the relationship between obsolete industrial infrastructure, gentrification, cultural production and cultural policies within a neoliberal context, characterised mainly by the lack of regulatory tools to manage real estate operations and citizen participation, particularly stressing the role of temporary uses of infrastructure and the design of methods for the collective generation of content and knowledge. These methods seek to produce encounters and engagement between members of Santiago's urban society that suffer spatial segregation, using design, architecture and art to catalyse spontaneous participation.

Continuing and expanding the reflection on the role of social movement Fundación Decide (Valentina Saavedra, Karen Pradenas, Patricia Kelly and Pascal Volker) authored Chapter 11 titled *Building the democratic city: a challenge for social movements* where they trace the evolution and the role of social actors that contest the production of the urban form shaped by the wholly complicit relationship of the State and real estate agents. The context in which urban development is being managed has generated discontent among the population, which has fostered the emergence in Santiago of various urban social movements that have revolved around the unleashing of various conflicts over territory. Reflecting on their limits and their strategies this chapter highlights that social movements were developing in a context of an absence of a common culture of struggle, but that non the less construct convergences in the claim for greater participation, democracy and equality, in a context of diversity and conflicting calls for more direct actions in alternative transformations of society, the State, and territory.

Finally in the last chapter titled *Especulopolis: a play in seven acts. A story of celebrations, displacements, schizophrenia, utopias, colonisation and hangover*, Grupo TOMA (Eduardo Pérez, Ignacio Saavedra, Ignacio Rivas, Mathias Klenner, Leandro Cappetto) present a speculative theatre play, as an attempt to build a continuous story through the different territories they have worked in during the last few years in Santiago de Chile. Grupo TOMA reflect on these contesting territories of engagement, highlighting the different logics and machinations neoliberal urbanism made of a constant atmosphere of lack of control, the multiple characters that have temporarily had certain impact on our practices, and the diverse territories in which the scenes have been mounted and soon dismounted, which have all increased the levels of contradiction of our work and our contexts.

At the crossroad of fiction, visual culture and architectural research Grupo TOMA provide an alternative resistive practice in *Especulopolis* contributing to making visible the paradoxes of neoliberalims in shaping city spaces and the complicit nature of architecture.

In the Afterwords, the editors interviewed Miguel Lawner, the former national secretary of planning in Salvador Allende's administration and one of the most influential urban planners in Chile. From his experience in the government of Unidad Popular until the present, he witnessed the neoliberalisation of urban planning in Santiago. The interview shed light the nature of neoliberal urban development, with somehow a positive tone, stressing that its end is near because it is no socially sustainable anymore.

Despite the easy immediacy of the poetics of the different chapters in this book, collectively the book is a call to arms tracing a possible alternative view of a renewed political project that contests Santiago's infinite totalising urbanisation.

The *cumplexus* that emerges is an urban territory in a multiplicity of forms with an impossible final synthesis, which cannot be captured by a multiple *savoir* and a plurality of looks. *Fabula Santiago* is produced by the multiplicity of urban processes influenced by the capitalist relationships, and is treated here – by all the authors – in their complexity and contradictions. They are seen at the same time as a place of oppression as well as transgressions where alternative social projects can be found, experimented and suggested. Hopefully this short series of reflections, written as speculative essays, will contribute to the current debate over the need to reclaim the political emancipatory project of architecture and urbanism against a technocratic, biopolitical and arrogant one. This is an emancipatory project that hopefully will reclaim the much-too-early abandoned critique of contemporary capitalism and its subsequent production of urban space. In doing so the book offer a few interventionist concepts or idée-forces that attempt to reconfigure the given matrix of references as they confront architecture's comfort zone, bringing 'uncertainty in place of purity' to use a Jeremy Till's language and to give some sort of shape and light to the promise of an urban society advocated by Henry Lefebvre. Advocating for a discrete, autonomous and artistic urbanism is seen inappropriately to contrast what Nadir Lahiji (2013:61) called "the desubjectivation of the political subjects in act of depoliticizing [architectural] discourses" calling for subversion to the process, which enables appropriation, well-being, solidarity, inhabitation and dwelling. As a result, practices such as urban activism, contested urbanism, and radical theory have been flourished in Santiago, developing a series of fables to oppose dissent and overthrow capitalism from everyday life. This book contributes to rethinking urbanism in order to eradicate neoliberalism from urban life, accomplishing the old desires of the whole generation of Marxist thinkers: unleashing an urban revolution and imagining a new urban society.

Fabula, the fable, is something that Giorgio Agamben (1993:61) reminds us is "freed from the mystery's obligation of silence by transforming it into enchantment: it is not participation in a cult of knowledge which renders him speechless, but bewitchment. The silence of the mystery is undergone as a rupture, plunging man back into the pure, mute language of nature; but as a spell, silence must eventually be shattered and conquered".

References

Agamben, G., (1993) *Infancy and history: The destruction of experience*. London: Verso, p. 60.

Lahiji, N., (2013) Political subjectivation and the architectural dispositive. In Lahiji, N., (ed.) *Architecture against the post-political: Essays in reclaiming the critical project*. Routledge: London, p. 61.

1 Foucault and Agamben in Santiago

Governmentality, dispositive and space

Camillo Boano

Neoliberalism means different things to different people. It is a 'slippery concept' examined from a multiplicity of conceptual categories and disciplinary realms: from cities to labour, from sexuality to race (Springer et al. 2016). It has "no fixed or settled coordinates [. . .] policy entailments, and material practices" (Brown 2015:20). In the recently published *Handbook of Neoliberalism* Springer et al. suggests that

> at a very base level [. . .], we are generally referring to the new political, economic, and social arrangements within society that emphasise market relations, re-tasking the role of the state, and individual responsibility. Most scholars tend to agree that neoliberalism is broadly defined as the extension of competitive markets into all areas of life, including the economy, politics, and society.
>
> (Springer et al. 2016:2)

Furthermore, Wendy Brown suggests neoliberalism "as economic policy, a modality of governance, and an order of reason is at once a global phenomenon, yet inconstant, differentiated, unsystematic, impure" (2015:20).

Despite the amorphous and polysepalous dimensions, neoliberalims is a material reality where all of us are immerse.

Adopting a Foucauldian perspective, neoliberalims seems representing a mode or reasoning, a discursive practice and a "*sui generis* ideological system" (Mudge 2008) at the crux of ideology, policy and governmentality or, to use Brown's words "a distinctive mode of reason, of the production of subjects, a 'conduct of conduct' and a scheme of valuation" (2015:21) emerged and grounded in historically specific economic and political conditions across the globe. It is worth quoting at length her provisional definition of neoliberalism as

> enacting an ensemble of economic policies in accord with its root principle of affirming free markets. These include deregulation of industries and capital flows; radical reduction in welfare state provisions and protections for the vulnerable; privatised and outsourced public goods, ranging from education, parks, postal services, roads, and social welfare to prisons and militaries;

replacement of progressive with regressive tax and tariff schemes; the end of wealth redistribution as an economic or sociopolitical policy; the conversion of every human need or desire into a profitable enterprise, from college admissions preparation to human organ transplants, from baby adoptions to pollution rights, from avoiding lines to securing legroom on an airplane; and, most recently, the financialisation of everything and the increasing dominance of finance capital over productive capital in the dynamics of the economy and everyday life.

(Brown 2015:28)

It is a normative reason that shape different governing rationalities and extend to all aspects of life developing both an epistemology as well as an attitude to the self.

Reinhold Martin (2016) uses the term neoliberal "as defined along two intersecting axes. The first, political-economic dimension of neoliberalism has been associated with the widespread deregulation, privatization" based on Harvey's inclusion of all human actions into the market, a "sociopolitical (or biopolitical) dimension has been defined by the philosopher Michel Foucault as the transformation of the modern subject, understood as *homo economicus*, into 'human capital', an 'entrepreneur of himself' (p. 59–60). Dardot and Laval (2014), argues that neoliberalism has entailed the reshaping of subjectivities through the promotion of particular ways of thinking about ourselves 'economically': as business enterprises, as efficiency impact, again in relation to Foucault's notion of *homo economicus*. All this has not only political implications but material and spatial. Again with Foucault, space is the medium and the locus where the intersections of powers and knowledge manifest, develop and reproduce. If space is the 'place' where the neoliberal phenomena operates, cities and urban space become the perfect battlefield for both critically understanding both its operation and on-going power. David Harvey defines neoliberal inefficiencies and subsequent economic disparities as a system of accumulation by dispossession (2007:178). A process that is spatial in nature and that starts with a spatial gesture of privatisation and commodification, wherein all public assets are subsumed as private goods becoming a new source of wealth and capital gain (Harvey 2007:160): space in all different form is put into production not only to produce wealth but to produce subject.[1]

Urban neoliberalism refers to the interaction of processes of neoliberalisation and urbanisation and how such ideology are shaping and producing the form, the image and the life in the cities. As Keil (2016:387) suggests "urbanization and neoliberalization are material and discursive processes that lead to real (and imagined) constellations through which modern capitalist societies are being reproduced". Neoliberal urbanism is then a descriptive category that is able to depict the spatio-temporal material and discursive practice and its operative analytical capacity of producing urban space. A material condition that designates a governmental technologies, discursive and spatial dispositifs that fuelled political imagination locally and globally that "penetrates the bodies of subjects, and governs their forms of life" (Agamben 2009:14) through accelerated production urban projects, seclusions and marginalisation, hyper-spectacular (Ortiz and Boano forthcoming) architectural forms, consumption spaces and housing policies of all sorts.

Neoliberal urbanism should be read in line to a Foucault-inspired critique that focuses on the recalibrated relationships of the citizen to the state and the corporate economy, or its 'governmentality' (Keil 2016:387). Foucault's governmentality as the new life-administering power dedicated to inciting, reinforcing, monitoring and optimising the forces under its control (Foucault 2003), assemblage that has an important role in depicting the spatial complicity and active role as the techniques and procedures for directing human behaviour, defined as an "ensemble formed by the institutions, procedures, analyses and reflections, the calculations and tactics" (Foucault 1977:20), Foucault viewed governmentality as a very specific and complex form of power that was effected through a range of 'technologies' and 'dispositives': an aggregate of physical, social and normative infrastructure – amongst which space, architecture and its manipulation – are put into place to deal strategically with a particular problem.

Even though Foucault emphasises that power cannot be localised in a state apparatus, the conception of the state is crucial in addressing how power operates. The state is conceptualised as a 'transactional reality' and part of 'practices of government'. The state is the result of an ensemble of power relations that produces a specific political knowledge to conduct and control populations. Actors use their "political knowledge" (Foucault 1977:67) embodied in "statistical accounts, architectural plans, bureaucratic rules, and graphs to represent data for political action" (Lemke 2007:48). Neoliberalism typically diminishes the role of the State, but as Peck argued, the "ideological shape of the State has not changed as much as neoliberal reformers would have us believe" (2004:397). Often rather than diminishing the State enjoy a rather expanded "elasticity, and the ability to, under the premise of reform, reinvent its roles and responsibilities in the project of development and the political economy of urbanism [. . .] through its collaborations with private investors" (Abu-Hamdi 2017:102).

When neoliberalism is understood as a political rationality that shapes the 'conditions of possibility' for thinking and acting in a certain way (Collier 2009), we understand it as a form of 'conduct of man' made by a diffuse power that "is embodied in every aspect of discourses, in formal routines, informal practices, and physical structures" (ibid). Therefore, the production of spaces in the neoliberal cities occurs through techniques, procedures and institutional arrangements in re-combinatorial processes and redeployments. Foucault insists that is made by a series of *dispositif*: an ensemble of discourses, institutions, architectural forms, regulatory decisions, laws, administrative measures, scientific statements, and moral propositions. Interesting for the argument here is the aim of the gesture of the governmental *dispositif* that for Foucault is essentially a gesture of normalisation. Foucault stated clearly this important concept in *Abnormal* where he posit,

> the norm brings with it a principle of both qualification and correction. The norm's function is not to exclude and reject. Rather, it is always linked to a

positive technique of intervention and transformation, to a sort of normative project.

(Foucault 2003:50)

That urbanism is a *dispositif* in itself is not a novelty in urban studies: planning policies and regulations, either holistic or selective, employ spatial devices – such as dimensions, location, separation, connection and housing typologies – that increase or decrease social difference and the distribution of welfare/well-being. One of the spatial dimensions of the overlapping of neoliberalisation and urban-isation has been the introduction of new and changing infrastructures in the form of what Graham and Marvin's named "splintering urbanism" (2001): sharply seg-regated, class-divided, privatised and access-controlled infrastructures in cities and suburbs. A massive modifications of infrastructures in water, transportation, communications and transport have not only alternated the urban and metropoli-tan landscape controlled and governed the access and the behaviours of urban dwellers but also altered set of modes of production and consumption till the development of new forms of urban 'smart' model (Datta 2015). As Keil suggests this new urban *dispositives* not only demonstrate

a particular techno-economic strategy which laid the groundwork for novel constellations of firms and workers in 'creative economies', it also prompted heretofore unseen techno-social and techno-spatial constellations [. . .] whose reliance on tech labour markets and (fast-moving, yet often precarious) turbo-consumerism has fed a deregulated explosion of inner city urbanism, some-times coupled with processes of displacement and gentrification in former inner city working-class neighbourhoods.

(Keil 2016:393)

The infrastructures of neoliberalism shape new forms of segregations through the combined action of land policies, real estate land speculations, urban displace-ment where the poor are driven from the "gentrified centres of the neoliberal city and reassemble in the 'in-between' spaces of inner and outer suburbs" (ibid), that expand and explode in the global production of a 'planetary urbanization' (Brenner 2014).

As briefly outlined above that following key authors as Springer, Brown as well as Dardot and Laval neoliberalism is a specific form of capitalism possessed and productive of its own apparatus of power, displayed and made possible through the central Foucauldian concept of governmentality and the one of *dispositive*. What is important in these reflections is what recently Douglas Spencer suggests that is a

less exclusive preoccupation with technologies of domination to a position more attentive to what he terms 'technologies of the self' [where] Foucault's agenda shifts from questions of how individuals are subjugated by power to ones of how subjectivity is actively produced

(Spencer 2016: 22).

The self and the individual both as subject and as conduct are quite an important element in the discussion on neoliberal urbanism where the market logic, its apparatuses and its mode of powers is "working to produce the mentalities and dispositions conducive to its continued operation" (ibid). As such it is not a disciplinary power as it not directly segregate subjects or impose normative conducts but to exercise of freedom: "Foucault's understanding of the neoliberal governmentality of the self corresponds with neoliberalism's own perspectives on how power should, in the interest of liberty, operate: not through the vertical application of external force but horizontally and immanently" (p. 23). The subject is not confined with limited action, not rendered dominated fully, but when

> neoliberalism rediscovers the care of the self, it is not to reduce domination to 'as little as possible' but to legitimate and extend its reach. The care of the self is not undertaken for the self, as a 'practice of freedom', but in order to maintain the economic order. The 'work on the self by the self' is not an autonomous practice, but one demanded by the conduct of the market to which the subject must accommodate and continually adapt itself.
>
> (Spencer 2016: 25)

Neoliberalims is then a form of existence or a form of life to use an Agambenian terminology or as per Dardot and Laval: "neo-liberalism is nothing more, nor less, than the form of our existence – the way in which we are led to conduct ourselves, to relate to others and to ourselves" (p. 3).

Techne oikonomike: Agamben's managerial paradigm

Aristotle made a fundamental distinction between politics and economics, *techne politike* and *techne oikonomike*, a set of decision for the public good, the commons, the elements of the collective living together. The *polis* emerges as the space of the many and because the man is 'a political animal' by nature, the politics emerge precisely because the existence of *polemos*, possible conflicts in such space. Precisely because politics is incarnated in the polis "the project of the city [. . .] holds the possibility of conflicts and the need for its resolution as its very ontological foundation" (Aureli 2011:3). *Techne oikonomike* on the other side, concern the very private realm of life, the administration of the quintessential individual space: the house, the *oikos* that for Aristotle is a complex real of relationships of its members being slaves, women, and children. The principle of economy is distinguished from the principle of politics in the same way the house (*oikos*) is separated by the *polis*. Such a complex set of tensions originated in the Greek city state create a two competing set of constituent elements: the private space of the *oikoi*, the agglomeration of houses as basic social space that ensure the reproduction of its members, and the public, the agora where confrontations over the nature of public goods happens. What seems evident is that urbanism has been a continuous, unclear, contingent and often-mutable construction of forms and ideas derived around such struggles. The two models of co-existence *polis* and *oikos*, *urbs* and *civitas* indicated two irreducible but complementary domains of human association. However the history of civilisation after the collapse of the Roman Empire, the distinction between *urbs* and *civitas*, not simply dissolved, rather the economic impetus of the private sphere, the *oikos*, took over the political ethos of the *civitas*. With the rise of the urban bourgeois, the advent of industrialisation and the rise of capitalist system the role of the *urbs* absorbed the *civitas*: a complete urbanisation a neutralised form material proximity, infrastructural and otherwise, that suppress the political character of the *civitas* in favour of what Giorgio Agamben define a managerial paradigm an economy turning it to the mere model of the *oikos*, the private administration of the house. As many argued however not only urbanisation have become a dominant reality globally allowing the manifestations of a varieties of urban situations and specific urbanisms but certainly have been the main locus of the production of capitalist relationship and the reproduction of injustice and exclusion presupposed along the fundamental substitution of politics with economics as a mode of city governance. In this total indistinction between private and public, political and economic a totalising, unlimited understanding of the city emerge, an urbanity completely understood as domestic space or using Aureli's words "the essence of urbanisation is therefore the destruction of any forms of limit, – [*a de-lirium*] a compulsive repetition of its own reproduction and the consequent totalising mechanisms of control that guarantees this process of infinity" (2011:16). What has started to be a dialectical dilemma a search of a possible equilibrium between *polis* and *civitas*, the possibility of encounters, of conflicts and confrontations, and the possibility of familiarity, security and identity, has been completely absorbed in an infinite process of urbanisation in despotic nature. Such infinite process of urbanisation, does resemble what Henri Lefebvre, theorised in the 1970, as 'complete urbanization' where he understood urbanisation as a complete process stretching out in time and space, transforming all aspect of the society and having a planetary dimension where not only urban morphology, space, limits and forms were changing but also the everyday life. Lefebvre use 'implosion-explosion' which certainly resemble the Agambenian dynamic indistinctness as "the tremendous concentration (of people, activities, wealth, goods, objects, instruments, means and thoughts) of urban reality and the immense explosion, the projection of numerous, disjoint fragments (peripheries, suburbs, vacation homes, satellite towns" (Lefebrve 2003:14), a totalising process that allow the generation of a complete new society: an urban society. Such urban society was not understood as an empirical object a real manifestation a simple totality, rather was conceived as a virtual object "something that will reveal itself only as the results of a contradictory historical process full of conflicts and struggles" (Stanek et al. 2015:14). This reflection opens a great and massive debate around the nature of the urban in both epistemological and ontological dimensions beyond the scope of this writing. However it does point out the conception of urbanisation as an incessant process, and indefinite one that both shape and it's been shaped by trajectories and rhythms, meanings and spaces, as an indeterminate filed of forces with its own complexity and contradictions that are bale to shape socioeconomic structures as well as micro practices and everyday

life and finally that is a process deeply embedded into the productive and repro-
ductive dialectics of the capitalist systems but is also a place where alternative,
resistances and transgressions can emerge. Giorgio Agamben suggests that "for
them [the Greek], "simple, natural life" (*zoe*) was not the affair of the city (*polis*),
but instead of the home (*oikos*), while bios was the life that concerned the polis"
(de la Durantaye 2009:204), a thresholds of indistinction that was already sum-
marised by Michel Foucault's intuition of biopolitics". What here is not novel is
what Agamben drawing from Foucault's disciplinary and controlled society, the
inclusion of *zoe* in the *polis* – a gesture that make life as such becomes a principal
object of the projections and calculations powers, but rather a

> process by which the exception everywhere becomes the rule, the realm of
> bare life – which is originally situated at the margins of the political order-
> gradually begins to coincide with the political realm, and exclusion and
> inclusion, outside and inside, *bios* and *zoe*, right and fact, enter into a zone of
> irreducible indistinction.
>
> (ibid:9)

Homo Sacer, the book that marked the definitive condition of global exception,
ends with the provocative conclusion:

> every attempt to rethink the political space of the West must begin with the
> clear awareness that we no longer know anything of the classical distinction
> between *zoe* and *bios*, between private life and political existence, between
> man as a simple living being at home in the house and man's political exis-
> tence in the city.
>
> (Agamben 1998:187)

Agamben argues, however, that the paradigm of providential *oikonomia* informs
and determines the whole political economy of modernity and the administrative,
"impolitical" notion of contemporary governmentality. In this urban *oikonomia*
we find a laboratory for observing the governmental machine and render visible
the true distribution of power that is articulated between power as government
and power as ceremonial, liturgical, and impolitical reality of the capitalist society
(Boano 2017). Agamben suggests that *stasis*, a civil war, takes place in a zone of
indifference between the impolitical space of the family and the political one of
the city. Transgressing this threshold, the *oikos* is politicised and, inversely, the
polis is economised, that is reduced to *oikos*. This means the very opposite of the
current application of the normal parlance of the word stasis which is often used
as a pejorative term to describe conditions of stagnation, fixity, passivity and inaction. Rather it means as Rivière (2017:81–82) "an enabler, but one that also set
out precise demands of relationship, moderation, and reconciliation, while holding the promise of new, energetic onward movement for all parties post-*stasis*".
For Agamben the system of Greek politics, the civil war functions as a threshold
of politicisation or depoliticisation, through which the house is exceeded in the

city and the city depoliticises in the family. The Athenian space then is constitute a political paradigm coessential to the city, that signify the "becoming political or the impolitical (*oikos*) an the becoming impolitical of the political (*polis*) (Agamben 2015:29); the stasis is not something that can never be forgotten or removed: it is the memorable that must always remain in the city and that, however, cannot be remembered through resentments. Just before closing the reflection, Agamben suggest that "we should conceptualise politics as a field of tensions whose extremes are *oikos* and the polis: in between them the civil war (*stasis*) define a thresholds in which the impolitical is politicised and the political is 'economicised'" (ibid). This threshold of indistinctions appears to qualify the nature of the managerial paradigm traced by Agamben back to the Greek *polis*. The discussion on *stasis* in the Agambenian translation of civil war or in the less violent, state suggested by Rivière confirm the diagnosis of modern politics as Foucauldian biopolitics as well as theological paradigm-oikonomico suggested by Giorgio Agamben

> through which a living system maintains the capacity to adjust itself to inevitable change and stasis as a state that demands full participation both for its proper resolution and so as to counteract the danger that a stasis shifts into the uncontrolled destruction of war
>
> (Rivière 2017:91)

In the current urban condition when *polis* is presented in the figure of a reassuring *oikos* – the comprehensive urban as absolute space of global economic management- the stasis, which can no longer be within the threshold between *oikos* and polis, becomes the paradigm of a conflictive status an unresolved tension.

Conclusion

According to Behrent (2014:157) free-market liberalism "arises when power realises that it has an interest as power in limiting power". Neoliberalism, in Foucault's conception, "has no need to hypothesize something outside of or beyond power, such as law, rights, or even "liberty", since liberty, in his view, is neither a "metaphysical entity [n]or a human attribute", but merely "a side-effect of power – as [he] put it, "the independence of the governed in relation to the governing'" (ibid).

But neoliberal ideology and spatiology is also a 'truth game' (Spencer 2016) as

> its accounts of human knowledge, social complexity and the economic market legitimate its management of individuals [. . .] that the economic market is better able to calculate, process and spontaneously order society than the state is able to [. . .] The function of architecture prescribed by this position is that of producing endlessly flexible environments for infinitely adaptable subjects. Neoliberalism is understood by Foucault as a form of governmentality

with its own particular apparatuses and techniques, its own means of 'taking care' of the self, though not for the self, but in order to render it entrepreneurial, to shape it in accord with neoliberal beliefs about the essential nature of the subject and its relationship to the putatively progressive and evolutionary forces of the market.

(Spencer 2016:4)

The complicit role of architecture in structuring, spatialising and determining such 'truth games' had then to become evident. The techniques of the management of human life includes everything from his birth to his death, the entry and exit of the territory, the crossing of the borders, preventive quarantine, protective custodies, eugenics, citizenships and so on. As Michel Foucault and Agamben have pointed out, the motor that triggers the apparatus of biopolitics is therefore no longer only the nexus connecting the juridical rule with the techniques of subjectivation, but the power of political economy at the centre.

Political economy here apparently does not refer to a system of rules or a science of knowledge, but to a paradigm that was associated with administrative activities, including management, arrangement, dispositif, organisation and execution of the order of things in the household, as what oikos-nomia suggests (Agamben 2011:17–18). *Oikos* designates private household space while polis refers to the public domain, and therefore oikos-nomias could mean the arrangement of household affairs.

Giorgio Agamben, once said that the true and urgent political task is to profane and deactivate the theologico-political machine in order to make room, beyond it, for a new use and imagine a completely new politics, detached and renewed from the one conceived in the society of mass hedonism and consumerism and capitalism The last image he used in one of his of earlier book *The Man Without Content* is illustrative, not only as it is a rare architectural, although generic, reference. He observed "it is only in the burning house that the fundamental architectural problem becomes visible for the first time, art, at the furthest point of its destiny, makes visible its original project" (Agamben 2009:172). The political house in flames of today's planetary state of exception is one in which Agamben believes its original structure can be glimpsed, and it is in this burning house that the perennial problems politics appear to him most clearly.

Note

1 Leshem in *The Origins of Neoliberalism, Modeling the Economy from Jesus to Foucault* (2016) suggests that "the most crucial among his multivalent contributions to the history of the economy was the insertion of patristic economic art into the history, linking what he [*Foucault*] called, in an atypical anachronism, pastorate or pastoral power and governmentality" (p. 5). Pastoral power does "not coincide with politics, pedagogy, or rhetoric. It is something entirely different. It is an art of 'governing men', [. . .] the modern state is born, I think, when governmentality became a calculated and reflected practice. The Christian pastorate seems to me to be the background of this process".

References

Abu-Hamdi, E., (2017) Neoliberalism as a site-specific process: The aesthetics and politics of architecture in Amman. Jordan. *Cities*, Vol. 60, pp: 102–112.

Agamben, G., (1998) Homo Sacer: Sovereign Power and Bare Life. Trans. Daniel Heller-Roazen. Stanford: Stanford University Press.

Agamben, G., (1999) *The Man without Content*. Stanford, CA: Stanford University Press.

Agamben, G., (2009) *What Is an Apparatus? And Other Essays*. Trans. David Kishik and Stefan Pedatella. Stanford, CA: Stanford University Press.

Agamben, G., (2011) *The Kingdom and the Glory: For a Theological Genealogy of Economy and Government*. Stanford: Stanford University Press.

Agamben, G., (2015) *Stasis La Guerra Civile come Paradigma Politico Homo Sacer II, 2*. Torino: Bollati Borlinghieri.

Aureli, P.V., (2011) *The Possibility of an Absolute Architecture*. Cambridge, MA: MIT Press.

Behrent, M.C., (2014) Liberalism without Humanism: Michel Foucault and the Free-Market Creed, 1976–1979, in Zamora, D. and Behrent, M.C., eds. *Foucault and Neoliberalism*. London: Polity Press, pp: 156–194.

Boano, C., (2017) *The Ethics of a Potential Urbanism: Critical Encounters between Giorgio Agamben and Architecture*. London: Routledge.

Brenner, N., ed., (2014) *Implosions/Explosions: Towards a Study of Planetary Urbanization*. Berlin: Jovis.

Brown, W., (2015) *Undoing the Demos: Neoliberalism's Stealth Revolution*. New York: Zone Books.

Collier, S.J., (2009) Topologies of power Foucault's analysis of political government beyond 'governmentality'. *Theory Culture and Society*, Vol. 26(6), pp: 78–108.

Dardot, P. & Laval, C., (2014) *The New Way of the World: On Neoliberal Society*. London: Verso.

Datta, A., (2015) A 100 smart cities, a 100 utopias [Response paper]. *Dialogues in Human Geography*, Vol. 5(1), pp: 49–53.

de la Durantaye, L. (2009) *Giorgio Agemben: An Introduction*. Stanford, CA: Stanford University Press, p: 204.

Foucault, M., (1977) The Confession of the Flesh (1977) Interview, in Gordon, C., ed. *Power/Knowledge Selected Interviews and Other Writings*, 1980. New York: Pantheon. pp: 194–228.

Foucault, M., (1980) *Power/Knowledge: Selected Interviews and Other Writings, 1972–1977*. New York: Pantheon.

Foucault, M., (2003) *Abnormal Lectures at the College de France 1974–1975*. London: Verso.

Graham, S. & Marvin, S., (2001) *Splintering Urbanism*. London: Routledge.

Harvey, D., (2007) *A Brief History of Neoliberalism*. Oxford: Oxford University Press.

Keil, R., (2016) Urban Neoliberalism: Rolling with the Changes in a Globalizing World, in Springer, S., Birch, K., and MacLeavy, J., eds. *The Handbook of Neoliberalism*. London: Routledge, Chapter 33.

Lefebrve, H., (2003) *The Urban Revolution*. Minneapolis: Minneapolis University Press, p. 14.

Lemke, T., (2007) An indigestible meal? Foucault, governmentality and state theory. *Distinktion: Scandinavian Journal of Social Theory*, Vol. 15, pp: 43–64.

Leshem, D., (2016) *The Origins of Neoliberalism, Modeling the Economy from Jesus to Foucault*. New York: Columbia University Press.

Martin, R., (2016) *The Urban Apparatus: Mediapolitics and the City*. Minneapolis: Minnesota University Press.

Mudge, S.L., (2008) What Is Neo-Liberalism? *Socioeconomic Review*, Vol. 6(4), pp: 703–731.

Ortiz, C. & Boano, C., (2018) Hyperupgrading Medellín: A Progressive Model for Spatial Justice? Politics of Informality through Spatial and Discursive Practices, in Rokem, J. and Boano, C., eds. *Urban Geopolitics. Rethinking Planning in Contested Cities*. London: Routledge, forthcoming in 2017.

Peck, J., (2004). Geography and public policy: Constructions of neoliberalism. *Progress in Human Geography*, Vol. 28(3), pp: 392–405.

Rivière , S. (2017). Stasis, Charging the Space of Change. *FOOTPRINT*, 10(2), 79–94.

Spencer, D., (2016) *The Architecture of Neoliberalims*. London: Bloomsbury.

Springer, S., Birch, K., & MacLeavy, J., (2016) *The Handbook of Neoliberalism*. London: Routledge.

Stanek, L., Schmid, C., and Moravanszky, A., (2015) *Urban Revolution Now: Henri Lefebvre in Social Research and Architecture*. London: Ashgate.

Zamora, D., & Behrent, M. C. (Eds.). (2016). *Foucault and neoliberalism*. John Wiley & Sons.

2 The neoliberal urban utopia of Milton Friedman

Santiago de Chile as its realisation

Francisco Vergara Perucich

Introduction

Neoliberalism is a comprehensive concept defining a series of social practices in which economic development is set as the main goal of humanity. In doing so, the neoliberal ideology requires the liberation of markets by deregulating its policies and fostering an engagement between the political and the economic elites preserving their hegemonic control over society. The success of neoliberalism requires politicians to develop a fierce defence of two principles: private property and entrepreneurial freedom. This defence is easier to conduct in liberal democracies under the reign of a representative democratic regime in which people place their power in the hands of a small number of representatives of society (parliament) whose decisions may be easily influenced by forces of the economic elites (see Figure 2.1). Recent evidence in the case of Chile demonstrates the comprehensive scope of neoliberalism in an exemplary liberal democracy, where economic power has acted coercively with political power in order to design public policies that besides fostering private property and entrepreneurial freedom, also had ensured the profitability of business in matters of the public interest.

Around the difference practice of Chilean neoliberalism, several scandals have exposed the mechanisms in which an entrepreneur approaches a politician offering advice in matters of public interest in exchange for funds for political campaigns. This has been the case for land regulations (Caso Caval), fishing (Ley de Pesca), international conflicts (Piñera y Bancard), pension schemes (Grupo Penta), education (Reforma educacional) and environment (Minera Dominga) just to mention few recent cases. The tentacles of this octopus named neoliberalism reach to every corner of human activity where it is possible to gain some profit. As per Pierre Bourdieu, neoliberalism represents the utopia (a becoming of a reality) of unlimited exploitation (Bourdieu 1998), and in the case of Chile, this reality has been a way of everyday life since 1975. Sadly for non-wealthy Chileans, neoliberalism became a concrete utopia (Lefebvre 2003) long ago; and its results nowadays are a vivid expression of somebody else's imagination. Neoliberalism is not an abstract form of action, or an invisible hand. Neoliberalism is the result of the theory and practice of a number of individuals whose ideas shaped this ideology: among theorists such as Friedrich Hayek, Milton Friedman,

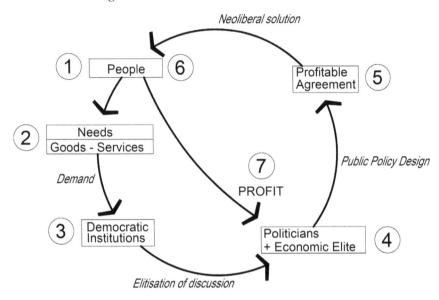

Figure 2.1 The scheme of the sequence of Chilean neoliberalism practice: 1. People have
needs 2. These needs may be of goods or services. These needs are organised
as a demand presented to democratic institutions (3), such as the congress,
mayors or central authority. The demand is discussed by the elite (elitisation of
discussion) which ends by excluding most of people from the decision-making
process. 4. The politicians and the economic elite gather to find a solution. The
meeting between both is not secret but neither is it exposed publicly. 5. After
designing public policy, politicians and the economic elite find a profitable
agreement, a neoliberal solution for the sake of people's needs (6). The solution
results profitable for politicians (in the form of votes) and incomes (in form
of money) for the entrepreneurial elite (7). For both outcomes, the exploited
resource comes from the people.

Ludwig For Mises, Walter Lippmann and Karl Popper, and in their implementers
and practical supporter such as Augusto Pinochet, Ronald Reagan and Margaret
Thatcher, to name a few.

In this chapter, I will introduce Milton Friedman's urban theory, whose way
to interpret a better society (the neoliberal society) also had a spatial and urban
form. Friedman was the mentor of the Chilean Chicago Boys (the economists that
oriented Pinochet to implement the neoliberal revolution), and it was Friedman
himself who sent a letter to Pinochet clearly stating eight points to transform the
Chilean economy, hence, his ideas about urban development are fundamental in
understanding the current status of Santiago's urban phenomenon. In doing so, I
will also reflect on some specific materialisation of Friedman's ideas in Santiago.
The evidence, as this book's content demonstrates fully, exposes how Santiago is
not only a neoliberal experiment, but also that it is the concrete representation of
a neoliberal utopia.

This chapter theorises on the background to the urban decisions and phenomena that compose neoliberal Santiago, and which inform its urban development. There is no direct transition from Milton Friedman's ideas about how a neoliberal city should be and how they were actually implemented. Neoliberalism in action is profoundly complex, it is an engineered complexity aimed at avoiding the public understanding of its twisted modus operandi, nevertheless, its ideology is simple and this chapter will attempt to unveil the logical thinking behind these neoliberal urban practices.

Ideological principles of neoliberalism and its spatial incidence

"The seller is protected from coercion by the consumer because of other consumers to whom he can sell. The employee is protected from coercion by the employer because of other employers for whom he can work, and so on. And the market does this impersonally and without centralised authority. Indeed, a major source of objection to a free economy is precisely that it does this task so well. It gives people what they want instead of what a particular group thinks they ought to want. Underlying most arguments against the free market is a lack of belief in freedom itself"

(Friedman 1982:20–21)

Freedom is the neoliberalism motto. The idea of freedom promoted by Friedman states that social relations ruled by the free market may help people to achieve their liberation from centrally controlled decisions (by the government for example), reducing the role of the state in personal life to its bare minimum. In Friedman's own words, economic freedom

is an essential requisite for political freedom. By enabling people to cooperate with one another without coercion or central direction, it reduces the area over which political power is exercised. [. . .] by dispersing power, the free market provides an offset to whatever concentration of political power may arise. The combination of economic and political power in the same hands is a sure recipe for tyranny.

(Friedman and Friedman 1980: 2–3)

While Friedman highlights the potential freedom that comes from reducing the size of the state, he hides the fact that the reduction of the state apparatuses also requires a deep transformation in the democratic system. This is seen in the Chilean case, when Pinochet reduced the size of the state in 1975, further weakening the democracy. Then, in 1981 after years of pursuing, exiling and killing detractors, Pinochet rebuilt a democracy using a neoliberal algorithm. The new model was tailored to free-market economics in domestic affairs and monetarism for macroeconomic development, consolidated by a political constitution designed by the Chicago Boys (Friedman's apprentices) and Jaime Guzmán, perpetuating a neoliberal regime by law in which private property and entrepreneurial freedom were the main principles.

Since then, neoliberalism has tried to convince society that it is possible to avoid coercion by just a 'civil' agreement between employer and employee, seller and buyer, which have to be enshrined by a democratic state. Therefore, the only role for that state is in defining a basic framework for social relations. Understanding that this ideology interprets society as a body of individuals instead of a collective entity, the effects on the modes of production of space was also redefined. The city is the politico-physical result of ideological struggles, a social product resulting from capitalists relations of exchange (Lefebvre 1991) and thus, in the case of Santiago, urban space is the spatial representation of neoliberalism.

The city, as a physical expression of social, political and economical relations, is subjected to the hegemonic ideology of its time. In the case of neoliberalism, the excessive promotion of the individual's realisation undermines the collective value of urban life. In concrete, this urban life is the subject of privatisation whose principle expression is the house: the elementary social space. As a consequence, the public space becomes a simple area 'between properties', unless it too is transformed into a private space. In a prior definition, under neoliberalism, the city may be seen as a network of private properties articulated by exchange interests (Figure 2.2). Private property, and its associated purchasing power, has become a symbol of happiness and success. Indeed, greater freedom is possible only for those who are smart enough to find happiness in what the market provides.

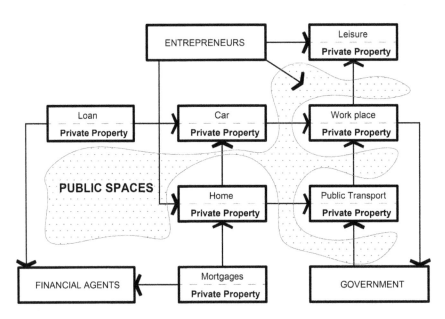

Figure 2.2 The diagram exposes a theoretical mapping of the urban relations in the neoliberal city: a network of private spaces in which public space has become a blurry leftover, an unnecessary function of everyday life unless it is transformed into a profitable support of activities.

Therefore, freedom depends on ones capacity for competing and defeating other members of a society in order to benefit more from what these social relations can provide. A sort of 'right of the stronger' originating in force (and a dangerous) interpretations of Darwin's theories (Spencer 1896). Individualism as a positive value triggers the existence of a new definition of the urban space not as a collective construction but as the consequence of a sum of social fragments (individuals, families, state and enterprises) that together are subscribed within a territory politically delimited and named as a city. Among these social fragments, only the state and the enterprises represent a collective force, which is also represented in the power that they hold.

However, neoliberal macroeconomic policy is not material but financial, meaning that currency becomes more important than objects, thus money fulfils social necessities more than space does. Alternatively, if one prefers, space has become the main asset for capital accumulation. Under the neoliberal macroeconomic rule, a house is useful only if its exchange value increases over time. Its spatial qualities, meanings or architectural significance are no longer important for the neoliberal ideology. Consequently, the quality of spaces deteriorates, design became a way to optimise profit, and the space becomes completely commoditised.

This radical change came from the economic crises of the seventies in which the Keynesian model faced its last days as the ruling political-economic theory. In this scenario, Friedman presented an alternative that seemed as ideal for contesting the apparent failure of a centralised state. In his words:

> The great advances of civilisation, whether in architecture or painting, in science or literature, in industry or agriculture, have never come from centralised government [. . .] Government can never duplicate the variety and diversity of individual action. At any moment in time, by imposing uniform standards in housing, or nutrition, or clothing, government could undoubtedly improve the level of living in many individuals; by imposing uniform standards in schooling, road construction, or sanitation, central government could undoubtedly improve the level of performance in many local areas and perhaps even on the average of all communities. But in the process, government would replace progress by stagnation, it would substitute uniform mediocrity for the variety essential for that experimentation which can bring tomorrow's laggards above today's mean.
>
> (Friedman 1982:11–12)

In the mind of Friedman, the implementation of a free-market model would result in more creative human relations. It is difficult to imagine that he never thought about the concentration of power in the hands of a few capitalists or the effects that a globalised world would have in his imagined future. However, for such a free-market society, the only role of the State was facilitating the exchange of services and products between producers and users, without interference. Nevertheless, for Friedman, if we lived in a free-market society, the individual efforts would be highly valorised and it would lead toward happiness and personal realisation. In this utopian society, everyone could thrive as entrepreneurs if they had determination. Friedman oversimplified complex social relations behind wealth and entrepreneurialism including, for instance, ignoring social origins, class and even cultural heritage.

Nevertheless, Milton Friedman thought that cities occupied a fundamental role in the production of an ideal free-market reality. Many of his aspirations are well represented in Santiago. Specifically, after the end of Pinochet's dictatorship, neo-liberalism was revitalised by the involvement of the State in the promotion of free-market economics. Consequently, a particular mode of urban design under neoliberalism resulted from what has been called the Chilean transition to democracy. In the production of public space, the Chilean state preferred to subsidise the private sector to develop public projects: thus the whole provision of social infrastructure is developed by private companies with public funds. Fernando Atria et al. (2013) defined this phenomenon as 'the privatization of the public sphere'.

Based on decades of economic theorisation, neoliberalism built its own 'concrete utopia' (Lefebvre 1972). Friedman's utopia of a happy society, in contrast to the decayed Keynesian post-war world, managed to convince several authorities, scholars and businessmen who were conveniently tempted to believe, almost religiously, in the free market. Thus, they also became preachers of the neoliberal regime as the medicine for a profoundly ill global economy. Forty years after its implementation, Chile is one of the most enduring places of neoliberalism (Henderson 1995; Duquette 1998)The Heritage Foundation positioned Chile as the place in America with the best free-market system, only surpassed by Canada (Heritage Foundation 2017). Surely, Friedman would be very interested to visit Santiago today. The everyday life of this city shows how his ideas on urban life went far beyond what he proposed. Santiago has become the concrete utopia of neoliberal urbanism.

Toward Milton Friedman idea of city

In Milton Friedman's related literature the use of qualitative data is scarce; numbers were his mantra. In spite of the fact that he was the chief commander of one of the most significant revolutions of the twentieth century (the neoliberal revolution), it is not easy to find ideas of how he imagined everyday life. Indeed, the few images that exist are subjugated to numeric data. After an exhaustive literature review, I am sure that his intentions were good, that he truly believed that free-market economics may liberate 'common' people, but also that he thought that the elite were entitled, and that it is a moral imperative, to compete to provide better goods and services. His failure was in not understanding the multidimensional complexity of human behaviour, the conscious rejection of the dialectic theory in social sciences, and for idealising the entrepreneurial class. Apparently Friedman did not include in his theorisation of everyday life the question of power, control and hegemony. Or, most likely, he intentionally avoided the topic because neoliberalism in the long term has been configured as a global mechanism for controlling human behaviours toward consumerism and advocating for debt.

Abstraction of social relations – to its bare minimum representation (numbers) – eliminates the richness and the complexity of urban life. The city imagined by Friedman was completely oriented to maximise productivity, consumerism and was imagined as completely controlled by the elite. Therefore, based on the two principles of private property and entrepreneurial freedom, urban design becomes a fundamental resource reproducing cycles of capital accumulations and in the creation of wealth. These connections between neoliberal principles and urban development are particularly important and are organised in a simple sequence: the state designs public policy for a particular need that facilitates the creation of businesses by opening an entrepreneurial opportunity and defining parts of the national land for exploiting it. Thus, the private sector and the state agree to work together in covering social need. While the state fulfils its role of building the spatial support for social development is also provides public funds to facilitate entrepreneurial freedom. The private sector and the state work together in mid-term and long-term contracts in order to ensure the creation of jobs, infrastructure and accommodation. The elite control these processes, the state ensures its contribution to society by building infrastructure and the private sector ensures the transformation of fiscal funds into entrepreneurial activity and finally, part of these fiscal investments are transformed into private profit. For example, on average, enterprises earn 27% profit from public-private partnership from building infrastructure and housing. The construction economist Sir David J. Hoare recommends a 9% profit the construction industry, which is in turn lower when the investments are larger. In Chile it is the reverse. Road maintenance contracts may generate more than 35% profits, while housing barely passes 15% profit. In both cases, the earnings are huge in comparison with other countries, demonstrating how profitable construction can be within a neoliberal period.

The urbanisation processes represent a significant resource for entrepreneurial freedom in social development. Therefore, the main demand Friedman had on cities was the urgency in privatising as many public affairs as possible in order to eliminate the bureaucracy of the state, converting it into a financial institution for fostering private initiatives, a resource of funds for the creation of wealth. In a way, this was the role that Friedman assigned to the state: a manager of funds and a promoter of direct relationship between the seller and buyer. Based on Friedman's arguments contained in his two manifestos *Capitalism and Freedom* published in 1962 and *Free to Choose of 1980* it is possible to create a preliminary theory of neoliberal urban design, as an imaginative exercise based in Friedman's interpretations of housing, transport, public spaces, urban life and how these urban components represent the principles of private property and entrepreneurial freedom.

On housing

One of the main critiques that Friedman had of the Keynesian development model was its control of a centralised state in economic life. For him, this model implied that adults were not capable of making their own decision correctly. In Friedman's interpretation, the state has to decide in the name of the majority, which in turn undermined individual freedom. In the particular case of housing (specifically public housing), he questioned the capacity of the state to deliver proper houses to people. Friedman stated that if individuals managed the same amount of money that the state used to construct houses, their decisions would have been different. Indeed, he stated that people could provide a superior house than what the state provides, using their own creativity for designing a solution to their accommodation needs (Friedman 1982). In concrete, Friedman argues that

> public housing is proposed not on the ground of neighbourhood effects but as a means of helping low-income people. If this is the case, why subsidise housing in particular? If funds were to be used to help the poor, would they not be used more effectively by being given in cash rather than in kind? Surely, the families being helped would rather have a given sum in cash than in the form of housing. They could themselves spend the money on housing if they so desired.
>
> (Friedman 1982:146)

In Chile, for example, the funds available for building a unit of social housing are around US$ 10,200 per family, while in the high-income districts the average cost of building a housing unit is US$ 400,000. It seems that Friedman was missing a lot of important data to make such a statement effective, such as land value, construction costs, access to design, just to mention a few limitations to what would be a contradictory condition in the freedom of housing design. What can a family in Chile do with US$ 10,200? Not much in the long term. The living cost per person in Santiago's downtown is around US$ 380 per month, which means that a family of four can afford only two years of living costs with the US$ 10,200 that the state invests in public housing. Also, there is the problem of location. Friedman forgot to address in any form access to services. How could free-market economics coordinate the allocation of goods if everything relies on the capacities of individuals? How can low-income communities compete with high-income members of society over locations if their access to capital is uneven? The neoliberal city increases the amount of low-income communities building their houses in the periphery exactly because it is in such areas that the market is less interested in investment and consequently it is cheaper to buy land. On the other hand, the neoliberal city concentrates the housing of wealthy sectors of society in certain areas, segmenting the demand for specific types of goods and services. Hence, for example, more expensive food is sold in wealthy areas while cheaper goods are trade in low-income areas. Because of this condition, the neoliberal city fosters residential segregation as a strategy to allocate specific kind of commerce for different types of people: the wealthy, the middle class, and low-income communities.

For Friedman, social housing is a problem because it generates 'problematic neighbourhoods'. Specifically he argues

> the income limitations quite properly imposed for the occupancy of public housing at subsidised rentals have led to a very high density of 'broken'

families in particular, divorced or widowed mothers with children. Children of broken families are especially likely to be 'problem' children and a high concentration of such children is likely to increase juvenile delinquency. One manifestation has been the very adverse effect on schools in the neighbourhood of a public housing project.

(Friedman 1982:148)

It is interesting to read how the stigmatisation of low-income communities was present in his discourse about how a good city should be defined. This argument stresses the strategic importance of segregation in the production of urban space. Expelling low-income communities from central and strategic areas of the city would follow the criterion of cleansing urban life and avoiding contested practices as in the case of squatting, for example. In Friedman's words:

> housing is better and more widely distributed in the United States today than when the public housing programme was started, but that has occurred through private enterprise despite the government subsidies. The public housing units themselves have frequently become slums and hotbeds of crime, especially juvenile delinquency.

(Friedman 1980:110)

Implicitly, Friedman states that public housing programmes are long term tools for the benefit of particular interests rather than tools to pursue a common good: "the central defect of these measures is that they seek through government to force people to act against their immediate interest in order to promote a supposedly general interest" (Friedman 1982). Friedman's theory suggests that neoliberalism aims to reach a state of freedom for everyone, but the unavoidable existence of poverty undermines free markets in practice. Under a neoliberal rule the just and equal city becomes an unfeasible utopia, but this is naturalised because even though poverty exists, some members of society benefit greatly from free-market economics

On transport

Friedman justified the existence of monopolies in the private sector against state regulations. In his words:

> All three [private monopoly, public monopoly and state regulations] are bad so we must choose among evils. Henry Simons, observing public regulation of monopoly in the United States, found the results so distasteful that he concluded public monopoly would be a lesser evil. Walter Eucken, a noted German liberal, observing public monopoly in German railroads, found the results so distasteful that he concluded public regulation would be a lesser evil. Having learnt from both, I reluctantly conclude that, if tolerable, private monopoly may be the least of the evils.

(Friedman 1982:31)

For Friedman, the public realm is particularly slow to adopt changes in technology, such as the case of trains or public transport, for example, while the private sector is more adaptable and is more capable to develop solutions for the common good. In concrete, along his texts, Friedman naturalises the privatisation of urban life. In doing so, he changes the logic of pursuing the common good as the main social objective, to a new one centred on pursuing profitable activities.

Friedman exemplified profit-extracting methods in the case of transport systems. For instance, he explains that highways may assist in granting tax relief especially in the way by which it is possible to transform a general tax on petrol consumption into individual payments depending of the use of some specific piece of infrastructure such as a highway: "city streets and general-access highways could be provided by private voluntary exchange, the costs being paid for by charging tolls" (Friedman and Friedman 1980:30). In Friedman's mind it results in a fairer system by paying directly at the moment of driving on a highway, instead of making the whole country contribute to it by paying taxes. In Santiago, this idea was followed in great detail through the urban highway concessions plan, which consisted of high impact infrastructure implemented during the Ricardo Lagos administration. For Ricardo Lagos, the concessions were a way to modernise the state with an infrastructural revolution (Lagos 2003). These highways were built with public funds but constructed, administered, and governed by private companies. These companies directly charge the end users via a microchip installed in every vehicle in Santiago. At the end of the month, users receive a bill emitted by the concessionary company. In this manner, the role of the State is almost invisible, acting only as the supervisor of the concession contract.

The concession model was also applied in Santiago's public transport through an emblematic project named Transantiago. The state acted as a centralised source of decision-making processes transforming public transport policies and developing a new system supervised by the state but executed by private transport companies.

> Aside from the serious technical errors caused by a miscalculation of the transport model and many other issues that have been broadly discussed elsewhere, the two most important aspects that contributed to the collapse of the system were first, that the system itself was not ready to be put into operation and second, that it did not recognise the importance of everyday life, and particularly everyday mobility, in people's life and in the city.
>
> (Jirón et al. 2016:600)

After a series of mistakes in Transantiago's design and implementation, the state invested in transforming roads and streets, building new bus-stops, buying new fleets of buses and then, through a public bid, assigning new bus companies that would help to operate the new system. Nevertheless, the government did not dare to transform the whole transport system into a public entity; it remained as a public-private partnership despite the yearly deficit of US$ 665 million. The costs of continued operation under neoliberal rule demonstrate that even before public scrutiny and its related questioning, free-market ideology prevails. This demonstrates another neoliberal principle: no matter the costs, the decisions made between politicians and the economic elite will prevail, hidden under the mask of a technical decision.

Parks and public spaces

Parks and public spaces are one of the few exceptions Friedman approved to be managed by the government. This exception is mostly due, explains Friedman, to the difficulty in controlling and determining who the users are and, in low attendance periods (winter), the difficulties in maintaining such areas by a profit-oriented entity. He argued that for

> the city park, it is extremely difficult to identify the people who benefit from it and to charge them for the benefits which they receive. If there is a park in the middle of the city, the houses on all sides get the benefit of the open space, and people who walk through it or by it also benefit. To maintain toll collectors at the gates or to impose annual charges per window overlooking the park would be very expensive and difficult. The entrances to a national park like Yellowstone, on the other hand, are few; most of the people who come stay for a considerable period of time. It is perfectly feasible to set up toll gates and collect admission charges. This is indeed now done, though the charges do not cover the whole costs. If the public wants this kind of an activity enough to pay for it, private enterprises will have every incentive to provide such parks.
>
> (Friedman 1982:33)

Despite this, Friedman expresses concerns regarding the control and management of this type of activities. This implies that it is difficult to generate profit from urban areas that are generally characterised by high costs of maintenance (water, gardening, cleaning, security) with low potential revenue. Instead, public management may require the externalisation of these maintenance activities, hiring private companies to do the work. Therefore through privatisation the park would be a free-access space but also a profitable initiative in which the government would have to invest in the private sector directly in order to preserve the quality of space. Nevertheless, this only happens in districts with funds available for such kind of expenditures. For example, in Santiago, the wealthy district of Vitacura has 18.3 square meters of green space per person while the poorest district of Pudahuel has only 1.3 square meters of green space per person. This is a significant difference that emphasises the point that the neoliberal city is uneven.

On urban life and social relations

As it may be repeated in the history, Milton Friedman was nostalgic for another era, that which existed prior to the Great War and the great depression. The early

capitalists that developed their businesses in the United States were great references for him. Their efforts were transformed directly into wealth because they
worked hard achieving high levels of prosperity, especially because there was a
lack of obstacles in developing their ideas and their entrepreneurialism. In his
view, historically private development had financed schools, universities, chari-
ties, hospitals, orphanages, museums, libraries, and other services for people. This
nostalgic view is where the term neoliberalism makes sense as a rebirth of those
principles that shaped the period of American industrial capitalism. The regulation
of everyday life – as Friedman interpreted the Keynesian period – undermining
the life of the entrepreneurial spirits that were aiming to thrive and move toward
a better era.

  Regarding urban management, one of the advantages pointed out by Friedman
was the lack of regulation and constraints for the private sector to produce significant developments in cities. In his view, entrepreneurial freedom may provide
buildings and landscape of great value for people (as the case of New York sky-
scrapers) whilst also being profitable for investors. In Friedman's interpretation,
cities are grounds of opportunities for individuals rather than a set of obligations
for the collective, and nobody should be restricted in following their individual
desires and aspirations. He questioned

> are those who make and impose such decisions equal to those for whom they
> decide? Are we not in George Orwell's *Animal Farm*, where 'all animals are
> equal, but some animals are more equal than others'? In addition, if what
> people get is determined by 'fairness' and not by what they produce, where
> are the 'prizes' to come from? What incentive is there to work and produce?
> How is it to be decided who is to be the doctor, who the lawyer, who the gar-
> bage collector, who the street sweeper? What assures that people will accept
> the roles assigned to them and performs those roles in accordance with their
> abilities? Clearly, only force or the threat of force will do
>
> (Friedman and Friedman 1980:135)

Thinking that under the reign of neoliberalism everybody has equal power was
at best naïve as it assumes that everybody has some sort of 'capital'. This is not a
common rule and only a few were lucky enough to have capital to invest in entrepreneurial initiatives. Furthermore, putting the entire fate of society in the hands
of those with entrepreneurial capacities would undermine the access to power
of those without access to these capacities. Nevertheless, for Friedman the city
should be a consequence of individual efforts, instead of a collective production.

  In this idea of the city imagined by Friedman, planning was unnecessary and
redundant, because people's desires would lead to good spatial transformation
processes, and inequality would remain as a common condition. Actually, he
justifies the existence of inequality in human history, regardless of the political
ideology behind decision-making processes. He recalls unequal spaces in Rus-
sia, China, and Cambodia as well as in his native United States, independently
of the political and economic system. Naturalising inequality was a strategy in

conceptualising a city in which those more advantaged in education and capital have the opportunity to produce great businesses while the less advantaged should struggle to find their own social position.

The logic of a naturalised inequality has its spatial representation, and neoliberalism resolves this inequality with more public-private partnerships to provide better spaces for the disadvantaged. For Milton Friedman (1980, 1982), quality is related to expenditure, which is why lower-income neighbourhoods tend to have poorer infrastructure since public resources fund them. But he proposes that if such infrastructure is privatised the quality of these works should become much better, because they have the capacity to generate profits. Under the gaze of Friedman, privatisation of urban life should offer better cities as a whole. If the city becomes a highly profitable business, the urban experience of citizens would be enhanced. Following this argument, Friedman did not hesitate in showing his critical position around the imposition of a uniform housing model by the state. For him, public housing in socialist societies tended to shape a boring city; while free-market economics delivered a diverse and thriving set of different spaces. Indeed, a contrast between a socialist city and a capitalist city was observed by Friedman himself when visiting Berlin:

> [The] most obvious example [of the difference between socialist and capitalist cities] is the contrast between East and West Germany, originally part of one whole, torn asunder by the vicissitudes of warfare. People of the same blood, the same civilisation, the same level of technical skill and knowledge inhabit the two parts. Which has prospered? [. . .] On one side of that wall the brightly lit streets and stores are filled with cheerful, bustling people. Some are shopping for goods from all over the globe. Others are going to the numerous movie houses or other places of entertainment. They can buy freely newspapers and magazines expressing every variety of opinion. They speak with one another or with strangers on any subject and express a wide range of opinions without a single backward glance over the shoulder. A walk of a few hundred feet, after an hour spent in line, filling in forms and waiting for passports to be returned, will take you, as it took us, to the other side of that wall. There, the streets appear empty; the city, grey and pallid; the store windows, dull; the buildings, grimy. Wartime destruction has not yet been repaired after more than three decades. The only sign of cheerfulness or activity that we found during our brief visit to East Berlin was at the entertainment centre. One hour in East Berlin is enough to understand why the authorities put up the Wall.
>
> (Friedman and Friedman 1980:55)

I wonder what Friedman would think of the spaces developed by capitalism such as Santa Isabel town in Santiago (see Figure 2.3). A deregulated area of the city in which diverse entrepreneurial initiatives were implemented in the form of housing projects whose aesthetic is completely homogeneous, monotonous and lacking of any kind of creativity.

Figure 2.3 Santa Isabel Street, an area where regulation was reduced to its minimum and free-market real estate development produced a series of monotonous buildings with scarce aesthetic innovation and not much creativity.

Conclusion: theoretical approach to neoliberal urban design

After reviewing the incipient insights of Friedman on urban development and cities, there are some conclusions that may lead toward the production of a theory of neoliberal urban design.

1   The neoliberal city does not need the state apparatus of urban planning because it is the free market that determines land value and the priorities for producing a fruitful urban space, in which an entrepreneurial environment fosters innovation and creativity. For success, it is necessary to have organised private agents to orient decisions about urban life, whose role is to promote the city as a matter of business. For example, there is no need to centralise housing production in order to provide a so-called public housing for the poor. A respectful relation between dwellers and builders would simply resolve these affairs. The state should facilitate such encounter lends cash to those that want to build their homes want to build their houses. The state should act more like a 'bank' for the poor and educate them in matters of entrepreneurialism, rather than acting as a paternalist institution for public developments. Only in this way can the urban poor approach a private entity to agree the construction of their houses. The private builders will face both challenges and unique opportunities in producing an innovative architectural model. Because of this competition, in the neoliberal city it is common to find great works of architecture, because building companies are doing their best to solicit more clients and in doing so diversify and invest in a phantasmagoria object aesthetically pleasant and '*a la mode*' Citizens compete localising themselves in the better areas of the city, reserved for the better exponents of the free-market society, or for those better off in negotiating with landowners.

2   Every urban activity is better if it is detached from fiscal regulations. For example, the market will facilitate the provision of good quality public spaces, as well as its maintenance. The state, rather than regulate, will coordinate these activities and promote a healthy competition between private enterprises dedicated to these kinds of works.

3   The neoliberal city is the place where people stop thinking in terms of common affairs, rather they focus on their own wishes and the means to realise them. This system assumes that the city works thanks to every individual doing his or her job in the best way, and consequently city services become outstanding. Individualism and lack of collective principles facilitate the objective of the *elite* whose entrepreneurial class remains highly associated and coordinated in order to commodify everyday life. Indeed, in the neoliberal city it is more accurate to talk about clients rather than citizens. It is a semantic and symbolic change of terms: a client obtains better services, treatment, and conditions from what a city may offer. Clients not only have rights but they also have choices.

4   The experience of living in the neoliberal city makes you feel at complete liberty. The neoliberal city is anarchic in regard to the unbounded levels of

freedom experienced by its inhabitants although the control over the disorder is in the hands of the capitalist system and the main principles of neoliberalism: private property and entrepreneurial freedom.

5   A neoliberal city has a government that acts as a technical agent. The only requisite of the state is to contribute to facilitating the relation between private actors (individuals or companies or both). Its main (and hopefully lonely) function is to lay down the rules of the game. The neoliberal city is the spatial manifestation of modern man's freedom.

Chile has fertile soil. In its lands you can sample a wide spectrum of fruits and great wines; in the ocean you can find a high diversity of fish and seafood. Indeed, Santiago is located in a central valley between the Andes and the Pacific Ocean, which used to be the territory of the Incas, Mapuches harvests, and productive uses in the early colonial years. Nowadays it is a metropolis that rather than reap, collects what is produced in the whole country. If the metaphor of Milton Friedman's neoliberal city elaborated throughout his work is a chef's recipe, Santiago has all the ingredients to cook an ideal neoliberal urban space. It is the empiric construction of Friedman's dreams. The neoliberal urban utopia is a reality in this particular physical space. Religiously, the followers of the intellectual legacy of Milton Friedman installed his convictions deep inside the Chilean culture, evangelising with the monetarist word of a fake god, transforming the way social relations occur from collective to individual, thus dissolving the collective sense of the city into a series of fragments. The production of space in Santiago adopted diverse methods that emerged from Friedman urban ideology, and some of them are well elaborated by the other authors of this book.

An apology to Santiago and a challenge for urbanists

How can we define the fundamental void in urbanism, whether the product of private intellect or public institutions? To the extent that it claims to replace or supplant urban practice it fails to examine that practice. But for urbanists, this practice is precisely the blind field I discussed earlier. They live it, they are in it, but they don't see it, and certainly cannot grasp it as such. With complete peace of mind, they substitute its representations of space, of social life, of groups and their relationships for praxis. They don't know where these representations come from or what they imply – that is, the logic and strategy that they serve. And if they do know, their knowledge is unforgivable; their ideological cover splits to reveal a strange nudity.

(Lefebvre 2003:153)

When Milton Friedman was about to receive his Nobel Prize in Economics in 1976, an activist interrupted the ceremony, yelling: "Friedman, go home! Friedman, go home! Long live the people of Chile! Freedom! Stop the capitalism!" Whilst the sounds of the activist voice rumbled in the whole auditorium, the face of Friedman exhibited a sort of guilt when the word Chile emerged from the throat of the anti-capitalist Swede in the audience. Sadly, the demand of the activist never saw the light. Neoliberalism prevailed over every social structure in Chile, which is most evident in Santiago. In spite of the fact that Friedman often denied his collaborations with Pinochet, the reality is that his ideology was dogmatically implemented during the dictatorship, and subsequently perfected in the return to democracy by the centre-left parties. The landscape of Santiago shows a scenographic urban setting of the neoliberal space. Just as 'The lord of the rings' film trilogy created a world of fantasies based on Tolkien's books, Santiago is the urban adaptation of 'Freedom to Choose' and 'Capitalism and Freedom'.

Nevertheless, it would be unfair to blame the people of Santiago for the aggressive neoliberalisation of their life. The invasion of this ideology was cleverly planned by the brilliant and Machiavellian mind of Jaime Guzman. Through a Constitution that embedded neoliberalism in every sphere of life and the privatisation of the public, Guzman ensured the success of neoliberalism throughout time. The repression and extermination of the opposition developed by the Dictatorship fostered fear among people to contest what the government says. Rather than believe in neoliberalism, it seems that people don't want to create trouble in society. The domestication through violence and threat was vital to implement this ideology. In this docile society, a blind field has closed the boundaries of possible progression towards a new future. Apparently, Santiago's people want a different social rule far from neoliberalism, the 'other model' as the specialists have named it.

An alternative to neoliberalism needs to be developed in order to demonstrate to people that the future life in Santiago can be reshaped. New imaginative projects should push the walls of this blind field, throwing the capitalist barriers down. A revolutionary attitude of urbanists is vital in order to unleash creativity and rethink urban life beyond what Friedman wished. Breaking his legacy will be impossible with the current social contract and urban trends, radical actions are urgent otherwise the capture of the social by capitalism will soon be total.

Without doubt, Santiago is not just another neoliberal city in a long list, but an exemplary model. Therefore, the actions of resistance and counterattack from urbanists and practitioners in this regard may deliver several lessons for other cities, aiming to finally overthrow neoliberalism from contemporary urban life.

References

Atria, F., Benavente, J. M., Couso, J., Joignant, A., & Larrain, G. (2013). *El otro modelo: Del orden neoliberal al regimen de lo público* (3a. ed., Debate. Actualidad). Santiago: Debate.

Bourdieu, P. (1998). *Acts of Resistance: Against the Tyranny of the Market*. New York: Free Press.

Bucknell, C., Muñoz, J. C., Schmidt, A., Navarro, M., & Simonetti, C. (2016). Impact of a loan-based public transport fare system on fare evasion: Experience of Transantiago, Santiago, Chile. *Transportation Research Record: Journal of the Transportation Research Board*, (2544), pp. 20–27.

Duquette, M. (1998). The Chilean economic miracle revisited. *The Journal of Socio-Economics*, 27 (3), pp. 299–321.

Exclusive interview: Milton Friedman on Reaganomics. (1981, Dec 5). *Human Events*, 41, p. 2. Retrieved from https://search.proquest.com/docview/1310020096?accountid=14511

Friedman, M. (1978, Nov 18). An interview with. *Human Events*, 38, p. 14. Retrieved from https://search.proquest.com/docview/1310012368?accountid=14511

Friedman, M. (1982). *Capitalism and Freedom*. Chicago: University of Chicago Press.

Friedman, M., & Friedman, R. (1980). *Free to Choose: A Personal Statement*. London: Harcourt Inc.

GSE (2015). [online] Retrieved from http://comunicaciones.udd.cl/mcom/files/2013/06/Informe-Actualizaci%C3%B3n-GSE-2012.pdf [Accessed 7 Mar. 2015].

Henderson, D. (1995). Economic 'miracles'. *Society*, 32 (6), pp. 59–67.

Heritage Foundation (2017). Country Rankings: World & Global Economy Rankings on Economic Freedom. *Heritage.org*. Retrieved 13 March 2017, from www.heritage.org/index/ranking

Hidalgo, R. (2005). *La vivienda social en Chile y la construcción del espacio urbano en el Santiago del siglo XX*. 1st ed. Santiago: Instituto de Geografía P. Universidad Católica de Chile/Centro de Investigaciones Diego Barrios Arana.

Jirón, P., Imilan, W., & Iturra, L. (2016). Relearning to travel in Santiago: The importance of mobile place-making and travelling know-how. *Cultural Geographies*, 23(4), pp. 599–614.

Lagos, R. (2003). *Discurso del Presidente de la República*. Valparaíso: 21 de Mayo de.

Lefebvre, H. (1972). *La revolución urbana*. Madrid: Alianza Editorial.

Lefebvre, H. (1991). *The Production of Space* (Vol. 142). Blackwell: Oxford.

Lefebvre, H. (2003). *The Urban Revolution*. London: University of Minnesota Press.

Piñera, J. (2015). Milton Friedman y sus recomendaciones a Chile: elcato.org. [online] *Elcato.org*. Retrieved from www.elcato.org/milton-friedman-y-sus-recomendaciones-chile [Accessed 10 Mar. 2015].

Spencer, H. (1896). *Social Statics: The Man Versus the State*. New York: D. Appleton and Company.

Tiznado-Aitken, I., Muñoz, J., & Hurtubia, R. (2016). How equitable is access to opportunities and basic services considering the impact of the level of service? The case of Santiago, Chile. *International Transport Forum Discussion Papers*, (2016–15), 1–30.

Valencia, M. (2007). La Ciudad de Libre Mercado: Neoliberalismo y transformaciones del espacio urbano metropolitano. *Revista de Diseño Urbano y Paisaje*, 3 (7), pp. 1–22.

3 Urban space production and social exclusion in Greater Santiago, under dictatorship and democracy

Matias Garreton

Introduction

Since the 1973 coup d'état, Chile has suffered a deep process of social restructuration (Giddens 1984), which has been imposed by political and exclusionary forms of violence. This transformation has involved a transition from the fear of military forces to a social consent that beholds unregulated markets as the principal mechanism for private and public goods distribution (Monckeberg 2001; Atria et al. 2013). Notably, a group of young economists with postgraduate studies at the Chicago School of economics, following Friedrich Hayek's and Milton Friedman's economic theories, exerted a decisive ideological influence over Pinochet's regime. As the State was considered an inefficient economic agent, key public services and enterprises were privatised, while subsidies were allocated in order to promote the access of insolvent populations to housing, health and education markets. Ever since, the capacities of the public sector to regulate economic activities in order to promote social benefits over private interests have been continuously eroded, due to constitutional and legislative restrictions to the scope of public action, limited budgets and a strong influence of private experts and interests over the design of public policies, (Garreton 2013).

In Chile, there is a close connivance of the economic and political elites, a phenomenon that is particularly conspicuous in urban policies, social housing and infrastructure projects. Under dictatorship, urban land limits were expanded and transportation markets were deregulated (Figueroa 2005; Poduje 2006), creating the initial conditions that allowed for a progressive capitalisation of these resources. After the recovery of democracy, a lucrative, subsidised and state-guaranteed concessions programme was created in order to develop transport infrastructures (Silva 2011), which was extended to a new urban transportation system in Greater Santiago (Garreton 2014). The Ministry of Housing and Urbanism, which was a powerful planning and social housing development agency before the dictatorship, progressively abandoned these tasks in favour of private investors, while specialising itself on the distribution of subsidies to insolvent families (Tokman 2006). Urban regulations were customised to stimulate construction and to boost housing markets, especially in central and pericentral areas (Lopez-Morales et al. 2012; Zunino 2006). All of these urban policies significantly contributed making up for huge housing and infrastructure needs accumulated under the dictatorship. They also allowed democratic governments to show that they were efficient administrators, in order to secure votes and to attract foreign investments. However, these goals implied a serious weakening of public capacities to regulate economic agents in key sectors for social welfare, thus aggravating and reifying inequalities through a differentiated access to housing and transportation opportunities.

Although there have been more visible social tensions and even scandals produced by the increasing power asymmetries in Chilean society – such as the massive students' protests of 2011 or the current judiciary processes for illegal political funding from several companies – our main interest is focused on the urban manifestation of social injustices. In fact, as "space is fundamental in any exercise of power" (Foucault 1984:252), we intend to highlight some key features of the long-lasting exclusionary urban structures that have been produced through political and socioeconomic domination. As it has been extensively documented in the 'neighbourhood effects' literature, this kind of adverse territorial conditions can have severe effects on the life prospects of their inhabitants (Frétigné 1999; Galster 2012; Sampson et al. 2002; Wacquant 2001). Thus, urban exclusion in Greater Santiago decisively contributes to the spatial accumulation and reproduction of social inequities.

The central thesis of this chapter is that the exclusionary urban policies implemented by Pinochet's dictatorship and by democratic governments since 1990, the public incentives for real estate development, and the marginalisation of vulnerable populations in violent urban environments are deeply entangled processes. We argue that these constitute an accumulation by dispossession design (Harvey 2003) that has evolved as a multifaceted but continuous process in Chile's recent history. Our objective is to show that the urban divide that is observed nowadays in Greater Santiago is not just an outcome of mechanical socioeconomic polarisation in an unregulated urban market, but mainly results from evolving forms of abuse of power that are intended for wealth hoarding. This accumulation by dispossession design is justified by the ideological argument that social policies are more efficient if they are boosted by private profits, involving a deliberate imagination, (un)planning and praxis, orchestrated by oligopolistic economic agents. The peculiar historical conditions of the implementation of neoliberal market discipline in Chile, directed by a small political-economic elite, sustain the thesis that this process has been developed with a high degree of self-conscious agency, actually being a neoliberal *delirium* that serves the purpose of hoarding wealth and reproducing privileges.

This chapter is organised as follows. We start with a brief exposition of accumulation by dispossession as a social, spatial, and historical trialectics synthesised in a conceptual model of wealth accumulation from land appropriation towards real estate development. This conceptualisation leads to an historical account that concretely shows how this design has been implemented in Chile, in two different but continuous and overlapping phases: land appropriation in dictatorship and real estate development in democracy. Next, we analyse the contemporary urban divide in Greater Santiago, following an historical process of forced eradication of low-income households to marginal areas, social housing massive developments in these sectors and formation of actual ghettos (Wacquant 2001), where low-income segregation and high levels of urban violence are observed nowadays. Our conclusion highlights the theoretical and historical inseparability of wealth and poverty production in the urban space of Greater Santiago.

Accumulation by dispossession: a social, historic and spatial *trialectics*

The combination of socioeconomic domination and urban structure in Greater Santiago can be analysed in the framework of Lefebvre's (1974) theory of capitalistic production as a spatial, historical and social trialectics, where all these dimensions are intertwined and reciprocally reinforcing. These relationships are particularly conspicuous in Chile, due to its recent history and the weakness of redistributive institutions (Lopez et al. 2013). Within a subsidiary State model, the public sector is constitutionally restrained to participate in any market where private providers exist, thus, public supply of primary goods is circumscribed to low-income groups that constitute an insolvent demand. Due to the lack of public funding, this produces a quality cleavage between high and low-income provision of essential services such as education and health, and marginalises public housing to peripheral, overcrowded and unsafe neighbourhoods.

The housing market in Chile is layered from a highly subsidised public housing, through progressive increments of households' contribution for property acquisition, up to an unsubsidised segment. Public grants to land acquisition are insufficient, so the location of these different kinds of projects is determined by the structure of land values, which generates a close spatial correspondence among household incomes, the geography of opportunities and the quality of local public services (Sabatini and Arenas 2000; Hidalgo 2007; Garreton 2013). As municipal income depends heavily on residents' wealth and the demand from vulnerable populations on basic public goods – as education, health and urban space – is concentrated in impoverished areas, local life quality deteriorates in these neighbourhoods while the opposite is observed in high-income sectors (Orellana 2009). In short, public institutions reinforce market trends that promote selective residential migration. As a consequence, socio-spatial segregation has become an uncontrolled vicious circle.

The inequalities that are reproduced by the redistributive weakness of local institutions are aggravated by the general dismantling of the regulatory capacities of public agencies and reinforcement of market discipline[1] (Brenner and Theodore 2002), due to reforms implemented during the military regime and after the restoration of democracy (Atria et al. 2013; Monckeberg 2001). Particularly, the unregulated urban market has been a key opportunity for progressive accumulation in real estate, first by land grabbing during the dictatorship (Hardy 1989) and more recently by the concentration of capital in a few huge real estate corporations that dominate the market in Greater Santiago (Lopez-Morales 2016). This political and economic design for the control of urban space has operated through a historic smooth transition from a 'forceful land appropriation' period towards a phase of 'accumulation in real estate'. Thus, social restructuration has been fuelled by a steady flow of wealth from 'commons dispossession' to a 'private capitalization' self-sustaining dynamic, being materialised in the social polarisation of urban space. These processes of accumulation by dispossession (Harvey 2003) can be synthesised in a conceptual diagram (Figure 3.1), which allows for an intuitive visualisation of their interconnection.

Indeed, land appropriation inflicted dispossession of common resources, eradicating families from properties that were well-located within environments with abundant employment opportunities and public services (lower-left dotted arrow in Figure 3.1). These premises were acquired by investors for a fraction of their future value, yielding substantial rent potentials for private capitals' expansion (wealth vector in Figure 3.1). More recently, this patrimony granted access to financial resources, which allowed to engage in massive high-rise developments to accumulate wealth as land capital gains and rental buildings (upper-right dotted arrow in Figure 3.1), thus maintaining sharp profit rates. As seen in Figure 3.1, each stage is intimately linked to the others, in a conspicuous example of a capitalistic growth cycle through urban commodification (Harvey 2010).

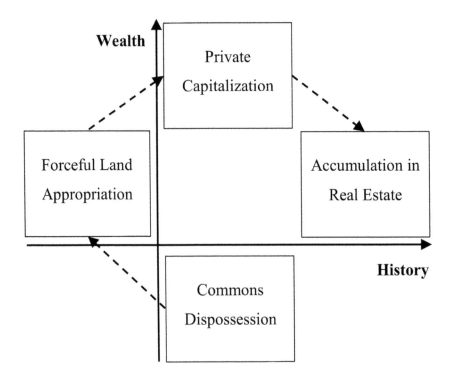

Figure 3.1 Urban accumulation by dispossession in Greater Santiago.

In sum, Greater Santiago's case can be considered as an unmitigated model of neoliberal strategies of accumulation by dispossession (Harvey 2003) in an urban context, which operates as a social, historical and spatial trialectics of capitalistic urban production (Lefebvre 1974; Soja 2010). Although these facets are articulated as a continuous process – where forceful land appropriation and accumulation in real estate evolve and can co-exist but predominate in different times – it is illustrative to describe both mechanisms in the context of different periods, under dictatorship and in democracy. Thus, the purpose of the next two sections is to show how this wealth hoarding design has concretely operated in Greater Santiago's recent history.

Forceful land appropriation

Forceful land appropriation constitutes the foundation of a highly lucrative real estate market that operates in Greater Santiago, boosted by public subventions and regulations that directly increase the profits of private investments. In recent history, this mechanism has adopted different forms, from the use of military force to legal procedures, either judiciary, economic or normative. After the *coup d'état* a massive urban restructuration was implemented in Chile and particularly in Greater Santiago (Figure 3.2), with the intent of segregating the population in more homogeneous low, middle and high-income sectors (Hardy 1989; Rodríguez and Rodríguez 2009). In the operations 'Confraternidad' I of 1976 and II in 1978 15,000 persons were relocated from high-income sectors to peripheral slums (Leyton, forthcoming), starting a 'National Urban Development Policy' until 1987, which violently marginalised 130,000 families all over Chile (Rodríguez and Rodríguez 2009).

These massive relocations were a brutal exercise of biopower[2] (Foucault 1976), an authoritarian decision that twisted the life trajectories of the eradicated families in order to impose two kinds of social control. First, working-class communities were considered a place of potential subversion, as they provided a territory for the organisation and concealment of revolutionary cells amidst the headquarters of political and economic powers in Greater Santiago. So, these communities were dismantled, and their members sent to different destinations, where rumours about the infiltration of military agents dissuaded the reorganisation of communities (Hardy 1989). As a consequence, families were dispossessed of their employment and social networks, and their sons and grandsons grew up in places of confrontation and mistrust. Second, Greater Santiago's land market segmentation was reinforced, both by the eradication of low-income families from wealthy neighbourhoods as by the redefinition of municipal circumscriptions following social homogeneity criteria (Rodríguez and Rodríguez 2009). High-income homogeneity is a main driver for increasing real estate prices and local institutions that can reinvest local taxes with low redistributive engagements intensified this trend, so this administrative restructuration paved the way for future speculation and high-rise development in high-income sectors (Hardy 1989; Lopez-Morales 2012).

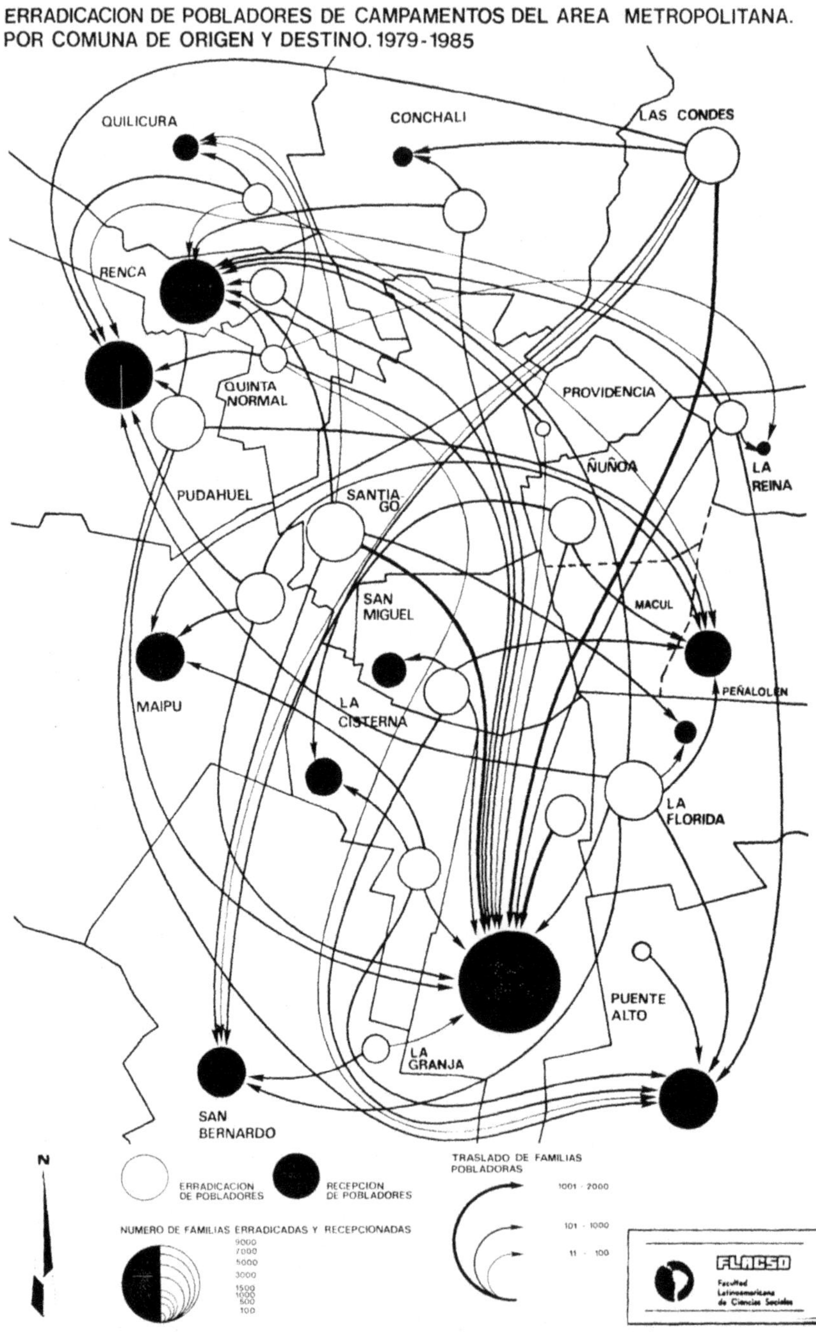

ERRADICACION DE POBLADORES DE CAMPAMENTOS DEL AREA METROPOLITANA.
POR COMUNA DE ORIGEN Y DESTINO. 1979-1985

Figure 3.2 Eradications in Greater Santiago under Pinochet's dictatorship.
Source: Morales et al. (1990).

With the restoration of democracy, more subtle ways were used to secure land for development, both legal and illegal. A striking case occurred in '*Villa San Luis*', a social housing project located in a high-income sector, which was inhabited by 1,038 working-class families, of which only 116 resisted the first waves of eradication in 1976 and 1978. A few months before the restoration of democracy, the property rights were fraudulently transferred to the Ministry of National Assets and afterwards to the Ministry of Defence (Lawner 2007). In 1995, the conservative mayor of *Las Condes* municipality changed land regulations in order to allow non-housing and high-rise projects in the sector. In 1996, *Villa San Luis* was sold to a realtor for US$ 89 million, for the development of the biggest project up to that date in Chile, estimated in US$ 800 million.[3]

The remaining 116 households received offers that soared from US$ 300000 up to a million dollars for their small apartments. In contrast, four hundred previously eradicated families filed a collective lawsuit but gave up with a pale compensation of less than US$ 4,000, while 500 were never found nor compensated. As this was negotiated, it could be discussed if in this case it is proper to talk about forceful appropriation, and we argue it is indeed, on the grounds of the enormous asymmetries of power between the involved parties. On one side, low-income families for which the prospect of a long judiciary process is extremely daunting, or who resist in a degraded environment among abandoned homes. On the other side, a powerful economic holding that had as investors some of richest and more politically influent person in Chile (Lawner 2007).

In short, even if forceful land appropriation was most clearly imposed in the dictatorship, several economic and institutional mechanisms sustain this process in Chilean democracy, with the counterpart of subsidiary housing policies that concentrate the excluded in impoverished and marginal areas. Thus, since the coup d'état there has been a flow of wealth from the public sector and low and middle-income populations, in the form of advantageous transactions of property that have yielded huge real estate gains. Moreover, this kind of land grabbing has also provided the conditions for a further stage of urban capital accumulation, which will be discussed in the next section.

Accumulation in real estate

Accumulation in Real Estate is the final stage of a design for wealth hoarding through the control of urban space, allowing to reinvest private capitals in land that has often been forcefully acquired, by violence or economic domination (Figure 3.1). This mechanism for private capitalisation is self-sustaining, obtaining profits from land rent speculation and the capture of public regulators. As capitals accumulate, the leverage over both of these processes is reinforced, thus enhancing the whole dynamic. The most apparent case among many examples of this mechanism are the high-rise development of housing in downtown Santiago (Figure 3.3) and the displacement of the Central Business District (CBD) of Greater Santiago (Figures 3.4 and 3.6).

Figure 3.3 High-rise housing in downtown Santiago.
Source: La Tercera.[4]

Towards the end of the dictatorship, downtown Santiago presented a notorious decay, having lost one-third of its population since a peak reached around 1950. The combined effect of the eradications and the 1985 earthquake had produced numerous vacant lots and wrecked buildings (Contreras 2011). In order to revert this situation, since 1992 its municipality implemented the plan for the repopulation of Santiago, identifying the owners of suitable land and connecting them with real estate developers, in order to facilitate land transactions. The state offered generous regeneration subsidies, and the municipality lifted building restrictions, allowing for more than thirty floors in some neighbourhoods. This plan was a success in terms of reverting the depopulation of Santiago, but the result has been criticised on the grounds of the inhospitable urban form that has been produced and because of the loss of functions in a traditionally diverse environment (Contreras 2011; Casgrain 2013).

With this brief account, I do not intend to evaluate this repopulation plan, as has been done elsewhere (Op. cit.), but I argue that it was mainly designed to provide a very advantageous opportunity for investing in real estate, rather than being shaped by social or urbanistic goals. Indeed, the explosive concentration of investments in Santiago's repopulation plan indicates that the returns on these investments were highly competitive even in the Chilean economic environment, which is characterised by strong incentives for capital attraction. Beyond realtors, this also includes investors in rental properties, who obtain a considerable income from a highly demanded sector where rents have soared in recent years. In fact, between 1992 and 2012, the resident's composition of Santiago changed from 0.9 to 1.5 tenants for each proprietor household.[5]

Following this residential expansion, huge investments have been made in office space in an axis that extends from downtown Santiago towards the east (Figures 4 and 6). This has displaced the economic centrality of Greater Santiago, reducing the distance of the functional CBD to the high-income cone, which is located in the northeast of Greater Santiago (Figure 3.6). Two huge developments have propelled this urban restructuration, each one consolidating a new secondary business centrality. The most recent, called *Nueva Las Condes* has been developed on the grounds of the aforementioned *Villa San Luis* and, being the seat of high-end office spaces of global companies, offers the most compelling example of accumulation by dispossession that I am aware of in Chile. The former, known as 'Sanhattan', a satirical contraction of *Santiago* and *Manhattan*, has become the main financial district of Greater Santiago, displacing the historical centre from this role (Figure 3.4). This development started with the Ministry of Housing and Urbanism Decree n° 20 of 1994 and the corresponding modifications of municipal regulations in the same area, which allowed the reconversion of a vast property of the former National Beer Factory and its surroundings into high-rise office buildings.

Successive height records have been broken in this sector, up to the recently finished *Costanera Centre*, which reaches up to 300 meters, also including a mall, two five-star hotels and two 'secondary' forty-story office buildings. This construction faced several lawsuits for conspicuous violations of the building permits until its developers announced the suspension of the project in the context of a downturn in economic activity after the 2008 subprime crisis. In 2009, in order

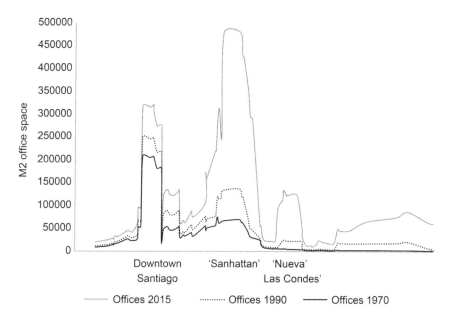

Figure 3.4 Sanhattan displaces downtown as the main CBD of Greater Santiago.

Source: Author's calculations based on SII[6] built surfaces cadaster.

Figure 3.5 Sanhattan skyline, the new CBD of Greater Santiago.
Source: El Mercurio.[7]

to sustain employment and investment rates in Greater Santiago, the Ministry of Transport and other public regulators issued several decrees and resolutions that allowed for the continuation of the works (CCHC 2012). Thus, the developers of this gigantic project managed to avoid paying for an important share of the mandatory road infrastructures that would have been necessary to absorb the additional traffic generated by these premises. This kind of regulation, which is normally applied in Chile, intends that the costs of absorbing increased traffic flows – which are attracted by new commerce, offices and housing – be discounted from the private profits that are generated by these developments. As this condition was not fulfilled, nowadays this sector suffers a severe and worsening traffic congestion.

A detailed analysis of the process of capture of public regulators by private urban investors in Chile (Garreton 2014; Lopez-Morales et al. 2012; Silva 2011; Zunino 2006) is beyond the scope of this brief account, but a pattern can be highlighted from these examples of massive investments. Land has been secured by violence, illegal procedures or overwhelming economic power, building regulations have been loosened by national and local authorities, and any irregularities have been ironed out by executive decrees, thus bypassing legislative procedures (Zunino 2006). This process is effective for capital accumulation, producing huge capital gains and agglomeration externalities, but I insist on the radical asymmetries that favour a progressive overconcentration of capitals at the expense of the common citizen. In short, implicit or explicit subventions and normative adjustments in key urban developments are mainly focused on capital attraction, and social benefits are misleadingly expected to be an automatic consequence of private investments.

In fact, the neoliberal presumption that public policy efficiency is dependent on private investments has allowed designing an organised set of practices for urban accumulation by dispossession (Figure 3.1) that has decisively contributed to a massive socio-spatial divide in Greater Santiago. Thus, privileged neighbourhoods concentrate investments and wealth while vast areas accommodate a numerous excluded population in violent environments. This neglected side of the coin will be briefly described in the next section.

Social exclusion and urban violence

In the previous sections I outlined few key factors around the complex historical processes of social restructuration, initiated by the neoliberal reforms of Pinochet's dictatorship, that have crystallised in the contemporary urban space of Greater Santiago as a massive pattern of socioeconomic segregation. In fact, this metropolis of 6 million inhabitants shows a high-income cone in its northeastern quadrant, which is conspicuously opposed to several low-income clusters distributed in a wide peripheral arc spanning the north, west and south of the agglomeration (Figure 3.6).

In order to elaborate a cartographic representation of these socio-spatial inequalities, I have superposed a segregation analysis with a crime hotspot analysis (Figure 3.6), both realised with ArcMap software. In this case, segregation was measured as a statistically significant spatial autocorrelation (calculated with an analysis of Local Moran indexes) of low-income and of high-income residential homogeneity. Likewise, the concentration of urban violence was ascertained through a hotspot analysis (identifying statistically significant clustering with Getis Ord indexes) of crime reports, considering drug-related offenses, illegal weapons use or possession, homicides, rapes, different kinds of aggressions, damages to property, robbery and theft. The superposition of the geographies of residential segregation and urban violence allows to show that the urban divide in Greater Santiago is not a purely economic phenomenon, as it also exposes low-income families to deeper forms of social insecurity and punitive policies in the form of a focused police action (Wacquant 2010). Moreover, the analysis of spatial autocorrelation and clustering suggests that segregation and violence are locally auto-produced phenomena, meaning that the concentration of poverty and crime could be a direct cause of their own reproduction in their surroundings (Jacobs 1961; Caldeira 2000).

Remarkably, the low-income segregation clusters in Greater Santiago almost perfectly match the hotspots of crimes in public spaces,[8] which suggest that both are spatially co-producing phenomena (Figure 3.6). Moreover, these areas also correspond to the destinations of the families which were violently eradicated during the dictatorship (Figure 3.2) or to massive projects of social housing which were developed in democracy. In fact, the sons and grandsons of the eradicated families have grown in places of confrontation and mistrust among neighbours,

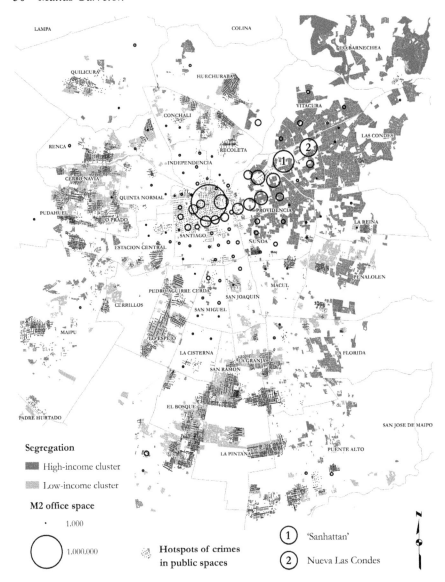

Figure 3.6 Segregation, Urban Violence and business districts in Greater Santiago.

Sources: Own elaboration based on Ministry of National Security offense reports, Internal Revenue Service cadaster of built surfaces, Census 2012.

having been displaced by State's violence or marginalised by subsidiary housing policies, which have forced their beneficiaries to accept the available accommodations even if they were in unwanted peripheral locations (Ducci 1997).

Moreover, within a strongly segregated educational system and facing highly unequal revenues in the labour market, there seem to be few incentives for unqualified citizens to adhere to a globalised cultural model. Instead, local cultures of exclusion seem to be developing in Greater Santiago, where illegal behaviours and insertion in a drug-dealing economy can be attractive ways for social integration (Ortega 2014; Sánchez-Jankowski 2003).

On the contrary, the high-income cone shows no relevant urban violence hotspots and has been favoured by the restructuration of Greater Santiago's CBD, as mentioned above. In fact, the '*Sanhattan*' and *Nueva Las Condes* developments appear as new employment sub-centralities that are strategically located in the midst of the main high-income cluster of the urban area (Figure 3.3). These developments are providing good job accessibility to high-qualification workers – by proximity and through toll-financed urban speedways – and an abundant labour supply to financial and skilled-services companies. Thus, high-income residential segregation is reinforced by functional autonomy and increasing land values, setting apart an upper class urban sub-system where there is no need to interact with the rest of the metropolis in a daily basis. In short, the spatial restructuration of Greater Santiago in recent years has accentuated the divide between excluded and violent areas and a safe, privileged zone where land values soar and where globalised capitalistic processes of accumulation can function in self-seclusion.

Conclusion

This brief account of some of the most salient processes that have reshaped Greater Santiago since Pinochet's dictatorship is certainly incomplete, but it clearly shows how key urban policies have been shaped under the neoliberal presumption that guaranteeing private profits is necessary for designing public policies, highlighting the dire social consequences that this has produced. The abysmal urban divide that is evident in this metropolis is a direct consequence of flawed planning, mainly due to the marginalisation of massive social housing developments and deregulation of high-rise construction, favouring capital accumulation by increasing land rents while failing to tax developers for the congestion costs that huge projects impose on their surroundings. This critical analysis emphasises that, even as public spending in social policies has increased, the restructuration of Greater Santiago has fostered regressive wealth transfers due to policymaking practices that are mainly designed to guarantee private profits. Understanding this wealth hoarding design is necessary in order to promote alternatives for just urban development (Fainstein 2010)

The Chilean neoliberal model of urban development was implemented in Pinochet's dictatorship and has been deepened by democratic authorities, as shown by the historical and geographical entwinement of social dispossession and clustering of urban violence in Greater Santiago, in stark contrast with areas of capital accumulation. Indeed, forceful land appropriation by military or economic force was a necessary step for accumulation in real estate, particularly in high-end developments. Both mechanisms must be understood within a continuous wealth transfer from impoverished groups towards a politic-economic elite (Matamala 2015); Monckeberg 2001), materialised through an urban capital growth cycle (Harvey 2010). All of these complementary processes (Figure 3.1) serve a purpose of wealth hoarding through the private control of urban development, under a deliberate design that is implemented by regulatory capture and that ignores the social costs that are imposed on disadvantaged groups.

Recent history shows how social exclusion in Greater Santiago has been aggravated by the forced concentration of low-income households in order to impose political control, to increase real estate gains or by the inadequacy of housing policies. I have briefly shown that the forcing out of *Villa San Luis* families was instrumental for the development of *Nueva Las Condes*, which became the most exclusive employment sub-centrality in the metropolitan area. This narrative exemplifies how the neoliberal urban policies implemented in Pinochet's dictatorship and during democratic governments has set off a social polarisation trend, which is self-reinforcing through the divergent spatial auto-production of prosperity and poverty. This is not just a 'natural' outcome of a deregulated market, but rather a result of power abuse for wealth hoarding by urban commodification, which has been fostered until today by public policies.

The consequences of this profit-driven approach of urban development are conspicuous in Greater Santiago's geography, where I estimate that one out of eight inhabitants resides in areas of low-income segregation and severe violence in public spaces while high-income groups develop a self-secluded city with specialised employment sub-centralities. This deepening urban divide can lead to a recrudescence of conflict and fear at a metropolitan scale, eroding the foundations of democratic co-existence. However, this kind of socio-spatial divide cannot be healed with subsidiary policies or with repressive police action, which characterise neoliberal urban development (Herbert and Brown 2006). We should be aware that the stigmatisation of the poor and the reinforcement of the penal apparatus are concomitant with the attrition of social welfare, both being instrumental processes for crafting neoliberal States (Wacquant 2010). Thus, rather than a glimpse of a turning point, this critical account should alert us of the risk of further intensification of this regime, fuelled by a 'bureaucratic field' (Bourdieu 2004) that has been captured by private interests while public capacities for investment and planning continuously erode.

I hope that the critical analysis of pro-entrepreneurial urban policies in Chile (Lopez-Morales et al. 2012), which are rooted in the social divides imposed in dictatorship and have been deepened by democratic governments, will help to build up collective pressure for the reinforcement of urban regulations and for the development of proactive socio-spatial integration policies (Fainstein 2010).

Notes

1 A sad example was the privatisation of water sources, in order to create a market for the administration of this resource, which has led to a large-scale appropriation by mining companies and export-oriented agriculture, to the overexploitation of sources and to endanger the supply for local populations and traditional agriculture.

2 Foucault develops the concept of biopower in a historical perspective, from the monarch's power over life and death towards the nation-state's power of sustaining and regulating life – or letting to die -, through punitive, health and welfare policies. In modern

societies, biopower is designed to discipline the bodies and to control the population, in order to make these "resources" available to capitalistic production, being an essential instrument for the development of modern capitalism. In a neoliberal context, biopower can be used to impose market discipline directly to individuals, through social insecurity and punitive policies (Wacquant 2010).

3 As it was triumphantly reported by the conservative newspaper "El Mercurio" on May 26th 1996.

4 Illustration of an article about constraining construction heights in downtown Santiago http://diario.latercera.com/2011/07/11/01/contenido/santiago/32-76090-9-plan-regulador-de-santiago-prohibira-nuevos-edificios-de-mas-de-16-pisos.shtml

5 Author's calculation with Census 1992 and 2012 data.

6 Chile's Internal Revenue Service: *Servicio de Impuestos Internos*

7 Illustration of an article that promotes *Costanera Center* as world-class office space www.edicionesespeciales.elmercurio.com/destacadas/detalle/index.asp?idnoticia= 201503301862480

8 The only exception occurs in downtown Santiago and following main transport corridors, where urban violence is related to a high density of floating population.

References

Atria, F. et al. (2013) *El otro modelo. Del orden neoliberal al régimen de lo público*, Santiago, Chile: Debate.

Bourdieu, P. (2004) From the King's House to the Reason of State: A Model of the Genesis of the Bureaucratic Field, Constellations, Vol. 11(1), pp. 16–36.

Brenner, N. & Theodore, N. (2002) Cities and the Geographies of 'Actually Existing Neoliberalism'. *Antipode*, Vol. 34(3), pp. 349–379.

Caldeira, T.P. & Do, R. (2000) *City of Walls: Crime, Segregation, and Citizenship in São Paulo*, Stanford: University of California Press.

Casgrain, A. & Janoschka, M. (2013) Gentrificación y resistencia en las ciudades latinoamericanas. El ejemplo de Santiago de Chile. *Andamios. Revista de Investigación Social*, 10(22), pp. 19–44.

CCHC (2012) Cronología de Sanhattan vista desde el Costanera Centre y sus impactos viales. Available at: www.cchc.cl/wp-content/uploads/2012/06/Minuta-CTR-N%C2%BA06-Cronolog%C3%ADa-Sanhattan.pdf [Accessed February 2, 2015].

Contreras Gatica, Y. (2011) La recuperación urbana y residencial del centro de Santiago: Nuevos habitantes, cambios socioespaciales significativos. *EURE*, Vol. 37(112), pp. 89–113.

Ducci, M.E. (1997) Chile: el lado obscuro de una política de vivienda exitosa. *EURE*, Vol. 23(69), pp. 99–115.

Fainstein, S.S. (2010) *The Just City*, New York: Cornell University Press.

Figueroa, O. (2005) Transporte urbano y globalización: Políticas y efectos en América Latina. *EURE*, Vol. 31, pp. 41–53.

Foucault, M. (1976) *La volonté de savoir*, Paris: Gallimard.

Foucault, M. (1984) *The Foucault Reader*. Ed: Paul Rabinow, New York: Pantheon Books.

Frétigné, C. (1999) *Sociologie de l'Exclusion*, Paris: Editions L'Harmattan.

Galster, G.C. (2012) The Mechanism(s) of Neighbourhood Effects: Theory, Evidence, and Policy Implications, in M. van Ham et al., eds. *Neighbourhood Effects Research: New Perspectives*, The Netherlands: Springer, pp. 23–56.

Garreton, M. (2013) Mobility inequalities in Greater Santiago and the Ile-de-France region: Housing and transport policies in metropolitan governance. PhD Thesis. Université Paris-Est: Paris.

Garreton, M. (2014) Derecho a la Ciudad y participación frente al centralismo en Chile. *Revista 180*, Vol. 18(34), pp. 4–9.

Giddens, A. (1984). The constitution of society: Outline of the theory of structuration. University of California Press.

Hardy, C. (1989) *La ciudad escindida*, Santiago, Chile: Alborada.

Harvey, D. (2003) *The New Imperialism*, Oxford: Oxford University Press.

Harvey, D. (2010) The Right to the City: From Capital Surplus to Accumulation by Dispossession, in Banerjee-Guha, S. (Ed.). *Accumulation by Dispossession: Transformative Cities in the New Global Order*, Thousand Oaks, CA: Sage Publications, pp. 19–32.

Herbert, S. & Brown, E. (2006) Conceptions of Space and Crime in the Punitive Neoliberal City. *Antipode*, Vol. 38(4), pp. 755–777.

Hidalgo, R. (2007) ¿Se acabó el suelo en la gran ciudad? Las nuevas periferias metropolitanas de la vivienda social en Santiago de Chile. *EURE*, Vol. 33(98), pp. 57–75.

Jacobs, J. (1961) *The Death and Life of Great American Cities*, New York: Vintage Books.

Lawner, M, (2007) *Demolición de la Villa San Luis en las Condes, historia de dos despojos*, Santiago, Chile: Centro De Estudios Nacionales de Desarrollo Alternativo (CENDA). Available at: www.cendachile.cl/Home/publicaciones/autores/miguel-lawner/miguel-lawner-documentos

Lefebvre, H. (1974) La production de l'espace. *L'Homme et la société*, Vol. 31(1), pp. 15–32.

Lopez, R. Figueroa, E. & Gutiérrez, P. (2013) *La parte del león: nuevas estimaciones de la participación de los súper ricos en el ingreso de Chile*, Santiago: Facultad de Economía y Negocios, Universidad de Chile. Available at: www.econ.uchile.cl/uploads/publicacio n/306018fadb3ac79952bf1395a555a90a86633790.pdf

Lopez-Morales, E., (2016) Gentrification in Santiago, Chile: A property-led process of dispossession and exclusión. *Urban Geography*, published online, pp. 1–23. Available at: www.tandfonline.com/doi/abs/10.1080/02723638.2016.1149311

Lopez-Morales, E. Gasic, I. & Meza, D. (2012) Urbanismo pro-empresarial en Chile: políticas y planificación de la producción residencial en altura en el pericentro del Gran Santiago. *Revista INVI*, Vol. 27(76), pp. 75–114.

Matamala, D. (2015) *Poderoso caballero: el peso del dinero en la política chilena*, Santiago, Chile: Catalonia.

Monckeberg, M.O. (2001) *El Saqueo de los grupos económicos al Estado de Chile*, Santiago, Chile: Ediciones B.

Morales, E. Levy, S. Aldunate, A. & Rojas, S. (1990) Erradicados en el régimen militar, una evaluación de los beneficiarios, FLACSO – Chile. Available at: http://cronopio. flacso.cl/fondo/pub/publicos/1990/DT/000226.pdf [Accessed October 20, 2014].

OECD, (2011) *Maintaining Momentum OECD Perspectives on Policy Challenges in Chile: OECD Perspectives on Policy Challenges in Chile*, Paris: OECD Publishing.

Orellana, A. (2009) La gobernabilidad metropolitana de Santiago: la dispar relación de poder de los municipios. *EURE*, Vol. 35(104), pp. 101–120.

Ortega, T. (2014) Criminalización y concentración de la pobreza urbana en barrios segregados: Síntomas de guetización en La Pintana, Santiago de Chile. *EURE*, Vol. 40(120), pp. 241–263.

Rodríguez, A. & Rodríguez, P. (2009) *Santiago, una ciudad neoliberal*, Quito: Organización Latinoamericana y del Caribe de Centros Históricos.

Sabatini, F. & Arenas, F. (2000) Entre el Estado y el mercado: resonancias geográficas y sustentabilidad social en Santiago de Chile. *EURE*, Vol. 26(79), pp. 95–113.

Sampson, R.J. Morenoff, J.D. & Gannon-Rowley, T. (2002) Assessing 'Neighborhood Effects': Social Processes and New Directions in Research. *Annual Review of Sociology*, Vol. 28, pp. 443–478.

Sánchez-Jankowski, M. (2003) Gangs and Social Change. *Theoretical Criminology*, Vol. 7(2), pp. 191–216.

Silva, E.R. (2011) Deliberate Improvisation: Planning Highway Franchises in Santiago, Chile. *Planning Theory*, Vol. 10(1), pp. 35–52.

Soja, E.W. (2010) *Seeking Spatial Justice*, Minneapolis: University of Minnesota Press.

Tokman, V. E. (2006). *Inserción laboral, mercados de trabajo y protección social*. Santiago: CEPAL.

Wacquant, L. (2001) *Parias urbanos: marginalidad en la ciudad*, Buenos Aires, Argentina: Manantial.

Wacquant, L. (2010) Crafting the Neoliberal State: Workfare, Prisonfare, and Social Insecurity. *Sociological Forum*, Vol. 25(2), pp. 197–220.

Zunino, H.M. (2006) Power Relations in Urban Decision-Making: Neo-Liberalism, 'Techno-Politicians' and Authoritarian Redevelopment in Santiago, Chile. *Urban Studies*, Vol. 43(10), pp. 1825–1846.

4 The politico-economic sides of the high-rise new-build gentrification of Santiago, Chile

Ernesto Lopez-Morales

Introduction

For the last decade, the gentrification effects derived from the privately-led, piecemeal high-rise renovation of the inner areas in the main Chilean cities have deserved increasing academic and political concern (Janoschka et al. 2014; Inzulza-Contardo 2012; 2016; Contreras 2011; Casgrain and Janoschka 2013; Lopez-Morales 2008; 2011; 2015a; 2015b; Lopez-Morales et al. 2016; Vergara-Constela and Casellas 2016). In Santiago, Chile, since 1990, its central area has witnessed an enormous amount of high-rise residential construction, as a supposedly environmentally efficient solution to counteract urban sprawl (Contrucci 2011). Even though, some local scholars argue that both central redevelopment and urban sprawl, for the last two decades, go hand by hand as the rate of suburban residential development has remained stable (De Mattos et al. 2014). Between 1990 and 2010, more than 250,000 new apartments were privately built in the 11 inner municipalities (of a total 38) of Santiago, aimed to the middle-income strata, for a total population of the city of 6.5 million. Indeed, this privately-led residential market has been very effective at attracting new population and property-led residential redevelopment into a number of inner city districts of Santiago that up to the nineties had considerably lost population and long been abandoned from private and public interest.[1]

Nevertheless this residential market has also meant that centrally located land and residence has become more expensive for the low-income population who originally lived there, making this space also inaccessible for new population belonging to the two lowest socioeconomic quintiles, that 15 years ago could have still been able to buy new apartments there. This market has generated the "exclusionary displacement" (Marcuse 1985; Slater 2009; Lopez-Morales 2015a) of the low-income resident population that, roughly speaking, belong to the two lowest socioeconomic quintiles of the country, through a form of "gentrification by ground rent dispossession" (Lopez-Morales 2011) of an important part of the local residents; I explain this phenomenon below.

However, some time ago the property-led market of high-rise residential renewal was strongly advocated by some international advisors. For instance, the International Development Bank advisor Rojas (2004) in his well-known book

'Volver al Centro' describes property-led, piecemeal redevelopment in Santiago as a desirable goal for a state policy that should manage to attract real estate and infrastructure reinvestment to central land and promote it as a socially inclusive policy. However, on the contrary, Santiago's housing market is probably one of the clearest examples of how private forces are ruling the Chilean urban economy. Redevelopers of the inner areas upgrade the socioeconomic composition of central neighbourhoods, obtain the highest margins of the potential ground rent that lies in those land plots by selling increasingly more expensive departments, and displace the most deprived households among low-income locals. Up to now, displacement has often occurred because as long as one or a few private firms enter a neighbourhood, original owner-residents who come to sell their land to real estate redevelopers receive a lowered price that does not come from competitive bidding but from a disadvantaged negotiation position that limits their post-occupancy options; 'financial culture' is often absent among local residents, as people usually do not know the exact value of the land they occupy or own, and much less they have the means to bargain with large-scale redevelopers (Lopez-Morales 2015a; 2015b).

In Santiago, the capital of the country, the whole economic power structure of central areas relies on this inequality among social and corporate economic agents. An example is given by Lopez-Morales (2015a), who shows the extent to which the ground rent per square meter of land is being accumulated by real estate redevelopers; this happens after the new units are sold, and due to the burgeoning housing prices they impose, this value can be often eight or more times greater than the price redevelopers paid to original residents for their land, which is often insufficient to meet the needs of housing relocation for original owner-residents (in the core municipality of the city, up to 50% landowners do not receive enough cash compensation for the land they sell to redevelopers; see Lopez-Morales 2015a). No land value capture policy exists in the country, unlike others in Latin America like Brazil and Colombia (Smolka 2013) as an eventual mechanism of redistribution of the land valorisation that takes place after the state provision of transport infrastructure like Metro, several public parks, or other public goods like schools and health centres that exist close to these renovating areas.

What was omitted by Rojas in 2004 is that urban ground rent does not grow 'naturally' anywhere; it requires that land is enabled and equipped with infrastructure and connected with the rest of the city through state-supplied networks, mobility and zoning laws. This is one of the fundamental laws in urban economics (Evans 2004). Therefore, the ground rent increases mostly due to state action in the provision of transportation infrastructure as well as the state monopolised changes in construction codes, and Floor Area Ratios (FAR) included in municipal-level master plans; the higher the FAR, the more profitable is the privately-led high-rise construction business. The provision of new transport access possibilities (since 1990 onwards, seven new or extended Metro Lines have been built or are under construction) enables certain territories to be more attractive to certain, usually the largest-scale real estate companies, but they have to pay higher prices if they want to buy that land and use it to host their projects.

The concept of ground rent has been largely theorised since Marx's Capital (who never carried out an 'urban' analysis proper), but a new wave of critical geographers have placed the concept at the centre of the debates about urban redevelopment and gentrification (Smith 1979; Clark 1987; Hammel 1999; Lees et al. 2008; Lopez-Morales 2011; 2015a; Lees et al. 2016, among many others). The nature of the ground rent is political, as its differential values are differentially captured according to each agent's economic and political power. Important questions derived from ground rent are how many parties and who exactly captures that value, to the benefit of whom, and what are the social costs its private capture generates. Following Neil Smith's thesis on rent gap (Smith 1979), I have previously advanced a more precise terminology that explains the intensive disputes on ground rent appropriation between original low-income residents (who only can absorb the smallest part of the rent gap) and upper-income redevelopers in the gentrifying areas (who almost monopolise the greatest part of the rent gap), namely "gentrification by ground rent dispossession" (Lopez-Morales 2011). In the case of Chile, there are extreme power differences between original residents and large-scale redevelopers who monopolise that rent, whilst the public policy usually encourages property-led redevelopment, support it through public investment in certain neighbourhoods, while at the same time the state seems to be blind to the gentrifying effects generated by the market of high-rise redevelopment (Lopez-Morales et al. 2012).

My argument here is that in Chile, as a country that grows and approaches unprecedented levels of development (with a GDP [PPP] per capita of about US\$ 23,500, the highest in South America[2]), land and housing policies are socially inefficient and tend to rise housing prices and increase segregation effects exclusively for reasons of the private accumulation of the ground rent by the largest-scale real estate private firms who dominate the housing market. This sole fact can be regarded as one of the crudest faces of the Chilean urban neoliberalism, which is regarded as one of the most rampantly unregulated sectors in Latin America (OECD 2012). By 2012, in Santiago Centro commune (the core of the Greater Santiago metropolis), four large-scale companies supplied half of the new units and so they have the largest stake in the market; comparatively, these firms' economic power is considerably higher than the almost forty other smaller construction firms operating there, and, obviously, the original owner-residents find problems when they come to negotiate land prices with the largest-scale firms. In the following paragraphs, I explain how and why this is a critical problem; and at the end of the chapter I suggest how a more comprehensive public housing policy and a multidimensional approach could ensure socioeconomic inclusion in many urban areas.[3] Also, I addressed the efforts made by the national state from the early nineties to subsidise intensively the private market of redevelopment, initially aimed to include an ample array of households ranging from low- to upper-income strata, but this market soon became exclusionary for the increasing prices of the unit supplied and the low cash compensation private redevelopers gave to original residents when they came to sell their land to construction firms. I also address the key role municipalities have at increasing the FAR, the rate of the building total floor size area and the size area of the plot where the building is constructed) in certain areas in order to increase the revenues to be obtained by private redevelopers. The privately-led, high-rise urban renewal in Chilean cities is not an efficient solution for the urban sprawl, but it increases that problem through the displacement of the poorest social segments to the peripheries for reasons of ground rent accumulation.

From inclusive to elitist urban renewal: the state-led gentrification of Santiago

During the last third of the military dictatorship, specifically in 1985, a massive earthquake hit the central area of Chile, creating an urgent need for a new policy of urban renewal that was later developed by the Ministry of Housing and Planning under the democratic regime (from 1990 onwards). This policy attempted to regenerate vast inner areas that at the time were deemed uninhabitable and derelict, while at the same time, this policy aimed to reverse the 'depopulation' of the 11 central and pericentral local communes of Santiago (Valenzuela 2003; Arriagada et al. 2007). For the years 1982, 1992 and 2002, these communes showed negative rates of population variation (even though by 2002, 40% of the metropolitan population of Santiago still lived there, and it mostly corresponded to the two lowest socioeconomic quintiles of the population). At that time, there had been little public and private investment to improve the living conditions in those neighbourhoods, which are characterised by one- and two-story buildings, many of them almost one century old. Currently, besides the original low-income population, these territories have also been progressively occupied by foreign immigrants who inhabit overcrowded, derelict properties, but compensate their poor living conditions with a very central location, especially since their massive arrival in the country in the late nineties (Borsdorf and Hidalgo 2013).

In 1991, seeking to counteract those negative population trends, the Ministry of Housing and Urbanism launched a subsidy aimed to benefit middle-income purchasers of new apartments located within an Urban Renewal Area in 8,500 hectares. The maximum amount to cover by the subsidy was 10% of the total sales price of the new units, and whose price should be up to UF 200[4] (currently, 213 times the minimum monthly wage). To this end, most municipalities' upzoned those areas in order to attract high-rise real estate activity by offering more profitable chances for investment. They also created ad hoc private-municipal agencies for promoting private and public land to the market for redevelopment. Almost all newly built, privately led projects have been located next to public services, parks and other state-built amenities, and connected to a growing number of transport networks and infrastructures such as Metro (urban underground), Bus lines and Transantiago (Bus Rapid Transit system implemented in 2007). Between 2000 and 2014, the FAR increased to a current average rate of 8.

However, 25 years later, although massive repopulation has been achieved for the central neighbourhoods of the metropolis (INE 2012, showed 40% population increase between 2002 and 2012) mostly because the effects of the high-rise housing market in these areas, the sales prices of these new residential units have also considerably increased. Nowadays, urban renewal subsidies are only covering 30% of the purchases of newly built apartments, because those prices are more expensive than the maximum allowed by the subsidy. This phenomenon is part of a general failure of the system of housing subsidies in the city. Concretely, the total number of subsidies issued for affordable housing is not matched by the number of affordable apartments and houses actually built by the private sector (for instance, 40% of beneficiaries of subsidies issued by the government aimed to buy new dwellings priced under UF 1,200 do not find the actual supply of homes). However, the price increase of apartments located in central areas has hitherto not been seen as a problem by the public sector. For instance, most central municipalities have kept attempting to 'seduce' and attract more real estate activity into their territories via upzoning their local master plans and offering building regulations that assure high ground rent absorption to private real estate firms. In fact, in ten of the 11 central and pericentral communes of Santiago, municipal-level master plans started to be created in the 2000s to upzone their land aggressively, while mandatory environmental assessments were made more flexible. But a major problem came when these ten communes started to compete against each other in order to attract real estate investments into their territories, generating an intensification of high-rise construction in certain areas, at the expense of devitalising the redevelopment in others, with a total lack of inter-municipal coordination. The externalities this market generates are high, as I explain below, because the real estate firms need to buy several adjacent plots, merge them together, demolish the existing structures and build in highest-rise allowed by ad hoc zoning laws. The National Law of Urbanism and Construction still allows increases in the FAR of the projects and offers tax exemptions (a reduced construction permit tax) to private construction firms when their projects are located in merged land plots, whereas the norm is the bigger the land plot to redevelop, the more substantial the public support in terms of increased FAR and tax exemption.

I have shown elsewhere (Lopez-Morales 2015a) how the profit made by large-scale private companies derived from the high-rise construction is often achieved at the expense of a low price paid to the original owner-residents for their land, a price that is insufficient to compensate the latter residents with enough cash to find replacement accommodation in similar neighbourhoods with equivalent amenities and centrality, after they sell the land they formerly owned, given the increased new housing prices imposed by private redevelopers. Thus, if in the nineties the assessment of the urban renewal market was positive, as it actually generated repopulation, improved new housing supply in central land, and a general revitalisation of the built environment. Currently, those positive effects are countered by the deterioration of the dwellings that surround newly built high-rise buildings (especially when they are under construction) whose height usually reaches from 20- to 30-stories. Hence, the buildings are generating shadow casts, and considerable losses of privacy, besides an increase in traffic congestion around the neighbourhoods. When low-income landowners come to sell their land, they lack any bargaining power because they usually have limited access to

Figure 4.1 High-rise residential buildings in gentrifying Santa Isabel area of Santiago
   commune (2015).

Source: Daniel Meza.

legal means and real estate professional advice, and because developers acquire
land plots in advance in order to avoid the entry of other competitors into these
areas, and therefore can exert extra pressure on the remaining landowners in the
same block (Lopez-Morales et al. 2015).

When high-rise residential redevelopers come to pay for the land they acquire, at least half of the original residents do not receive enough income to afford new replacement dwellings in the same neighbourhoods they live in; hence, residential exclusion is the norm for the original households who belong to the two lowest socioeconomic quintiles (Lopez-Morales 2015a). In a recent study conducted with 157 new high-rise projects located in six communes (Santiago, Quinta Normal, Recoleta, Independencia, Ñuñoa and Macul) and 756 residential households who live surrounding those projects (Lopez-Morales et al. 2015). It was found that the average ground rent paid to original residents barely exceeded UF 11/m², although there is also a high variation in the values of the floor price paid during the period, with highs of UF 25/m² and a minimum below UF 5/m², with a standard deviation of 5.23. In contrast, profits made by the private redevelopers of these renovating areas (discarding all financial, construction, land, marketing and sales costs) easily exceeds four times that land value paid and often reaches a value of UF 8. That is, for every one UF redevelopers invest in buying land plots to build in high-rise buildings, they recovered UF 4 to 8 as pure profit. Certainly, this revenue is a very lucrative market so far, although this condition is permanently denied by real estate companies and their union organisations.

Meanwhile, prices of new apartments supplied in the central and pericentral areas of Santiago are reaching a significant increase of prices. In Santiago Centro commune, it was accounted maximum selling prices of new units at UF 73 per square meter built. This means that for a 50 m2 apartment, the selling price ascends to UF 3,650 (397 times the minimum wage of the country). However, this is a commune that for decades has hosted middle-income and lower-income population. In 2000, the maximum price of a department of the same size and in the same area was UF 1,800. In just 14 years, there has been an increase of 100% of the maximum prices of new housing in this commune. Remarkable increases were also seen in other central communes, that by 2014 reached unprecedented levels: San Miguel (UF 53 / m2), Estación Central (UF 50 / m2) and Independencia (UF 57 / m2), as recently reported by the economic brunch of the *El Mercurio*, the most traditional and influential newspaper in the country. The problem is that the change on prices also inflates renting prices, and generally produces an overall increase in housing prices in the city. Consequently, this phenomenon is radically displacing the poorer segments of inhabitants towards other districts and distant peripheries of the urban. In the Santiago Centro, 60% of the original resident households, i.e., inhabiting properties that have not been renewed, receive a family income generated by three times the minimum wage or less, which is about the first three quintiles of the population (Lopez-Morales et al. 2015).

The leading private real estate firms have achieved such a level of control over the urban renewal market that these companies are currently handling prices by controlling the supply of housing, i.e., producing less housing that what is needed in Santiago and other major metropolitan centres, and otherwise redirecting their investments towards more profitable niches like the cities of Iquique and Antofagasta and other Latin American metropolises like Lima and Bogota. In spite how it looks like, this is not an illegal procedure, but it is a voluble market behaviour

Figure 4.2 Renewed and derelict dwellings in Santiago (2016).

that demands a more resolute public sector, one that goes beyond the current role of 'subsidy supplier' the Chilean state currently performs. It is in Chile and Santiago in particular where a whole new system of production of affordable housing is needed. A recent report by Adimark,[5] one of the leading firms that conduct urban economic studies in Chile, showed a noticeable socioeconomic upgrade in at least two central communes of Santiago, like Santiago Centro and San Miguel; these districts currently show a higher presence of the highest socioeconomic income deciles than fifteen years ago, and this is substantially regarded as effect of the increasingly expensive market of property-led, high-rise residential redevelopment that spreads over these areas.

Conclusions

The empirical data from Santiago exposes how the differential exploitation of the ground rent is ultimately a political/class-based process. High-rise redevelopment in Santiago rests on the big amount of landownership among low-income population, the extremely unequal economic power relations between the original population and the redevelopers, and the dominance of high-rise construction in the redevelopment process, all of which are drivers to class-led residential displacement.

Three politico-economic issues co-exist in this redevelopment process. First and foremost, this method of gentrification is probably the most efficient device for amplifying capital within the secondary circuit of the built environment, multiplying the return in the form of profit once high-rise redevelopment has occurred. Second, it responds to the production, uneven accumulation, and disputes over ground rent in redeveloping urban areas, comprising a specific 'urban' form of creative destruction that erases many social networks and destroys the quality of life in affected neighbourhoods. Third, the gentrification of Santiago responds to what has come to be called 'urban entrepreneurialism' (Lopez-Morales et al. 2012; following for instance Harvey 1989) namely the multisided and usually intertwined roles of the state and assorted holders of economic capital in the production, distribution, and representation of urban exclusion and segregation.

In most international studies displacement is often 'invisible' to simple empiric observation and to public policy (see the seminal work by Slater in 2009 based on Marcuse's 1985; more recent work by Freeman 2006; Wyly et al. 2010); in Santiago, displacement comes as the true profit margins 'achieved' by the inner city owner-resident population after the selling of their land and thus the purchasing power they acquire to afford their replacement residential relocation elsewhere, with at least with similar or better conditions, a process that can be deemed gentrification (Lopez-Morales 2011; 2015a; 2015b; Lopez-Morales et al. 2016). It is particularly striking to see how the state, on the one hand, ignores the very high levels of ground rent accumulation by real estate firms (not to mention the residential exclusion derived from it) whilst on the other hand allows the very high FARs achieved by those developers. To analyse this form of ground rent exploitation allows an ex ante and inductive visualisation of displacement processes derived from real estate pressure, according to the pre-established guidelines for demographic and real estate market behaviour, thus appreciating what seems invisible to the empirical study or analysis of traditional public policy. The gentrification of Santiago may look different from the most classical narratives of gentrification coming mainly from the Global North (Lopez-Morales 2015b), but it is quintessentially the same, namely, the forced replacement of a class by another higher and more powerful class. In Chile, gentrification is nothing more than the extreme polarisation of an already polarised urban society. The latter does not mean that private economic profit is the only or main causal factor of gentrification, but I claim that the ground rent private accumulation explains fundamental questions about gentrification, like who really makes the changes in the central neighbourhoods, and at the expense and for the sake of whom these changes are done.

Socio-spatial segregation in Chile is still very high (Ruiz-Tagle 2014), and therefore it is required to consider a more socially inclusive urbanism and to strengthen the state with new supra-municipal powers. These powers should operate on the whole metropolitan area, in order to set standards for social integration, limit high-rise construction up to a certain level, and avoid the concentration of high-rise construction in certain places only, among other urgent measures. These new powers need to be subtracted from municipalities who currently, and chaotically, monopolise them. For instance, the definition of maximum FARs for every zone. These new supra-municipal regulatory planning instrument also require approving participatory instances when setting the new rules, following the Law of Citizen Participation, passed in 2011 (Gobierno de Chile 2011) but that hitherto has not been yet implemented by the public sector and municipalities in the country. Also the state could go beyond its current role as a mere housing subsidy issuer and assume a more direct role in the real estate market; for example, participating through newly-created non-profit, public-private real estate agencies, in order to prevent the enormous mismatch that currently exists between land prices paid and new apartments sales prices, both freely fixed by the private sector.

Some good examples of anti-gentrification activism in Chile now can be seen by the *Movimiento de Pobladores en Lucha* who have struggled to create a social real estate firm and so have managed to self-build affordable housing in well-located land in Peñalolén commune; this operation has barely made no profit with achieved far higher spatial and building standards than many residential units sold by private real estate firms (Castillo 2013). Another case of anti-gentrification activism occurred in Pedro Aguirre Cerda commune where a highly effective institutionalised insurgency by local residents achieved to counteract the state attempt to upzone their neighbourhoods between 2003 and 2005 (Lopez-Morales 2013).

As it is the state who provides almost all the urban opportunities for privately-led, real estate redevelopment, it is also needed to implement a system of land value capture above certain level of ground rent achieved by the private firms, or above certain FAR, considering for this total revenue after sales of real estate products (Smolka 2013). This can be seen not only as a way to solve the inequality generated from the polarisation of the absorption of the ground rent, but also as a source for financing a new state housing policy, in order to afford social housing located in central land, for instance in neighbourhoods which at the moment are considered 'expensive' by private redevelopers, in a similar way as it is done in cities like Sao Paulo in Brazil through ZEIS, and in a different way, in Cali or Medellín in Colombia (Smolka 2013). Both cases provide positive results in reducing segregation, and in generating greater socio-spatial cohesion. All this requires a coordinated and inter-sectorial governance regime that exceeds the current scheme of competitive municipalities Chile has nowadays.

The real estate market in central areas of the main cities of Chile has produced repopulation and an active real estate sector. No-one could deny its positive impact at attracting population to the formerly depopulated central areas. However, its effects in terms of excluding certain socioeconomic strata are high, especially that one that has remained living in these central neighbourhoods for a long time. Chilean private real estate firms receive high profits whilst the income received by local population is low; housing as a right in Chile is being totally replaced by the concept of housing as a commodity. There is no housing regulation but a form of self-regulation of a financial market and the housing sector depends on those fluctuations. Chile's inner city piecemeal, property-led urban renewal reveals how advanced urban neoliberalism works in this country.

Chile's high-rise urban renewal economics can be deemed an example of neoliberalism in one of its crudest forms. Urban and housing governance in Chile is increasingly entrepreneurial, as municipalities independently and speculatively manage to 'supply' flexible zoning and construction conditions to the private housing construction sector. Over recent decades, the supply of new private housing in Santiago has been focussed primarily in central neighbourhoods and has become increasingly expensive and thus less accessible to the lowest income segments. The evidence shows that there are high levels of 'exclusion by price' that the housing market generates, as the evidence shows there is nothing natural about segregation but this is therefore reinforced by market rules, leading important fractions of urban society to being displaced or excluded from the urban environments in central areas, in the places they have traditionally inhabited.

Notes

1 According to census data released by the National Statistics Institute (INE 2012), between 2002 and 2012, the Santiago Centro commune showed a population increase from 214,000 to 308,000 inhabitants, as an effect of the piecemeal residential redevelopment market in this district.
2 www.imf.org/external/data.htm
3 Several of these ideas and possible solutions come from my participation in Chile's National Committee for Urban Policy that functioned from 2012 up to the present, where I represented the University of Chile; some of these outcomes were also published in a book (Lopez-Morales et al. 2013).
4 Although the Chilean official currency is the Peso, the Indexed Unit of Account (UF) is a unit of account constantly adjusted to inflation, so that the value of the UF remains constant. By 2015 it is equivalent to approximately CLP\$ 25.000 or US\$ 40. Prices of land, houses and real estate financing instruments are defined in UFs in Chile.
5 www.latercera.com/noticia/tendencias/2015/05/659-630172-9-estudio-muestra-como-ha-cambiado-el-mapa-social-de-santiago.shtml

References

Arriagada, C., Moreno, J. C., and Cartier, E. (2007) *Evaluación de Impacto del Subsidio de Renovación Urbana: Estudio del Área Metropolitana del Gran Santiago 1991–2006.* Santiago: MINVU.

Borsdorf, A. & Hidalgo, R. (2013) Revitalization and tugurization in the historical centre of Santiago de Chile, *Cities*, 31: 96–104.

Casgrain, A. & Janoschka, M. (2013) Gentrificación y resistencia en las ciudades latinoamericanas. El ejemplo de Santiago de Chile, *Andamios*, 22.

Castillo, M. (2013) Producción y gestión habitacional de los pobladores. La autogestión de vivienda en Peñalolén y La Pintana, *Santiago de Chile, Boletín CF+S*, 54: 133–145. Available in: http://habitat.aq.upm.es/boletin/n54/amcas.html [Accessed in 17 August 2015].

Clark, E. (1987) *The rent gap and urban change: Case studies in Malmö 1860–1985.* Lund: Lund University Press.

Contreras, Y. (2011) La recuperación urbana y residencial del centro de Santiago: Nuevos habitantes, cambios socioespaciales significativos, *EURE*, 37(112): 89–113.

Contrucci, P. (2011). Vivienda en altura en zonas de renovación urbana: Desafíos para mantener su vigencia, *EURE*, 37(111): 185–189.

De Mattos, C., Fuentes, L., & Link, F. (2014) Tendencias recientes del crecimiento metropolitano en Santiago de Chile. ¿Hacia una nueva geografía urbana?, *Revista INVI*, 29(81): 193–219.

Evans, A. W. (2004) *Economics and land use planning.* Oxford: Blackwell.

Freeman, L. (2006) *There goes the 'Hood': Views of gentrification from the ground up.* Philadelphia: Temple University Press.

Gobierno de Chile (2011) *Ley 20.500 "Sobre asociaciones y participación ciudadana en la gestión pública"*. Available in: www.leychile.cl/Navegar?idNorma=1023143

Hammel, D. J. (1999). Gentrification and land rent: a historical view of the rent gap in Minneapolis. *Urban Geography*, 20(2), 116–145.

Harvey, D. (1989) From Managerialism to Entrepreneurialism: The Transformation in Urban Governance in Late Capitalism, *Geografiska Annaler. Series B, Human Geography*, 71(1): 3–17.

Inzulza-Contardo, J. (2012) 'Latino-Gentrification'? Focusing on Physical and Socio-economic Patterns of Change in Latin American Inner Cities, *Urban Studies*, 49(10): 2085–2107.

Inzulza-Contardo, J. (2016) Contemporary Latin American gentrification? Young urban professionals discovering historic neighbourhoods, in special issue 'Latin American Gentrifications'. In: Lopez-Morales, E., Shin, H. B. and Lees, B. eds. *Urban geography*. 37(8), 1195–1214.

Janoschka, M., Sequera, J., & Salinas, L. (2014) Gentrification in Spain and Latin America – A Critical Dialogue, *International Journal of Urban and Regional Research*. 38(4), 1234–1265. doi:10.1111/1468-2427.12030.

Labbe, F., Carrasco, E., & Mathews, S. (2012). *Resultados preliminares Censo de Población y Vivienda 2012*. Santiago: Instituto Nacional de Estadísticas Chile.

Lees, L., Shin, H.B., and Lopez-Morales, E. (2016) *Planetary gentrification*. Cambridge: Polity Press.

Lees, L., Slater, T., & Wyly, E. (2008) *Gentrification*. New York: Routledge.

Lopez-Morales, E. (2008) Destrucción creativa y explotación de brecha de renta: discutiendo la renovación urbana del peri-centro sur poniente de Santiago de Chile entre 1990 y 2005, *Scripta Nova*, 12(270).

Lopez-Morales, E. (2011). Gentrification by Ground Rent Dispossession: The Shadows Cast by Large Scale Urban Renewal in Santiago de Chile, *International Journal of Urban and Regional Research*, 35(2): 1–28.

Lopez-Morales, E. (2013) Insurgency and institutionalised social participation in local-level urban planning: The case of PAC comuna, Santiago de Chile, 2003–2005. In: Samara, T., He, S. and Chen, G. eds. *Locating right to the city in the global South: Transnational urban governance and socio-spatial transformations*. New York: Routledge. Pp. 221–246.

Lopez-Morales, E. (2015a) Assessing exclusionary displacement through rent gap analysis in the urban redevelopment of inner Santiago, Chile, *Housing Studies*. doi:10.1080/026 73037.2015.1100281

Lopez-Morales, E. (2015b) Gentrification in the global South, *City*, 19(4): 557–566. doi:http://dx.doi.org/10.1080/13604813.2015.1051746

Lopez-Morales, E., Arriagada, C., Gasic, I., & Meza, D. (2015) Efectos de la renovación urbana sobre la calidad de vida y perspectivas de relocalización residencial de habitantes centrales y peri centrales del AMGS, *EURE*, 41(124): 45–67.

Lopez-Morales, E., Arriagada, C., Jirón, P., & Eliash, H., eds. (2013) *Chile Urbano hacia el Siglo XXI: Investigaciones y reflexiones de Política Urbana desde la Universidad de Chile*. Santiago: Editorial Universitaria.

Lopez-Morales, E., Gasic, I., & Meza, D. (2012) Urbanismo Pro-Empresarial en Chile: políticas y planificación de la producción residencial en altura en el pericentro del Gran Santiago, *Revista INVI*, 28(76): 75–114.

Lopez-Morales, E., Shin, H. B., & Lees, L., (2016), Latin American gentrifications, *Urban Geography*. 37(8): 1091–1108

Marcuse, P. (1985) Gentrification, abandonment and displacement: Connections, causes and policy responses in New York City, *Journal of Urban and Contemporary Law*, 28: 195–240.

OECD (2012) *Working Party on Territorial Policy in Urban Areas. National Urban Policy Reviews: The Case of Chile*. Available in: www.oecd.org/officialdocuments/publicdis playdocumentpdf/?cote=G OV/TDPC/URB(2012)13&docLanguage=En (retrieved in 20 July 2016).

Rojas, E. (2004) *Volver al centro: la recuperación de áreas urbanas centrales*. New York: Banco Interamericano de Desarrollo.

Ruiz-Tagle, J. (2014) *Bringing Inequality Closer: A Comparative Urban Sociology of Socially Diverse Neighborhoods*, Unpublished PhD Thesis, Chicago, IL: University of Chicago.

Slater, T. (2009) Missing Marcuse: On gentrification and displacement, *City*, 13(2–3): 293–311.

Smith, N. (1979) Toward a theory of gentrification: A back to the city movement by capital not people, *Journal of the American Planning Association*, 45: 538–548.

Smolka, M. (2013) *Implementing Value Capture in Latin America: Policies and Tools for Urban Development Policy Focus Report Series*. Cambridge: Lincoln Institute of Land Policy.

Valenzuela, M. (2003) Programa de repoblamiento comuna de Santiago: Un programa de gestión urbana, *Urbano*, 6(8): 53–61.

Vergara-Constela, C. & Casellas, A. (2016) Políticas estatales y transformación urbana: ¿hacia un proceso de gentrificación en Valparaíso, Chile?, *EURE*, 42(126): 123–144.

Wyly, E., Newman, K., Schafran, A., & Lee, E. (2010) Displacing New York. *Environment and Planning A*, 42: 2602–2623.

5 Urban universalism

The housing debt in the context of targeted policies

Camila Cociña

Introduction

A series of conversations with Juan Arbona, a good friend and colleague from Puerto Rico, led me to the decision to stop talking about neoliberalism, and start referring to it as a neoliberal project. It's not just an ism (with a neutral suffix). It's a political and ideological project that was implemented – through more or less violent and dramatic processes – over most countries of the so-called Global South. And in Chile, as a paradigmatic laboratory of most neoliberal policies, this is particularly evident; it's not a spontaneous order that filled a vacuum of ideology, as the very notion of liberalism would have you believe, but a body of ideas that constitutes a project. Just to be clear, this is not an attempt to present a conspiracy theory, but to analytically understand that, as a project, it has various dimensions, scales and agents, with elements interacting with economic, political and social spheres. As talking about the neoliberal conditions of our cities has become synonymous of talking about a little bit of everything, this project-dimension helps to understand that there are particular elements that constitute such a condition.

This reflection looks to explore a very particular aspect of the neoliberal project: its logic of targeting public policies, and its relation with the urban form. It argues that this definition about the nature of social policies is at the root of many of the consequences of urban exclusion, and is at the base of the production of cities 'for the rich' and 'for the poor' as two separated and parallel systems, and therefore needs to be revisited.

It will be organised as follows; first, there will be a discussion about the nature of neoliberal policies and the distinction between targeting and universalism, briefly analysing the consequences of these models in terms of inequality; secondly, a discussion on the paradox of housing and urban policies from a universalist perspective, as housing is identified as one of the main creators of cities at different scales, and at the same time one that presents a dilemma in understanding it from universalist perspectives; then, it will discuss the specific Chilean urban context as a paradigm of targeting, and its particular consequences on the urban form of Santiago in terms of segregation and inequality. And finally, it will offer a reflection on the challenges for urban and housing policies from a universalist perspective, introducing the idea of 'Urban Universalism', a specific way to understand universalism for housing policies, as a political and analytical frame that may help to reduce inequalities and segregation, particularly in the city of Santiago.

Targeting and universalism

David Harvey defines neoliberalism as the "theory of political economic practice that proposes that human well-being can best be advanced by liberating individual entrepreneurial freedoms and skills within an institutional framework characterised by strong private property rights, free market and free trade" (2005:2). In practice, the expansion of such a theory of political-economic practice, took place through the processes of transformation that occurred towards the end of cold war across different parts of the world. In the case of developing countries, the neoliberal project arrived mainly through the implementation of Structural Adjustment Programmes (SAPs), as part of the requirements of the IMF and World Bank during and after the 1982 debt crisis. Neoliberal reforms implied structural transformation such as the opening of national economies to international financial markets, the privatisation of welfare services, the decrease of state's attributions and deregulation (Mohan 1996).

Along with those changes, there was a shift in the nature of social policies. As Horton and Gregory point out,

> precisely who welfare policy is supposed to apply to very much depends on your underlying philosophy. Is welfare provision a necessary evil, a temporary phenomenon for those in need, or is it a positive mode of social provision and interaction, which, far from undermining citizenship status, also helps to create it?
>
> (Horton and Gregory 2009:53)

Neoliberal policies tend to choose the first option.

Under neoliberal transformations, most national states reinforced and strengthened the idea of targeting, which implies that the "eligibility to social benefits involves some kind of means-testing to determine the 'truly deserving'" (Mkandawire 2005:1). In the context of a major criticism of the welfare state, especially to the dependence of individuals on the state that it breeds, the implementation of targeting policies emerged as an ideologically coherent tool to reduce the state's attributions, and as a useful mechanism to involve private market supplying services to the 'less needy' groups, who would be left outside of the targeting policies scope. In practice, targeting has become not just a ruling principle for social policies, but also a criterion for evaluation: from this perspective, the better targeted a policy is, the most efficient use of resources in supplying assets and services to those who otherwise cannot access to them, and this would have a better performance in the task of reducing extreme poverty.

But targeting is also an object of criticism from more progressive sectors, claiming for the need of universalism in areas such as education and health; universal policies imply that "the entire population is the beneficiary of social benefits as a basic right" (Mkandawire 2005:1). The main argument behind universalism is that targeting policies diminish the condition of social services understood as rights, and imply a perverse process of segregation through the development of services such as education and health 'for the poor' and 'for the rich' as two separate systems. Additionally, since these are typically social policies built on targeting principles to tackle the problem of poverty and not inequality, there are no policies pursuing such an end (Atria 2011). Over time, targeted welfare tends to become less egalitarian because it commends less political support than universal principles. In other words, services targeted just for the poor will be always worse than those designed for everyone (Horton and Gregory 2009).

In the case of Chile, neoliberal targeting policies were implemented in the seventies and eighties, much earlier than in most developing countries and even before the SAPs promoted by the Washington Consensus (Gilbert 2002); Chile became a laboratory in terms of neoliberal policies, and they were implemented in a very radical and pure way. This is particularly clear in education and health; it is not the aim of this chapter to discuss the specificities of these two systems, but merely to acknowledge that targeting policies in both cases have been particularly strong, concentrating the action of the state just in low-income groups and perpetuating the separation of a private provision for richer groups; in both cases, these targeted systems are now facing a deep crisis.

In the case of education, the Chilean system is considered one of the most segregated in the world (GIESCR 2014), and this has been at the core of sociopolitical claims over the last few years (Atria 2012), putting free universal education as a key element to reduce segregation in the classrooms; these demands that started from social movements, have now been incorporated as part of the educational reforms promoted by the government since 2014. In the case of health, even though some reforms towards universalist principles were implemented a decade ago, introducing universal guarantees for some illness through the Plan Auge, the system is still far from universalist models such as the NHS in the UK, and the questions about the importance of providing public health for the rich, those who can pay for it, is starting to be part of the public debate (Sanhueza 2014).

Even though universalism is still far from being central in the public debate in Chile, some elements of it have become key in education and timidly in health. Universal guarantees are becoming a more explicit principle in facing one of the main national drawback, as is the reduction of inequalities, and therefore there is a need to expand their scope beyond education and health to other social spheres such as housing policies, which have consolidated segregated urban patterns over the last decades.

The paradox of housing and urban universalism

Is it possible to do this, to apply universalist principles to the housing field? Urban and housing production presents a particular challenge. Housing policies are probably one of the most emblematic cases of targeting, as houses are usually provided to low-income groups only, even in countries led by more universalistic principles. However, as we will discuss here, housing needs to be understood as more than houses, and therefore there is room for some universalistic principles.

Housing should not be mistaken as merely a shelter as refuge from the outside, a collection of walls and a roof. Housing is multidimensional and multiscalar, as its footprint go far beyond its physical dimensions, determining social, economic and cultural realities of people, neighbourhoods and cities; housing design and policies affect the kind of physical arrangements that take place within a family, at the time that influence the way in which the physical structure of the cities is socially produced. Housing is a means of city production that affects its multiple scales, from the very intimate sphere of the body, to the kind of socio-spatial relations that we build as society (Blunt and Dowling 2006). Housing is not an object, but a complex process (Turner 1976) and for most people the primary asset, without which it is impossible to produce other assets (Moser and Dani 2008). At the city level, housing projects are not just about building individual units, but about shaping neighbourhoods, bringing infrastructure, consolidating communities and therefore producing cities. Housing should be defined in these terms: as the set of efforts put together to provide homes, which includes not just the private space, but the city and social relations built along it. Housing should be a key component of the city as an indivisible right.

Understood as a city builder, housing production has a specific type of agency, which goes beyond the effects it has in individuals. Particularly, this brings about the idea that housing agency is basically a spatial and urban agency, and therefore housing policies must be conceived as city policies. This supposes a particular challenge, questioning the policy's nature as a provider of individual answers -and therefore requiring targeting solutions.

That said, the nature of housing policies from this perspective presents a particular paradox, a dilemma that is not easy to solve: housing policies must be attended with targeted actions (to build houses), being at the same time part of the process of city shaping (to collectively produce cities), that can be understood as a right from a universalist perspective.

Yet, even if we define that the object of social policies should be the inclusion of everyone in the development processes, and that universalism is more effective than targeting in achieving it, housing policies present a complicated dilemma: the claims for universalism presented above cannot be applied to housing policies, or at least not in the same way that in education or health. In countries opened to the market, a policy of "free housing for everyone" would not make sense. In fact, housing as a right is at the same time synonymous with a private project, and requires a targeting action to give answer to groups that otherwise cannot access to it, and not to the society as a whole. But this does not mean that the logic of universal guarantees should not be applied to the housing sector, it just implies that it has to be applied in other ways: with the construction of housing we are basically building cities, and cities must be understood from the perspective of universalism; otherwise, we are producing cities 'for the poor' and cities 'for the rich'.

The question is therefore the following: how can housing policies, which must be attended with targeted actions, be part of the process of city as a right from a perspective of universal guarantees? It is in the recognition and construction of the multidimensionality and multiple scales of the housing project where the idea of Urban Universalism lies: it implies the recognition of a universalist approach to the city, in which some kind of positive discrimination is used as a tool for inclusion, embedded on the view of the city as a universal right. It is a return to the discussion of the right to the city (Harvey 2008), in which the idea of universal policies is used in housing as a way to tackle segregation and inequalities, and to build cities for everyone.

Chilean housing and urban production: the paradigm or targeting

This discussion may seem highly theoretical, but it is a necessary one in the Chilean context. As was said above, targeting as a principle was implemented with a hitherto unseen radicalism in Chile during the eighties, and perpetuated in the following decades.

The focus since the nineties in most Chilean social policies (health, education, housing) was to increase the services coverage and decrease deficits. In the case of housing, it was through a successful financial system structured by subsidies provision (individual vouchers), and the management and construction of housing by the private sector, that allowed that between 1990 and 2000, an average of 90,000 families obtained a subsidy each year (Salcedo 2010). This model proved to be effective in cutting the quantitative housing deficit, and by 1993, "a Chilean-type model, or at least elements of the Chilean model, had become acknowledged best practice" (Gilbert 2002:310).

The scenario after three decades of such a successful financial model has different faces. The positive numbers and quantitative success contrast with the quality of the city produced, as Santiago is considered the most segregated city of the OECD members (OECD 2013), which can be explained in part by the constant process of exclusion of urban land that the private-led housing policy has created. While poverty and housing deficit decreased at similar rates, inequality remains as one of the highest of the region (see Figure 5.1).

The product of the capital housing subsidy model was the construction of extensive areas of housing for the poor on cheap land to increase private profits, socially and functionally homogenous, in which the houses were understood by the private sector as a profitable commodity, and the citizens as state-subsidised customers through targeted policies. The fact that this was a successful and efficient economic policy for financing housing but not necessarily a successful social policy has been acknowledged by many authors; a key contribution to this discussion was the reflections of Alfredo Rodríguez and Ana Sugranyes (2004) regarding the emergence of what they called the problem of those with roof, in contrast with the historical constrains regarding those without access to a formal shelter.

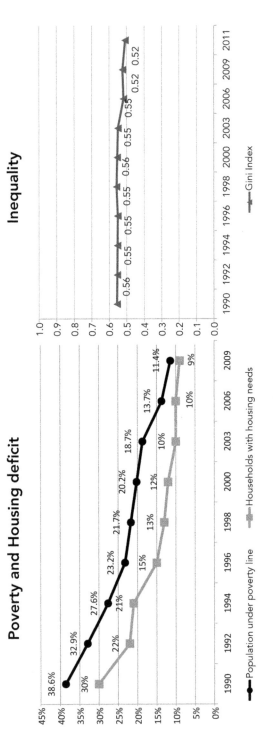

Figure 5.1 Reduction of poverty and housing deficit over the last decades, and inequality index.

Source: Own elaboration based on data from CASEN Mideplan; Ministerio de Desarrollo Social; and Trading Economics.

There is a general debate about what has been called the 'the dark side of a successful housing policy' (Ducci 2000), in which an exemplary financial policy has reproduced and deepened social problems. Some authors have studied particularly the extreme process of segregation that this set of policies has reinforced (Sabatini et al. 2001; De Mattos et al. 2004; Salcedo 2010), as housing policy is recognised as one with the ability to build houses, but no city (Castillo Couve 2004). Particularly relevant is the phenomena of ghettoisation of areas of the city as a product of the social homogeneity enhanced by housing policies (Sabatini and Brain 2008), and the idea that a 'new urban poverty' (Tironi 2003) has emerged as a consequence of it. These debates have also influenced policy makers, with the development of policies and programmes that look to revert some of these processes and recover areas built from this approach. In sum, there is a general questioning about to what extent home ownership and targeting actions have actually contributed to decrease social problems, as housing production has been mistaken as an agent at one scale (individual level), forgetting its multiple agencies at city level with disastrous consequences.

The phenomenon in Chile is not an isolated one, and can be regarded as an early adaptation of what has become a new generation of housing policies centred on private provision and subsidies as the main available public instrument, that "almost invariably have been made possible by the production of housing of very minimum spatial and building standards in peripheral land with very low levels of urbanisation" (Fiori and Santa Rosa 2014:2). In Chile, the voucher system became a perfect mechanism for materialising targeting principles in housing policies, and as in the case of education or health, for perpetuating separated systems

Figure 5.2 Social housing built during the nineties in the outskirts of Santiago, being demolished in 2015 by a public programme, given the physical and social problems of the area.

for the rich and for the poor. In the case of the city, vouchers have strengthened segregated patterns of development, as the production and control of surplus is the main driving force of urban development.

The need for Urban Universalism in housing: land and process

It is in this context where the question of Urban Universalism becomes key: after decades of building and consolidating a city for the poor and a city for the rich is worth asking how universalist principles can help to shape a city for everyone. Urban Universalism means to understand that, even though some targeting actions are required in the field of housing, the construction of cities (the main outcome of housing production) needs some universal guarantees to avoid the consolidation of segregation patterns.

Countries that seem to be successful in their social policy management, have given account of the necessary complementarities between universalist and targeting principles. In practice, it seems like "all welfare states contain a mixture of targeted and universal welfare provision" (Sefton 2008:612). For housing, its multiscalar nature requires an approach where "overall social policy itself has been universalistic, and targeting has been be used as simply one instrument for making universalism effective; this is what Theda Skocpol has referred as "targeting within universalism", in which extra benefits are directed to low-income groups within the context of a universal policy design" (Mkandawire 2005:17).

There are some aspects of the city in which this is easier to understand and observe; one is public transport, as slowly cities and societies understand that public transport systems cannot be designed just for those who cannot afford cars, but for everyone, as a means to decrease congestion, pollution, and improve quality of life in general. In Chile, public transport policies are still seen as targeted to those who cannot access to cars (Echenique 2009:80), with consequences in the design of mobility infrastructure (as highways) and in the quality of the service of public transportation, for the reasons we discussed above: services targeted just for the poor will be always worse than those designed for everyone (Horton and Gregory 2009).

But as we have said, for housing this is not that obvious; it is necessary to understand housing policies embedded in the production of city as a collective good to enlarge their capacity of action, whilst being supported by targeted efforts. There are some possible pathways that one could take to work with Urban Universalism in the case of Chile, which would require different approaches from the private sector (with more regulation and incentives for innovative ways of involvement); civil society (promoting organisation and strengthening capabilities); and for the public sector (questioning its subsidiary role to the private sector and involving it actively in land markets from its different government scales).

Regarding this last point, there are two key elements of housing that need to be addressed to grasp its multidimensional condition: the importance of the economy of land and the understanding of housing as a dynamic process. Land should be at the core of the discussion of housing and universalism, as often land markets are the main reason behind our inability to ensure universal urban guarantees. This is why it is important to think of the consequences of involving the public sector in the land market. If the state at different levels (central, regional, municipal) could participate (investing in well-located land as it does for the construction of public goods), it could build affordable and social housing integrated to services that the 'legitimate desires of profit' of a private company would never allow. This would imply neighbourhoods and districts more socially integrated, and the consequent synergies of the process of sharing services and spaces by different groups, sharing also the taxation towards municipalities that is again re-invested in the city.

An effective involvement of the state at its different scales in land markets, along with an understanding of housing as a process, require a deep transformation not just regarding public institutions such as SERVIU and its subsidiary role, but also in terms of decentralising through capacities, power and resource redistribution – and not just privatisation and redistribution of responsibilities, as it is usually misunderstood. It implies a questioning of the subsidiary logic, the commodification of housing, and a process of empowerment of local governments and civil society organisations able to develop sustainable projects that contribute to the city as a right; it also requires the implementation of adequate scales of actions for metropolitan areas such as Santiago, that do not have metropolitan authorities. The production of housing with a focus on land and defining it as a dynamic process contributes to an understanding of the city from a universalistic perspective, as it moves away from the static and individualistic perspective of housing units as isolated commodities.

Conclusions

Through this chapter we have discussed the targeting principle as one of the aspects of the neoliberal project, and particularly the implications of targeted policies in terms of segregation and inequality. Recognising the limitations of universalism in fields such as urban policies, we have presented an understanding of housing as multiple in scale and nature, looking for spaces of universalistic principles in housing production. The Chilean case, as a paradigm of neoliberal policies materialised through a voucher system, has helped to illustrate the urgent need of universalism behind social policies such as housing.

Segregation and inequality are impossible to tackle from a residual targeting perspective, as they require an understanding of social services as rights, incorporating universal guarantees in every sector, and moving away from a subsidiary state towards one that is a duty-bearer and guarantor of rights. If we want housing policies to help reduce inequalities and not consolidate them, combat segregation and not deepen it, some universalist principles in the understanding of land and the urban process need to be considered, as those described above. Housing is not synonymous with just building houses, although the principles behind the neoliberal project make us think the contrary. We need to move away from that, and

Urban Universalism may be a simple but powerful analytical and political frame to start; after all, it's just about producing cities for everyone.

References

Atria, F. (2011). Las cosas cambian cuando les pones un "tu": sobre universalismo, focalización y regresividad. Documentos de Trabajo. [Online] Available from: www.uai.cl/images/sitio/facultades_carreras/esc_gobierno/documentos_de_trabajo/universalizacion_2011.pdf [Accessed: 5/02/2015].

Atria, F. (2012). *La mala educación: Ideas que inspiran el movimiento estudiantil en Chile.* Santiago: Catalonia/CIPER.

Blunt, A. & Dowling, R. (2006). *Home.* Oxford: Routledge.

Castillo Couve, M.J. (2004). Renovación de las Población es mediante la radicación de allegados. Una alternativa a la expansión de Santiago de Chile. *Informes De La Construcción,* 56(491), 7–1.

De Mattos, C., Ducci, M.E., Rodríguez, A., & Yáñez, G. (eds.) (2004). *Santiago en la globalización ¿Una nueva ciudad?* Santiago: Ediciones SUR, Libros EURE.

Ducci, M.E. (2000). Chile: The Dark Side of a Successful Housing Policy. In Tulchin, J.S. & Garland, A. (eds.) *Social development in Latin America: The politics of reform.* Boulder, CO: Lynne Rienner.

Echenique, M. (2009). Corto y largo plazo. In Cociña, C., Quintana, F. & Valenzuela, N. (eds.) *Agenda Pública: Arquitectura, ciudad y desarrollo,* 78–93. Santiago: Cientodiez.

Fiori, J. & Santa Rosa, J. (2014). Towards an international comparative analysis and exchange of practices of a new generation of mass housing policies. Presented at the 7 World Urban Forum, Networking Event: "New Formal Housing Policies: building just cities?", Medellin, Colombia.

Gilbert, A. (2002). Power, Ideology and the Washington Consensus: The Development and Spread of Chilean Housing Policy. *Housing Studies,* 17(2), 305–324.

Global Initiative for Economic Social and Cultural Rights (GIESCR) (2014). Alternative Report Submitted by the Global Initiative for Social and Economic Rights and the Sciences Po law school Clinic. [Online] Available from: http://globalinitiative-escr.org/wp-content/uploads/2014/11/101114-ChilereportCESCR-GI-ESCR-privatisationineducation-FINAL.pdf [Accessed: 6/02/2015].

Harvey, D. (2005). *A brief history of neoliberalism.* Oxford: Oxford University Press.

Harvey, D. (2008). The Right to the City. *New Left Review,* N.35, 23–40.

Horton, T. & Gregory, J. (2009). *The solidarity society: Why we can afford to end poverty, and how to do it with public support.* London: The Fabian Society.

Mkandawire, T. (2005). *Targeting and universalism in poverty reduction.* United Nations Research Institute for Social Development. [Online] Available from: http://tinyurl.com/mkandawire [Accessed: 01/08/2014].

Mohan, G. (1996). SAPs and Development in West Africa. *Geography,* 81(4), 364–368.

Moser, C. & Dani, A. (2008). Asset Based Social Policy and Public Action in a Polycentric World. In Moser, C. & Dani, A. (eds.) *Assets, livelihoods and social policy.* Washington: The World Bank.

OECD (2013). OECD Urban Policy Reviews, Chile 2013. [Online] Available from: www.keepeek.com/Digital-Asset-Management/oecd/urban-rural-and-regional-development/oecd-urban-policy-reviews-chile-2013_9789264191808-en [Accessed: 30/06/2014].

Rodríguez, A. & Sugranyes, A. (2004). El problema de vivienda de los "con techo". *Eure,* 30(91), 53–65.

Sabatini, F. & Brain, I. (2008). La segregación, los guetos y la integración social urbana: mitos y claves. *Eure*, 34(103), 5–26.

Sabatini, F., Cáceres, G., & Cerda, J. (2001). Segregación residencial en las principales ciudades chilenas: Tendencias de las tres últimas décadas y posibles cursos de acción. *Eure*, 27(82), 21–42.

Salcedo, R. (2010). The Last Slum: Moving from Illegal Settlements to Subsidized Home Ownership in Chile. *Urban Affairs Review*, 46(1), 90–118.

Sanhueza, C. (2014). Universalismo: ¿por qué financiar a los ricos?, in Conversaciones sobre Políticas Sociales, Blog de Claudia Sanhueza. [Online] Available from: http://voces.latercera.com/2014/10/02/claudia-sanhueza/universalismo-por-que-financiar-a-los-ricos/

Sefton, T. (2008) Distributive and Redistributive Policy. In Moran, M., Rein, M. & Goodin, R. E. (eds.) *The Oxford handbook of public policy*, 607–623. Oxford: Oxford University Press.

Tironi, M. (2003). *Nueva Pobreza Urbana, Vivienda y Capital Social en Santiago de Chile, 1985–2001*. Santiago: PREDES Universidad de Chile, Ril Editores.

Turner, J.F.C. (1976). *Housing by people: Towards autonomy in building environments*. London: Marion Boyars.

6 The mobility regime in Santiago and possibilities of change

Nicolás Valenzuela Levi

Introduction

If our analytical effort about Chile's capital departs from the idea of exploring the nature of the 'Neoliberal Santiago', it means that there have been 'other' stages in past moments of history and, of course, diverse potential futures. We have access to several analyses that characterise the historical (Gárate 2012), political (Garreton 2012) economic (Atria et al. 2013), legal (Atria 2013) and socio-cultural (Moulian 1997; Araujo and Martuccelli 2012) effects of the implementation of the – so called – 'neoliberal' experiment in Chile. In addition, research that look into Santiago as a case of a neoliberal city have documented different faces of neoliberalism's effects on the urban space (De Mattos et al. 2004; Rodríguez and Rodríguez 2009; Hidalgo and Janoschka 2014), and on specific aspects of urban life (Han 2012; Rodríguez et al. 2012).

However, when it comes to discuss power relations at a metropolitan level beyond general trends, specific urban mega-projects or particular local conflicts, discussions tend to focus on the distance between Santiago's reality and intendedly consensual visions on what 'good governance' or 'good practices' in metropolitan government are (Valenzuela 2015; Orellana 2009; OECD 2009). They do not explore a political economy perspective on the problem of the current – neoliberal – balance of powers and the possibilities of overcoming it. The obvious reason that one can give to explain this is the absence of any clear alternative to neoliberalism in the realm of 'the possible' (De Sousa Santos 2010; Mangabeira Unger 2010). This chapter is an attempt to use the discussion about mobility (Sheller and Urry 2006) and the city as an opportunity to produce an exploratory and very limited-in-scope approach on this problem of political economy and institutional change (Polanyi 2001; North 1990; Khan 1995).

In order to do so, we will use a framework based on institutional political economy (Chang 2002), which means to pay attention to how power relations determine institutions that define the roles of the state, markets and civil society.

On the one hand, this allows us to understand how institutions are shaped and organised in particular regimes (Kantor et al. 1997) that balance the powers of governments, financial capital, different local and national levels of political representation and state bureaucracy, and, of course, people. Kantor et al. (1997)

define typologies for understanding metropolitan political economy in forms of regimes that "function to bargain out the terms of cooperation between the public and private sectors in a liberal-democratic political economy" but also to bargain "for political support within popular control systems in which elections, referenda, and other democratic mechanisms require public approval of projects" (Kantor et al. 1997: 349–350).

For these authors, regimes vary depending on market positions, intergovernmental environments and democratic conditions. The market position of a city is understood as 'advantaged' when it has access to public investment resources, and as 'disadvantaged' when it relies on attracting private capital. An intergovernmental system will be 'integrated' when there are strong links between different levels of the state, and 'dispersed' when local contexts operate separately from the central or regional level and consequently need to bargain with other levels of the state to have access to resources. Popular control will be 'strong' when there are democratic formal and informal institutions in place that empower the local political community and make authorities accountable, and 'weak' when these forms of control are scarce. On the other hand, the concept of political settlements (Khan 1995, 2010) provides us analytical tools to understand the present regime as a result of power dynamics and relations of force (Gramsci 1999) between different groups. The political settlement determines institutional arrangements, which we call regimes, based on a particular balance of powers. Khan's (1995) idea of this political settlement is grounded on the notion of institutional transition and change, which implies to consider transition costs that emerge as a result of attempting to modify these power relations. We will, therefore, look at the groups whose power interact and the actors that play different roles in the dynamics behind Santiago's neoliberal mobility regime.

In both the analysis of the regimes and the political settlements, outputs from the functioning of the state and markets are expected to be produced and allocated according to each group's relative power. Part of our analysis will try to illustrate disputes regarding these outputs. In Chile, mobility is becoming increasingly important in distributional terms. For instance, regarding income inequality, the poor have to deal with a new importance of mobility and connectivity within the material conditions that allow them to survive and be part of an urbanised society. In Chile, 'transport and telecommunications' surpassed 'food and not alcoholic drinks' as the main item in the average expenditure per household since the mid-2000s (Instituto Nacional de Estadísticas 2013).

Another example comes from investment and financial capital: during the same decade of 2000, foreign direct investment in public-private partnerships (PPPs) for infrastructure reached a peak and even surpassed the mining sector (Ministerio de Obras Públicas 2003) in a predominantly mining and transnational-capital-friendly country such as Chile (Palma 2012). During 2016, the discussion about the 2017 National Budget regarded PPPs for transport infrastructure as one of the country's main policies for attracting investment and enhancing economic growth, as stated by the president herself (Bachelet 2016).

Mobility plays an increasingly important role in the general political settlement that defines Chile's neoliberal institutional arrangements. Nevertheless, mobility in specific can be institutionally understood while comprehending the settlement that conditions it as a particular dimension of urban life in its social, economic and political dimensions. In what follows, firstly, the concept of the regimes will be used to understand how mobility is institutionally produced in Santiago. A first section will be used to try to draw a map of the mobility regime's actors. After that, another section will map disputes that illustrate both the current regime's characteristics and possibilities of change. We will then close the chapter with some final remarks.

These two mapping exercises attempt to produce a reflexive-practical perspective. On the one hand, these maps aim to be useful in the elaboration of possible practical strategies for change. On the other hand, this perspective is based on my own experience as an activist first, and then as Director of Planning in the Municipality of Providencia between 2012 and 2015.[1] In that sense, these reflections emerge as results of an exercise that get close to 'militant research' (Halvorsen 2015) or 'action-research' (Wicks et al. 2016) in processes of institutional change and political involvement. In this way, we aspire to be part of a tradition started by Gramsci (1999), when he focused on studying the 'relations of force' and the role of the 'organic intellectual' in the organisation of social change.

Actors

The dispute over Santiago's mobility policies involves a diverse group of actors. Following the aim of trying to communicate the predominant nature of their interests easily, they are classified here in three typical sectors, which are 'government', 'civil society' and 'markets'. However, some actors are difficult to classify. Therefore their position lays in between the main sets. Their interests and actions intersect with those from subsets of actors inside the three sectors. Their role will be specifically discussed afterwards. Figure 6.1 shows the result of the mapping exercise.

Government

In the government sector, mapped actors illustrate the centralised nature of Santiago's governance regime (Valenzuela 2015). National ministries such as Housing and Urbanism (HU), Public Works (PW), and Transport and Telecommunications (TT) have a direct saying in the city's mobility policies. The HU ministry is in charge of investment on local and metropolitan roads, while PW on highways and the Metro lines. TT, by contrast, is in charge of operating the transport system that is based on the infrastructure implemented by the other national authorities and their centrally-appointed regional officials. For instance, the TT minister directly designates the metropolitan buses system's director and participates in the Metro's board. The central government appoints both Metro's executives and the Intendente (Regional Intendant).

Mayors from 52 municipalities that are part of the Metropolitan Region, on the other hand, are the next levels of executive democratic representation below the

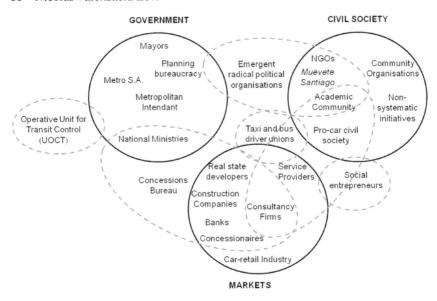

Figure 6.1 Map of actors in Santiago's mobility regime.

National Government. They have recently been involved in unprecedented political mobilisation and executive actions regarding mobility policies. One example is their alliance with civil society for demanding lower public transport fares for pensioners (Valenzuela 2016a). Another instance is the agreement between eleven mayors to create an integrated bike-hire service and its subsequent implementation in 2014.[2]

This last case is useful to illustrate the presence of other governmental actors: a community of planning bureaucrats that have been involved in efforts between mixed government levels in order to implement innovations or improvements that promote sustainable transport. Through formal and informal interactions, they have been building a new basis of knowledge for policymaking in the field of mobility. The inter-municipal bike-hire system was technically and administratively possible thanks to innovations made by this group.[3]

This group, however, takes care of matters related to one specific metropolitan area, although it is mostly part of hierarchical relations which make them dependent on the central authority. Their composition and nature are another samples of the importance of national powers over regional, metropolitan or municipal levels among Santiago's governmental actors. An influential exception is made by Santiago and Providencia's municipal teams, which led the bike-hire process and became a national role model regarding non-motorised transport policies.[4] However, although they can be seen as an exception to the hegemony of the State's central level over Santiago's metropolitan and local actors, they show the enormous gap in terms of capacities that are available to only two local governments, located exactly where national powers are, in comparison to other municipalities in the country and even in the same city of Santiago.

Finally, especially with the imminent democratic election of regional authorities,[5] the Intendente – so far directly appointed by the President – has been increasingly trying to get involved in transport's public discussions. Especially since 2014, Santiago counted with a proactive Intendente. In the case of the bike-hire system, he was key in the political side of the process. Since there was no precedent in such an inter-communal service before, the planning bureaucrats came up with an administrative solution that required that each one of the eleven city councils voted in favour of delegating the management of a public bid to one of the municipalities.[6] Although the Intendente and his team weren't administratively part of neither the bid nor the subsequent service contracts, they were strategic partners (political) for part the implementation process.

Civil society

In the civil society sector, there are both emergent actors and traditional ones getting involved in mobility disputes. For example, we can account recently formed NGOs and informal organisations. The most notable actor in this sector is Muévete Santiago (Move on Santiago). They work as a federation-assembly that gathers different organisations and movements, which emerged during the last decade, especially – but not only – around pro-cycling activism. Muévete's biggest achievement was bringing the World Bike Forum to Santiago during 2016, getting notable public exposure and giving political relevance to their demands – including a presidential promise about transforming the historically neglected Mapocho River into a cycle-park[7] (Intendencia Metropolitana de Santiago 2016).

Other actors, although are not new, have been recently getting involved in mobility discussions. For instance, neighbourhood-based pensioners' organisations were the starring actors behind demonstrations that demanded lower fares in the public transport system (Valenzuela 2016a). These organisations, called *clubs de adulto mayor* (Elderly Clubs) have been one of the few growing forms of local civil society organisations in Chile, especially since the country's inactive older population started to grow in the last two decades. The first actors demanding such type of fare reductions were high school and university students from the middle of the nineties to the emblematic mobilisations in 2006 and 2011 (Ponce-Lara 2013). The involvement of pensioners, as well as the demand's territorial organisational logic, is new elements. This territorial aspect of their emergence facilitated an alliance between them and many mayors since the older population has become increasingly important en the Chilean elections (Contreras-Aguirre and Morales-Quiroga 2014).

The academic community has usually been present and highly considered in Santiago's transport policy discussions. The most important change is the growing number of transport engineers that are challenging car supremacy's hegemony in mobility discussions. These changes in the scientific community have to do with the global debates on climate change (Ackerman 2009) and inequality

(Milanovic 2011), on one side, and, locally, with the social and political impacts of Transantiago's failure in 2007[8] (Ureta 2014), on the other side.

Also, different forms of protest have been increasingly common since Transantiago was implemented in 2007. They usually take form by calling for boycotting fare payments. This kind of unsystematic protest is not new in Santiago, but they have not led to a permanent organisation and action regarding transport, despite early expressions of discontent such as a famous revolt in 1957 called the *Huelga de la Chaucha* (The pennies strike) (CEME 2005). Then, as most of the today's examples, the protest was organised against the increase in public transport fares.

An intriguing comparison could be done with housing. The first land occupation in La Victoria in 1957 is considered as the beginning of the *pobladores* movement for housing (Garcés 2002). It was the start of an organised movement that lasts until today. Another comparison could be done reviewing the connection between the 1955–1956 bus boycotts related to the civil rights movement and the contemporary existence of the Bus Riders Union in Los Angeles, California, in the United States (Lipsitz 2004). The causes of Santiaguinean transport-related civil society's passivity seems to be an important topic for further action and research.

Markets

The markets sector is constituted by a diversity of actors, some of whom perform in a coordinated way in order to maximise their gains, many of which depend strongly on the current form of mobility policies in Santiago. One example are car-related retailers, which ground their business model on an ability-to-pay created by consumption loans provided by the financial sector (Zúñiga 2014), and are important advertising buyers in the mainstream national media – whose business-models, including the case of the only state-owned TV channel, are founded on selling advertising space (Salas et al. 2009).

Another instance is the vertical integration between real estate developers and construction companies, which have been organised together during more than half a century in the Chilean Chamber of Construction (Álvarez 2015). Constructors and Developers are coordinated with banks and highway concessionaires for promoting a Public-Private Partnership agenda in Santiago (Icare 2014). Consultancy firms, as well as service or product providers, are mixed with the academic community, which implies some times to have the same people playing different roles within these three types of actors and between the markets and the civil society sector.

The problem of scale is a key to understanding different actors in this sector, particularly among mobility service providers: the motivations from small and medium-sized enterprises can significantly vary in respect to transnationals, and many times be in conflict.

Cross-sector actors

To finish the discussion on this first map, we can see the existence of three particular actors that appear to be having a catalysing role in the dynamics of each sector. The first one is the Ministry of public work's Concessions Bureau. This organisation was created inside the government at the end of the nineties, had a key role in boosting Foreign Direct Investment through PPPs for infrastructure projects (MOP 2003; Engel et al. 2009; Bitrán and Villena 2010), was involved in emblematic corruption scandals at the beginning of the 2000s (Balán 2011), and also became a cornerstone in the design of Transantiago's conflictive implementation before 2007 (Ramírez et al. 2007).

These days, the Concessions Bureau and complementary bodies such as the 'Concessions Board' keeps playing a central role in decisions on transport investment in Santiago, based on the idea of PPPs and incentivising the participation of national and transnational capital in Santiago's infrastructural development (Valenzuela 2016b). The concessions system, governed by this bureau, is strongly and deeply installed in mainstream political elites' imaginary as a motor of Chile's economic development (Bachelet 2016). It is a knot in Santiago's neoliberal institutional settlement. Building an alternative to what it represents and what it achieves regarding infrastructure investment must be a central task for any counter-hegemonic project.

The second of these intermediate actors is a group of what these days is called 'social entrepreneurs'. At a local level, there are several new entrepreneurial activities that have been forming a new socio-productive fabric, bike stores, small manufacturing companies, service providers such as the ones behind the bike-hire system and bike taxies, different sorts of apps, groups of professionals involved in transit education, non-profit consulting organisations, technology importers and distributers, and so on. They denote both how the State's step back from many roles related to the provision of public services – as it is common under neoliberal hegemony – and demand for social innovation in the specific field of mobility services. Designing a new mobility regime in Santiago, or anywhere else, urges to produce capacities and institutional spaces for the production of innovation, especially since mobility and connectivity technologies are inherently an evolving phenomenon. These social entrepreneurs are part of a grey area where limits between for-profit and non-profit motivations are ambiguous, as it is also the case with taxi and bus driver unions.

Finally, we can likewise find new radical political organisations that have emerged after 2011's student protests (Fleet and Guzmán Concha 2016). Revolución Democrática (RD), for instance, a new political party founded in January 2012 mostly by student unionists, counts within its militants a number of Muévete Santiago's activists, urban planning bureaucrats and academics. In Providencia, RD was a key in the 2012 municipal election, which led to Josefa Errázuriz government and then to achievements regarding several metropolitan transport policies and discussions. Our team in Providencia played a crucial role in the bike-hire system's implementation, as well as in the promotion of public transport in general. There have been previous cases of political parties that have had presence in the different sectors and have coordinated determined agendas, however, the case of RD illustrates the social and political importance gained by mobility, included the emergent influence of social leaders that come from mobility-related organisations, and also a certain demand for both coordination between sectors and recognition of the people's mobility needs.

Summarising, regarding the actors, neoliberal hegemony can be understood as a concentration of power among the markets sector, especially regarding real estate and financial capital. As a consequence, the State works as a facilitator of the big corporations' agenda. In these terms, the social and political work needed to change the regime involves both strengthening civil society and disputing control over the State, for which effective political strategies are needed.

Disputes

After having developed and illustrated a map with actors, we can now do the same with disputes. While adopting the notion of disputes, I am trying to illustrate ongoing conflicts or contradictions that express both the current state of affairs and possibilities of change in Santiago's mobility regime. These disputes entail a potential appeal for being used as a driver for political action. In another simplification – as it was with the 'sectors' in the previous map – the map here is divided into three spaces that imply different forms of political action: 'communications', 'collective organisation' and 'state policies'. As it was already mentioned, if the Actor's Map tries to explain the nature of each one's interests, the Disputes' Map tries to explain the type of work needed to change relations of force in each space. The type of organisation, action and value that is needed in media communications, for instance, is not the same as for community organising, or to change the regime set by formal institutions put in place by state policies. They are all, however, inter-related. Although, within any group that aims to change the regime, each space might need a certain division of work and specialisation, their efforts need to be strategically coordinated.

The mapping exercise that can be seen in Table 6.1 involves conflicts, contradictions, hegemonic views and alternatives regarding neoliberal transport policies. All these elements can allow us to do, inductively, a series of connections in order to synthesise the main disputes.

For instance, in the case of communications, the main dispute is the notion of mobility as a public or a private good. The relations of force in this space are difficult to measure. Doing it is directly related to resources used by neoliberal capitalism to influence the public discourse and people's perceptions. At least, one needs to pay attention to two variables. On one side, perceptions, such as the population's understanding of public transport as a commodity or as a social right, or aspirational values assigned to different means of transport (Barker 2014). On the other side, how these same concepts are part of authorities' discourses when they address the public (Ureta 2014).

The space of collective organisation is characterised by tensions between public versus privatised, and democratic versus non-democratic production of mobility policy, infrastructure and services. It has to do in general with the role of civil society, but, in particular, with the degree of democratic accountability of decision-making processes, with how industrial processes behind mobility services are organised, and finally with how mobility is articulated by socio-technical systems that produce effects on communities – for instance, in terms of socioeconomic segregation.

All these different topics imply groups which gain or lose power for decision-making, bargaining or seeking for rents. Although their relative power strongly depends on which sort of state policies is set in place, this space of collective organisation is where we find the actors themselves interacting and influencing different

Table 6.1 Disputes in Santiago's mobility regime

Space	Disputes	Neoliberal hegemonic view	Post-neoliberal alternative
Communications	Official discourse about Public Transport	Public transport as a commodity.	Public transport as a social right.
	Ideological use of different transport modes	The car as a sign of status obtained through credit. Cycling as backwardness.	Promotion of low-carbon, non-polluting, healthier and cheaper modes, as a cultural value.
Collective Organisation	Forms of organisation among the public transport users	Transport as a managerial and non-political phenomenon. Rejection of links between social movements and the state.	Co-production of mobility. Strong civil society in partnerships for the development of policies and services.
	Decision-making	No democratic accountability of decision-making regarding transport.	Democratic accountability of decision-making regarding transport.
	Segregation produced by transport policies	Collateral damage	Unacceptable
	Social-industrial fabric of transport	Deregulated, finance-led, technologically precarious. The presence of rent-seeking.	Use of revenue to reinvest, strategic planning, a central role of the public sector. Industrial policies linked to mobility. Promotion of innovation.
State policy	Land regulation regarding public space for mobility	Minimum. Car-oriented.	Maximum. Oriented to multiple modes and especially promotion of the non-motorised ones.
	Modal integration devices and coordination costs	Lack of integration and coordination costs transferred to users. No incentives for inclusion of less profitable modes.	Integration and coordination as a function of the public sector. Promotion of sustainable modes.
	Role of public transport	Targeting subsidies to specific users and understanding of public transport as a market failure.	Public transport as a strategic decision for sustainability and as a universal social policy.
	Financing mobility services' investment and operation.	Regressive, oriented to groups with higher ability to pay. Transportation costs transferred from capital to labour.	Progressive, oriented to reduce inequality gaps. Not based on users' ability to pay. Transportation costs transferred from labour to capital.

spaces. It is in the collective organisation space where one can verify what Kantor et al. (1997) identify the three key variables to characterise a metropolitan governance regime: who has the stronger market power for investment decisions between capital and governments, how strong is popular control over decision-making, and how integrated and collaborative are relations between different levels of government.

Finally, in the space of state policies, we can find different institutions that take place in the form of laws, government programmes, executive acts, tax collection, public budgeting and PPP mechanisms. The main cleavage entails the tension between mobility institutionally understood as markets or as commons. The kind of state policies that can define a regime could involve, for instance, land regulation, coordination between different transport modes, targeting of public transport services, and transport financing models. Concerning the latter, for instance, Santiago's regime entails an extreme dependency on private capital. Alternative financing models could be the Colombian 'valorisation charge' (Doebele et al. 1979) for funding public infrastructure investment or the French 'transport contribution' (Mirgalet 2011) for financing public transport systems' operation.

Moreover, the spaces of communications, collective organisation and state policies are inter-related. The same can be said regarding the disputes that have been identified here. Dialectics regarding 'mobility as a public or private good', 'privatised and non-democratic versus state-led and democratic production of mobility infrastructure and services', and 'mobility institutionally understood as markets or commons' are simply different expressions of the same core tension. What is in tension is the nature of the mobility regime, which expresses and is disputed in each space: the general public's notion of mobility, the way in which it is organised, and state institutions that formalise these relations. The state of affairs cannot be defined as an imminent emancipatory change, but neither can it be considered a consensus. The exercise of doing this map shows how on-going disputes are expressing possibilities of regime change.

Final remarks

The value of the maps is that they allow us to understand Santiago's regime as a dynamic phenomenon, and therefore not an incontrovertible reality. Although there is a clear hegemonic position that transforms Santiago in an orthodox example of neoliberal mobility, there are disputes in place, which can develop towards unpredictable directions. Using the framework provided by Kantor et al. mobilisation (1997), on the one hand, Santiago has a disadvantaged market position in relation to its dependence on private capital, which gives the financial and real estate sector an enormous power. On the other hand, a dispersed and non-integrated governmental system is linked to a weak popular control. These two characteristics are key to understanding possibilities of change. Other cases in which these regimes changed in Latin America included social and political mobilisation that strengthened popular control and subsequently reconfigured the State's relation to private capital and how political power is distributed between different levels of government (for a review on the cases of La Paz and Medellin, see Valenzuela 2016b). Although processes as such are not present in Santiago, the maps show actors and disputes that could have the potential to gain power. That will depend on this different actors' agency soon.

Change in regimes faces transition costs (Khan 1995), and depend on the relative economic and political power of different stakeholders that sustain a particular political settlement developed under a neoliberal rule. That is the case of the mobility regime in Santiago. As we already stated, it is evident that a neoliberal hegemonic view remains dominant on how this regime is configured. Nevertheless, the lack of consensus around this regime is evident as well. Understanding the map of actors interacting and establishing relations of force between them is useful to comprehend the nature of their interests. Additionally, mapping different disputes, each of which implies a particular form of specialised political work, can provide a view on the amount and character of resources needed to be deployed in order to produce change. Knowing the actors' interests and having an operationalised notion of efforts needed to modify their current power relations are the foundations for setting a strategy for change. The exercise done here is only an initial attempt to produce reflexive-praxis within actors that aim for changing the mobility regime. Both further action and research are needed to be done in order to comprehend and eventually challenge the neoliberal mobility regime in Santiago.

Notes

1 Providencia is one of the municipalities located in the centre of Santiago. In its case, it concentrates a relevant part of the central business district. Although it has around 150,000 residents, its daily floating population reaches 2,000,000 people. It also plays a strategic role in terms of transport, since Santiago's geographical conditions make it the gateway to access the eastern part of the city, where most of the jobs are concentrated.
2 See the discussion below.
3 See note 6.
4 Since the sixties, Providencia became a national leader regarding urban planning. In particular, its Department of Urbanism became famous under the leadership of Germán Bannen, who was awarded a National Urbanism Price for its contributions from the Municipality. More recently, during Josefa Errázuriz' administration, a particular leadership in terms of sustainable mobility was recognised by institutions such as the South American Development Bank, with its Price for the Best Urban Development Initiative in 2013. In Valenzuela (2013) I propose the notion of the 'School of Providencia' to refer to this tradition and its new developments.
5 In October 2016, the Chilean Senate voted in favour of the democratic election of 'regional governors'.
6 The absence of preceding experiences was sorted under the lead of a joint team formed by the legal advisors from the municipalities of Santiago and Providencia. They discussed the administrative solution at a national level with the National Government's Comptroller and the National Public Procurement System. In order to open one single public bid for hiring one single service, local councils had to vote in favour of delegating the power for doing it to one municipality, which in this case was Santiago. After the bid, each municipality would sign different contracts, since there is not a single legal entity that can be the principal for the eleven municipal jurisdictions.
7 This Project emerges as a proposal from cycling activists, and became a symbol in the demands raised by Muévete Santiago and the municipalities of Santiago and Providencia.

8 Transantiago is the questioned system of public transport of Santiago. Originally was imagined as a Bus Rapid Transit system but after ten years and several upgrades, people still express a feeling of rejection for its implementation and functioning.

References

Ackerman, F. (2009). *Can We Afford the Future? The Economics of a Warming World*. New York: Zed Books.

Álvarez, R. (2015). *Gremios empresariales, política y neoliberalismo. Los casos de Chile y Perú (1985–2010)*. Santiago: Lom.

Atria, F. (2013). *La constitución tramposa*. Santiago de Chile: LOM Ediciones.

Atria, F., Larraín, G., Couso, J., & Benavente, J. M. (2013). El otro modelo. DEBATE.

Araujo, K., & Martuccelli, D. (2012). *Desafíos comunes. Retrato de la sociedad chilena y sus individuos*. Santiago: LOM Ediciones.

Bachelet, M. (2016). Discurso de la Presidenta para el proyecto de Presupuesto 2017. Retrieved October 10, 2016, from www.gob.cl/presidenta-presento-proyecto-presupuesto-2017/

Balán, M. (2011). Competition by Denunciation: The Political Dynamics of Corruption Scandals in Argentina and Chile. *Comparative Politics*, 43(4), 459–478. http://doi.org/10.5129/001041511796301597

Barker, J. (2014). Aspirations for Automobility: Family Geographies and the Production of Young People's Aspirations for Cars. *Families*, 3(2), 167–183. http://doi.org/10.1332/2 04674314X13965329386888

Bitrán, E., & Villena, M. (2010). El nuevo desafío de las concesiones de obras públicas en Chile: hacia una mayor eficiencia y desarrollo institucional. Estudios Públicos.

CEME – Centro de Estudios Miguel Enríquez. (2005). 2 de abril de 1957: Chile huelga general, incidentes y disturbios por alza de locomoción colectiva. Prensa de la época. La Tercera. Retrieved from www.google.co.uk/url?sa=t&rct=j&q=&esrc=s&source= web&cd=1&cad=rja&uact=8&ved=0CCAQFjAAahUKEwill-yCoNbIAhUCPBQKH a95B14&url=http%3A%2F%2Fwww.archivochile.com%2FMov_sociales%2FDoc_ gen%2FMSdocgen0025.pdf&usg=AFQjCNHm1zF1SdeI9nwzyxEW5xTxc9sKqQ&bv m=bv.105814755,d.bGg [Accessed 20 September 2015]

Chang, H. J. (2002). Breaking the Mould: An Institutionalist Political Economy Alternative to the Neo-Liberal Theory of the Market and the State. *Cambridge Journal of Economics*, 26(5), 539–559. http://doi.org/10.1093/cje/26.5.539

Contreras-Aguirre, G., & Morales-Quiroga, M. (2014). Young people and electoral participation in Chile 1989-2013. Analyzing the effect of the voluntary vote. Revista Latinoamericana de Ciencias Sociales, Niñez y Juventud, 12(2), 597–615.

De Mattos, C., Ducci, M. E., Rodríguez, A., & Yanez, G. (2004). Santiago en la globalización: ¿Una nueva ciudad? Santiago: Ediciones Sur.de Sousa Santos, B. (2010). *Descolonizar el saber, reinventar el poder*. Montevideo: Ediciones Trilce.

Doebele, W. A., Orville, F., Grimes, S. J. S., & Linn, J. F. (1979). Participation of Beneficiaries in Financing Urban Services: Valorization Charges in Bogotá, Colombia. *Land Economics*, 55(1), 73–92. http://doi.org/10.2307/3145959?ref=search-gateway:88ba811 e5f07f7c421b6085ad72ad3c2

Engel, E., Fischer, R., & Galetovic, A. (2009). *Renegociación de concesiones en Chile*. Santiago: Centro de Estudios Públicos.

Fleet, N., & Guzmán Concha, C. (2016). Mass Higher Education and the 2011 Student Movement in Chile: Material and Ideological Implications. *Bulletin of Latin American Research*, n/a – n/a. http://doi.org/10.1111/blar.12471

Gárate, M. (2012). *La revolución capitalista de Chile*. Santiago: Ediciones Universidad Alberto Hurtado. http://doi.org/10.1111/ehr.12106/full

Garcés, M. (956AD). Tomando su sitio. El movimiento de pobladores de Santiago, 1957–1970. Santiago de Chile, Ed. LOM. 450 p., 2002.

Garreton, M. A. (2012). *Neoliberalismo corregido y progresismo limitado: los gobiernos de la Concertación en Chile 1990–2010*. Santiago: Editorial Arcis/Consejo.

Gramsci, A. (1999). *Selections from Prison Notebooks* (pp. 1–846). London: The Electric Book Company Ltd.

Halvorsen, S. (2015). Militant Research against-and-beyond Itself: Critical Perspectives from the University and Occupy London. *Area*, 47(4), 466–472. http://doi.org/10.1111/area.12221

Han, C. (2012). *Life in Debt: Times of Care and Violence in Neoliberal Chile*.

Hidalgo, R., & Janoschka, M. (2014). *La ciudad neoliberal*. Santiago de Chile: Serie Geolibros.

Icare. (2014). II Congreso Empresa y Sociedad. Cooperación Público Privada: Buscando espacios de colaboración Estado – Empresa – Sociedad. Retrieved from www.icare.cl/congreso/2014/eys/feys2014.pdf

Instituto Nacional de Estadísticas. (2013). *VII Encuesta de Presupuestos Familiares* (pp. 1–37). Santiago de Chile: Instituto Nacional de Estadísticas.

Intendencia Metropolitana de Santiago. (2016). Presidenta Bachelet hace importante anuncio sobre Mapocho Pedaleable. Retrieved October 10, 2016, from www.gobiernosantiago.cl/presidenta-bachelet-hace-importante-anuncio-para-las-ciclovias-de-la-region

Kantor, P., Savitch, H. V., & Haddock, S. V. (1997). The Political Economy of Urban Regimes a Comparative Perspective. *Urban Affairs Review*, 32(3), 348–377. http://doi.org/10.1177/107808749703200303

Khan, M. (1995). State Failure in Weak States: A Critique on New Institutionalist Explanations. In C. Lewis, J. Harriss, & J. Hunter (Eds.), *The New Institutional Economics and Third World Development* (pp. 71–86). London: Routledge.

Khan, M. (2010). *Political Settlements and the Governance of Growth-Enhancing Institutions*. London: SOAS.

Lipsitz, G. (2004). Learning from Los Angeles: Another One Rides the Bus. *American Quarterly*, 56(3), 511–529. http://doi.org/10.1353/aq.2004.0037

Mangabeira Unger, R. (2010). *La alternativa de la Izquierda*. (S. Villegas, Trans.). Fondo de Cultura Económica.

Milanovic, B. (2011). *The Haves and the Have-Nots: A Brief and Idiosyncratic Guide to Global Inequality*.

Mirgalet, L. (2011). Tarifas, subsidios y sistemas tarifarios: El caso de las ciudades francesas (pp. 1–26). Presented at the Conferencia de Transporte Sustentable, Calidad del Aire y Cambio Climático, Rosario, Argentina. Retrieved from http://cleanairinstitute.org/download/rosario/gp3_3_03_lucas_mirgalet.pdf

Ministerio de Obras Públicas. (2003). *Sistema de Concesiones en Chile 1990–2003*. Santiago de Chile.

Moulian, T. (1997). *Chile actual: Anatomia de un mito*. Santiago de Chile: Santiago: LOM-ARCIS Ediciones.

North, D. C. (1990). *Institutions, Institutional Change and Economic Performance*. Cambridge: Cambridge University Press.

OECD. (2009). *Estudios Territoriales de la OCDE: Chile 2009*. OECD Publishing.

Orellana, A. (2009). La gobernabilidad metropolitana de Santiago: la dispar relación de poder de los municipios. *EURE (Santiago)*, 35(104), 101–120. http://doi.org/10.4067/S0250-71612009000100005

Palma, J. G. (2012). *Why Has Productivity Growth Stagnated in Most Latin American Countries since the Neo-Liberal Reforms?* Oxford: Oxford University Press. http://doi.org/10.1093/oxfordhb/9780199571048.013.0023

Polanyi, K. (2001). *The Great Transformation*. Boston: Beacon Press.

Ponce-Lara, C. (2013). La socialización política en el aula: Comparación entre las movilizaciones de Francia y Chile. *Revista Latinoamericana de Ciencias Sociales, Niñez y Juventud*, 11(2), 603–615.

Ramírez, P., Minay, S., & Skoknic, F. (2007, November 4). El recorte que mató al Transantiago. Retrieved October 10, 2016, from http://ciperchile.cl/2007/11/04/el-recorte-que-mato-al-transantiago/

Rodríguez, A., & Rodríguez, P. (2009). *Santiago, una ciudad neoliberal: SUR Corporación de Estudios Sociales y Educación*. Escuela de Dirigentes Sociales.

Rodríguez, A., Saborido, M., & Segovia, O. (2012). *Violencias en una ciudad neoliberal: Santiago de Chile*. Santiago: Ediciones SUR.

Salas, V., Hernández, D., Pastén, W., & Poblete, P. (2009). Mercado de la publicidad en Chile. Working Paper Series Boletín De Estudios Sectoriales.

Sheller, M., & Urry, J. (2006). The New Mobilities Paradigm. *Environment and Planning A*, 38(2), 207–226. http://doi.org/10.1068/a37268

Ureta, S. (2014). Normalizing Transantiago: On the Challenges (and Limits) of Repairing Infrastructures. *Social Studies of Science*, 44(3), 368–392. http://doi.org/10.1177/0306312714523855

Valenzuela, E. (2015). *Descentralización Ya*. Santiago: RiL editores.

Valenzuela, N. (2013). La Escuela de Providencia. In Márquez, J. (2013) *Senderos en el Bosque Urbano* (pp. 9–20). Santiago: Ediciones ARQ.

Valenzuela, N. (2016a). El Derecho a la Conexión: imaginarios, luchas, derechos e instituciones. Revista ARQ, No. 94 (Imaginarios).

Valenzuela, N. (2016b). Soberanía Urbana: Estado Conector, Infraestructura De Transporte Y Procesos Constituyentes en Colombia, Bolivia Y Chile (pp. 1–18). Presented at the Congreso Internacional Contested Cities, Madrid.

Wicks, P. G., Reason, P., & Bradbury, H. (2016). 1 Living Inquiry: Personal, Political and Philosophical Groundings for Action Research Practice. In *The SAGE Handbook of Action Research* (pp. 14–30). 1 Oliver's Yard, 55 City Road, London England EC1Y 1SP United Kingdom: SAGE Publications Ltd. http://doi.org/10.4135/9781848607934.d7

Zúñiga, D. (2014).Mercado automotriz chileno: un análisis empírico. Available at: http://www.repositorio.uchile.cl/handle/2250/116653

7 Retail urbanism

The neoliberalisation of urban society by consumption in Santiago de Chile

Liliana De Simone

Introduction

In urban studies, it is a current debate that changes in global processes of production and consumption – lead by the expansion of the neoliberal market model – have restructured the ways in which contemporary cities are transformed, represented, and perceived. Nevertheless, the many ways in which consumption has transformed the urban realm is not still completely understood. This mainly because this processes lay within an economic system that blends local and global scales as never happened in history before, making quite difficult to understand the forces laying beneath everyday consumption practices in the city.

Baudrillard original works on consumer society, back in the Seventies, laid the foundations for a symbolic and physical interpretation of the act of buying in contemporary societies (Baudrillard 1998 [1970]). The *Systéme des objects* (Baudrillard 1978 [1968]) his first work about the role of merchandise in contemporary society, described the new socio-technical order emerged as the novel ground for everyday life organisation. For Baudrillard, the relation between goods and its social meanings stands as a cultural change brought by modernity, in which consumption replaced production as the central model for social relations and value reproduction (Baudrillard 1998: 115).

While many researchers have focused their works on the production processes that are reconfiguring the geographies of power and capital around the globe (Harvey 2012; Sassen 1991; Soja 1989), not many studies have addressed the role that spaces for consumption have had in this process. Retail infrastructure has been understudied as an iconic element of a global urban society, even if it plays a major role in the processes of mass production and collective consumption. The multiplication of spaces for mass consumption (as shopping malls, retail centres, and commercial infrastructure in general) has set a new territorial dimension for the organisation of the urban under new marketisation aims. Urban retailisation understood as the infiltration of the retail logics in the production of the urban environment, has set new standards in the planning, financing, and management of cities.

Furthermore, retail infrastructure stands today as an iconic element of the global urban society in which collective consumption crystallise new social interaction patterns, as well as it reflects the relations between global capital and local urban configurations.

By adopting a leading role amongst other public and private infrastructure, retail-ised urban spaces construct experience and place in a neoliberal manner, in which the private sector builds and operate private areas with the expectation to be perceived and consumed as public by consumers. By one hand, retail promoters have managed to spread urban projects within the city by installing urban planning strategies, aiming to promote consumption practices the door of entrance for a daily urban experience. In the other hand, local governments have sustained retail developments as the key projects to administrate downtown areas, leaving retailers the duty of guarding public space. This chapter argues that the retailisation of urban spaces have inaugurated a way of creating new concepts of urbanity in neoliberal societies. It describes how this process can be observed in the recent evolution of retail geographies in Chile, and proposes that this particular configuration between global capitals and markets, with local territories and routines, can be referred to as a retail-lead urbanism.

Chilean cities are a key laboratory in this process and have been the arena for experimentation for retail urbanism, even replicated abroad. After the radical liberalisation of urban legislations and the economic opening to free markets during the seventies and eighties, Santiago saw a radical explosion in the number of retail developments. As the detractors, as well as the supporters of this neoliberal change, have claimed, Chilean social life revolves today around consumption and retail spaces, which has changed the meaning of commercial space for all citizens (Moulian 1999; Larrain 1996).

By examining the current distribution of retail infrastructure in Santiago, this chapter describes the processes that conducted the ideological consolidation of the neoliberal logics at the local scale and through consumption activities in retail spaces. I will highlight the transformations in meanings and functions of Chilean shopping malls, and the results in a multidimensional consumption experience that restrained the city and transformed the notion of 'right to the city' into 'right to the mall'.

In a first place, I will offer a theoretical background to understand the role of consumption spaces in the neoliberal urbanism debate, followed by a historical revision of the genealogy of foreign retail infrastructure in Santiago de Chile, and I'll conclude with a consideration around the current tensions of Santiago's consumption urban society.

Consumption spaces roles in the consolidation of a neoliberal everydayness

Neoliberalism is often conceptualised as a process of marketisation, in which the state and local governments provide public goods through the increasing involvement of private sector (Birch and Siemiatycki 2016; Peck and Tickell 2002). In the entanglement of the state and the markets in planning, financing and operating services and facilities within the city, neoliberalism has been expanded globally as a logical order of capital and power. In this entanglement corporate money has a significant role in the provision, management and functioning of duties that were previously commanded by the State. Nevertheless, neoliberalism's historical analyses have often dismissed the spatial dimension of its reproduction (Hackworth 2007), as well as its dialectical relation with the geographical expression of global production/consumption processes.

The radical reforms on civic legislation, economy, urban policy and civil rights, performed by Augusto Pinochet dictatorship during the seventies and eighties, made of Chile a country that is widely known as a neoliberal laboratory. The primary goal that drove the neoliberal Chilean mindset was to find and promote any possibility of private business opportunity that may lie in the tasks traditionally managed by the State. The public health system, retirement pensions, primary education, public housing and urban planning, among others aspects, were seen as arenas where to liberalise markets. And by that, the neoliberal revolution set in Chile was set in order to let capitals reproduce under private hands, in a process that – as the media widely diffused it – will eventually 'trickle-down' wealth to lower incomers by the creation of new jobs by the richest.

Under this process, the social production of urban space in Chile remained restrained to market-oriented intentions. Its aims were to promote economic dynamism through a strong real estate market, an intensification of internal consumption through increasing consumer loans and mortgage credits, and the privatisation of formerly public systems of public health, basic education and pensions. Domestic consumption became then a primary national business, which nowadays produces rates of return satisfactory enough to keep the good health of the national economy. Moreover, the influx of global capital into retail real estate completes a successful business structure for the Chilean economy, now exported to other Latin American countries under a retail development model.

The articulation of domestic consumption practices and its urban entanglements in the city within a neoliberal local governance – summed up with foreign financial capitals injected into local real estate markets – is what I defined as the retail urbanism. As a combination of retail business performed in the city in the last thirty years, retail urbanism is both the medium and the result of neoliberal mindset.

With retailers' technical expertise in building successful shopping centres and with the support of local authorities, eager to attract national and foreign capitals, the urban resultant of retail urbanism is a city meant for consumption as its lucrative primary activity. An activity that triggers speculative land markets, volatile stock markets, and symbolic and social value in constant redefinition by global fashion trends. In this 'city of consumption', every other urban function (e.g. education, recreation, transportation, culture or health) are contingent to the retail spatial configurations, which agglutinate all these former services into complex urban master plans.

Retail urbanism has three possible dimensions that affect urban realm. On one side, it is the visible face of global consumption economies and the landing hubs of global networks of logistic and distribution of delocalised mass production (mainly located in Asian countries). Shopping malls, big boxes, and retail-ised historical downtowns are the physical infrastructure for global production and consumption networks. This dimension includes the speculative nature of real estate and land markets, which lie under the marketisation of the urban development and becomes involved whenever retail infrastructure is located in a local territory, affecting properties prices and triggering speculative processes of urban financialisation.

On the others, transnational investments funds, global retail, corporate chains, securitisation of leasing flows in local and foreign stock markets, just naming a few, are all part of the financial instruments that lays in a single shopping mall located in a city. In the Chilean case, retailers are also allowed to manage banks and give mortgage loans to its customers, without the requirements usually made by banks. The urban outcomes of the banking dimension of retail become even harder to grasp, as the funds that come from abroad through investments funds and corporate chains are relocated in millions of consumer's loans. The millions loaned by retail and invested in private housing are another evidence of the impacts of retail urbanism in the city.

At last, there is a third cultural dimension of retail urbanism that has to do with is meaning in a consumption society. The social meaning of consumption in a globalised world makes every shopping mall a 'door' that opens to the rest of the world. Global fashion trends and standardised architecture make retail infrastructure an artefact of globalisation (de Mattos 2001). The location – or absence – of this infrastructure impacts substantially in the society that dwellers can create.

Having said this, by retail urbanism I am referring to those retail-oriented urban strategies, implemented in urban lands as the result of multi-sectorial business investments. It proliferates within a lax legislation that comes from a neoliberal urban policy setting, and which combines different geographical and temporal scales of production of value and goods, within a cultural framework for the circulation and reproduction of symbolic value. Retail urbanism, therefore, is one of the many resultants of the urban neoliberalisation, as well as it is a mechanism of production of value, in a dialectical socio-spatial process that lays in consumption as its main motor – and no longer production as the engine for wealth reproduction (Soja 1980, 1989). By this, every shopping mall is at the same time a place for shopping goods, brands, and values (cultural dimension); a place where investors rent from lands speculation and urban renovation (urban dimension); a place where financial capital goes through and beyond, using mortgage, loans and securitisation tactics (financial dimension). These 'places' of consumption restructure the city through a retail urbanism.

These arrangements of consumption produce a generic but segregated landscape, which must be understood beyond the contextual dimension of every shopping mall. As artefacts of an urban economy – well attached to global forces of production – retail urbanism also responds to the storage and logistic geographies. Warehouse buildings, storage districts, global distribution logistics networks made of ports and airports, expressways and toll-roads are other expressions of retail urbanism since they are necessary for the massive distribution of goods within the city. Usually, they are segregated from the consumption geographies, but nevertheless, they respond to the same phenomena.

Moreover, global advertising campaigns (oriented to the reproduction of what is valued), massive billboards; thematic festivals; sports, musical and cultural mega-events run by global brands, are other expressions of retail urbanism. They transform the urban in order to promote and locate consumption practices within the cities.

And more than ever, post-consumption disposal conflicts, meaning by this the physical and symbolic destruction of value, needed for a re-creation of new consumer goods, are therefore vital for the survival of a market-oriented society. And again, within the urban arena, these are urban conflicts that respond to the dynamics of retail urbanism, as we are describing them here.

Retail as a medium for the urban to be express, produced and consumed, also determined the way a citizen is transformed into a consumer. The cycle of productions and consumptions of value and goods constructs and determinates space from a consumption logic – in which consumption is a production force in itself. This reflects the context of a cultural order that shifted from the figure of the citizen to the figure of the consumerist as the subject of rights and duties (Bauman 2000, 2007). To paraphrase Bauman, in the absence of work and production as major indicators of class and identity – what I do is what I am – consumption became the new way to mediate with society, and it's hierarchies of access – what I buy is what I am. By this, the validation of individual as members of society goes through the mediation with consumption as a civilising process, in which retail spaces paradoxically become the places for performing the right to be part of society at its core. Therefore, to consume becomes a social validation action. The dialectical materialism that traditionally put production forces like the ones that structure class is no longer valid, or at least, cannot be the primary indicator of value reproduction and class relations (Soja 1980).

Retail urbanism as a theoretical framework is born from a Lefebvrian sociospatial analysis used for understanding contemporary urban consumption. As Soja pointed out, the spatial analysis of the social production of space rely on the production relations expressed in the territory (1980: 208). By acknowledging consumption as a productive force of capital and social relations, with a particular structure of organised space – as retail Urbanism points out – it's evident that we need to inverse the importance that has been given to productive activities over consumption activities. As the least studied manifestation of the same dialectic process of capital reproduction, consumption is an area still to address from Marxist approaches. Retail organisation in space is thus both social and spatial, and it represents a dialectically defined component of the general relations of production.

The socio-spatial structure of consumption in a retail urbanism generates a type of urbanity mediated by consumption practices. Within this, retail urbanism creates territorial inequalities that cannot longer be examined only from the traditional approach of spatial analysis of class and production (Soja 1980: 210–211), that commonly focus on where do people works and where they reside. We must include new epistemologies in the urban analysis that allow us to study contemporary consumption practices as a productive force – of capital and space – in itself, that also focus on the importance of where do people buy, how and why, as well as how is the cityscape that these practices create.

Approaching retail urbanism as a productive force to study the socio-spatial logic of consumption raise awareness of consumption as a spatial productive force, in Lefebvrian terms (Lefebvre 1991), and not only as an abstract resultant of spatial processes between capital and its agents. The territorial dimension of consumption as a productive force is accomplished within a new global hierarchy of spaces and places, as pointed out by Lefebvre, which re-scaled the discussion of national economies around the globe by pointing out cities as the major economic hubs for capital reproduction (Lefebvre 2003).

Retail urbanism, therefore, exceeds singular urban areas. It cannot only be addressed to cities, but it may be rather comprehended as an urban phenomenon of planetary effects, motivated by the institutionalising of neoliberalism as an economic, politic and, at large, cultural model. Even if we have studied shopping malls as standardised and globalised artefacts, the spatial organisation of retail in the city and its urban outcomes varies from city to city. Retail urbanism is then a spatial production process that uses 'decontextualised' architecture, systematically build by global placemaking industries, and invigorated by the local and regional market-oriented policies that neoliberal deregulation forged around the world. Brenner and Theodore referred to this as the synchronisation of financing markets, the de-localisation of productive processes, the fragmentation of workforces, the homologation of aesthetics and taste trough global media and advertising, and the incremental promotion of standardised consumption practices worldwide (Brenner and Theodore 2002).

As Brenner and Theodore have pointed out, the new scenario in urban production is characterised by the demolition of many institutional constraints upon the increasing participation of market logics in the commodification of public goods, exploitation of local workers and territories, and liberalisation (or total abrogation) of urban policies and planning strategies. These trends, when put together, can be one way to analyse the reproduction and intensification of uneven development in cities all over the world. But retail urbanism lightens up to other symbolical values that lay down on consumption as a cultural process in itself, as we begun discussing it through Baudrillard works. Retailisation and retails urbanism explain the cultural backgrounds where this daunted processes of uneven development collide with a commoditised reality that we can only understand through the analysis of the entanglement between the symbolic meaning of goods, and its promises of a better and happier everyday life through consumption practices. To look at both sides of the same reality are keys to understanding the current dispersion of retail in cases as the Chilean one.

Conflict and naturalisation in Chilean consumption spaces

Retail-oriented projects and the distribution of retail infrastructure represent the multiscalar dynamics of neoliberalism, which confront values, perceptions, and representations of culture through the production of consumption landscapes. This approach abandons the sociological and anthropological tradition that analyses consumption as alienated phenomena, and by which shopping places are a suburban sub-product of this postmodern de-naturalisation of urbanity (Amendola 2000; Augé 1995). Retail infrastructure is no longer approach as a suburban invention in response to the suburban's population consumption practices. We see these spaces of consumption as a *dispositif* for the global dissemination of a normative discourse around value and goods, using Foucault's, amplified by Agamben's recent works (Foucault 1977; Agamben 2006). As a *dispositif,* retail infrastructure would denote to the various institutional, physical, administrative mechanisms and knowledge structures that enhance and sustain the exercise of power within the social body.

In the Chilean case, the installation of shopping malls can be seen as part of a revolutionary ideological and spatial discourse: by re-programing, the hierarchy of accessible spaces within the disputed city, consumption infrastructure repurposed the meaning of public space thought a commoditised lens. The shopping mall, become a dispositive that – besides to the many changes applied by the dictatorship of Augusto Pinochet (1973–1989) – enabled the establishment of a neoliberal society trough everyday actions and discourses around the very urbanity: retailisation as the urban epitome of the neoliberal society.

Chile is the country with more meters of shopping malls for every inhabitant in all Latin America and the Caribbean region, with a density of retail areas within the city similar to developed countries (Kearney 2016; Cushman and Wakefield 2014). Every major city Chile has a regional mall, and in the past years, people who live in towns without a shopping mall had organised in popular movements demanding to local authorities to 'bring' a mall developer for their city. In some cases, local authorities rely on mall developers to provide public amenities and even basic services to their communities, in a case where privatised space and urban development is not seen in contradiction with the rights to the city (Miller 2016). The arrival of the shopping mall to Chilean cities became a paradigmatic example that allows us to understand how neoliberalism permeated daily life. By providing safe, comfortable and nice spaces where to gather with others (besides of shopping for goods), shopping malls reorganised the hierarchies of accessibility in the socially segregated Chilean city. Located in dense areas and connected to public transport systems Chilean shopping malls and promote multiple uses besides shopping, becoming physical and symbolically more accessible than any other public access building within the city. Through this, malls in Chile managed to include services, amenities and public offices, like hospitals, medical clinics, kindergartens, universities, cinemas, museums, art galleries, metro stations, bus stations, municipality offices, ministerial bureaus, and banks. By creating the dashboard that connects citizens/consumer to the market that provides all private and public amenities, the shopping mall became a dispositive that enables the neoliberal way of urban life. By becoming part of the daily routines of thousands of Chileans, retail transformed the city patterns into a new form of urbanity, one mediated for and through consumption, which can explain why Chile has become the leading country in retail development in the South and Central America region. The irruption of retail as the arena for any urban activity, ones that could have been previously linked to traditional city areas, has changed in a radical way how centralities are conceived, planned and managed in Chilean urban planning.

The conflicts between the new social roles of shopping malls and the dynamics that they trigger on the neoliberal markets reproduce many of the capitalism's contradictions when observed at a local scale.

The study of consumption spaces encloses itself an epistemological conflict. From what points of view should we approach consumption in the contemporary cities? Should we see them as a production force of urban inequalities? Or as the landing hubs of global flows of power and capital? Or maybe as the conflictive re-signification of private space as pseudo-public space? Studying the physical arrangements of consumption, it's important to relieve the gravitations that retail space generates in the global market system, as they have a central role in the circulation of capital on a scale that surpasses local production, local consumption, and local taste. But then again, we cannot ignore the independent appropriations that users of these spaces make in everyday actions. Far from being non-places (Augé 1995), consumers' constructs an experience that is unique, authentic and with high symbolic value, which changes the original configuration of cities and the inhabitant's practices (Cachinho 2014; Kärrholm 2013). This multidimensional way of addressing consumption is a key to understanding the dual reinterpretation of consumption spaces in Chile, and how they gained importance as a social centrality.

In Chilean cities, retail urbanism has brought many conflictive disputes and discourses about something we can call the 'right to the mall'. In the neoliberal Chilean society, to have access to goods and retail space is being seen as a right that authorities and the State must ensure to all the citizens. So to have a mall developer interested in opening a new shopping mall in some remote town, far away from the capital city, is seen by the people as a victory of inclusion, as has been studied in very new research (Miller 2016). The case of Chiloé Island's first shopping mall is eye opening on this matter. Located in a remote area recognised by its cultural heritage, architectural history, and unique culture, Mall Paseo Chiloé in Castro inaugurated an intense national debate in 2014. With great local support, the mall's opening was seen as the realisation of promises of progress and development for the city. Marches and protest by islanders, broadly covered by national television, seek to fight back to the intentions to shut down the project by central authorities. Santiago's architects, planners, intellectuals and political authorities declared the huge conflicts that such a big mall could bring to a small and protected touristic city of only 50.000 inhabitants. Many opinions published in editorials denounced consumerism abomination that the mall rising symbolised to the remote Chilote culture. The debate raised many arguments about touristic conservation, heritage, and global culture, still on-going. The academic opinions became confronted with the local rights to participate in a national discourse of consumption, promoted for decades as one of the pillars of the social neoliberal restructuration. To have a mall nearby – or better said, to have the right to have a mall in every city – is one of the main symbolic effects of retail urbanism in Chilean urban culture (De Simone 2015, 2016).

Besides the campaign to shut it down, the shopping mall opened anyway, even with UNESCO persons leading the opposition process. The consumption space connects Chilotes with products and aesthetics that are far away from their cultural landscape, and by doing so, it opens a window from where locals confront their sense of remoteness and disconnection. In a post-colonial discourse, Chilotes occupy the mall's spaces in ambiguous and contradictory ways, as Miller pointed out (2016). Mall supporters have a nuanced understanding of what the mall now means for cultural identity at Chiloé, but they demanded its opening at all stands. Based on the evidence gathered by Miller, we can describe this as a conflict between the local's ideals of Chiloé's post-colonial positionality relative to Chile, against the centralism spread by Santiago's powers around the regional periphery. Upon the asymmetries of this 'power geometries' (Massey 1993), Chilotes reappropriated the global meaning of shopping malls as their own space for everyday life.

Rewriting the neoliberal city's history through consumption spaces

The contradiction between the cultural interpretations of shopping malls and the real uses of its spaces has been present since the first retail project arrival to the country.

In a society that was extremely reformed by the shocking liberalisation of its economy during the dictatorial years (1973–1989), the enclosed and protected space of shopping malls in Chile represented meanings far beyond their functions as retail centres, which cannot be interpreted under the analyses of Postwar consumerism and suburbanisation in North America driven by the white, middle-classes.

The installation of the first shopping centre in Chile in the early eighties, just a decade after the 1973 Military Coup, was used as a statement of political success. Its urban evolution in the past decades as an urban sub-centrality in Santiago shows how retail urbanism has been used as a cultural process since its arrival in Chile.

In the process of urban mutations and hybridisations of the former ways of shopping, the new generation of commercial spaces redefined the economic function of retail during the seventies and eighties in Chilean cities. They established a new scenario for social interaction, not without receiving critiques from political detractors, who saw in these places the embodied architecture of a newly arrived neoliberalism from the US. By inventing innovative commercial layouts, by one hand, or importing foreign retail formats, by the other, retail investors changed the role of commerce in Chilean cities during the years of the dictatorship, in a process that was referred to as the 'Angelinisation of Santiago'. The phrasing denoted the political and aesthetical opposition to the arrival of the North American way of life to Chile, and the retail types were its main evidence (Salcedo and De Simone 2013; Iribarne and Friedmann 1984).

The first enclosed shopping mall, Parque Arauco Shopping Centre (1982) – brought to Chile by American and Brazilians investors, and supported by the Junta

Militar, launched the race of building shopping malls for the masses. It established a revolution in local retailing. Centrally managed and car-oriented, the US shopping mall model changed the way traditional Chilean commerce was handled and perceived.

The enclosed shopping mall arrived as a big monolithic box, with no windows, and surrounded by a big parking area. With total climate control, the enclosed shopping mall was originally designed to be fitted to the new suburbia of cold Minnesota, US, back in the '50. But it was replicated in Santiago's tempered new urban developments, close only 8 kilometres from the historical, still prosperous downtown. The dissonances in the local project of the first imported mall were gradually adapted to the Chilean commercial practices. Open areas for strolling on Sundays evenings, places where to sit and gather at open air, and replicas of traditional plazas inside the mall, were implemented looking after the people's acceptation of the foreign space. The media and political propaganda promoted the opening as part of the new urban scenario brought by the social restructuration of the neoliberal reforms. The goal was to install a liberalised economic system, paired with new spaces for the novel consumerist, as the time the conservative values and traditions were promoted as the main if not only, a way of socialisation. The exaltation of the traditional family as the key centre of society, and the main core for a reunion as the private family house positioned the mall was the extension of these conservative values. The new mall, with a suburban aesthetic but localised in a central urban area, had an instrumental nature for the pervasiveness of the neoliberal logic implemented by the military dictatorship. In the context of a city full of soldiers with guns, controlling the pass of everyone who dare to walk around, the "openness" of the consumption spaces to everyone who could get there was a radical affirmation of the construction of a neoliberal scenery and a neoliberal routine for the new consumerist citizens.

As a symbolic artefact of the arrival of neoliberalism, the figure of the shopping mall was also used as a repository for veiled criticisms from the opposition wing. Many saw in it a plausible target for other ethical and moral judgments coming from the extreme Marxism, by one hand, and the Catholic and traditionally ascetic Chilean aristocracy, by the other (Salcedo and De Simone 2013). Authors like Pedro Lemebel (2003) and Alberto Fuguet (1990) critically placed their characters in the mall's corridors as aliens in a new city, as people who felt, by radically different reason in both authors, detached from the new consumption culture that emerged from the radical neoliberal social change. The cultural translation of neoliberalism into Chilean manners took some decades to become naturalised. In the early 'eighties, one largely side of Chilean society saw shopping centres as the physical artefacts that embodied the "structural social change" that took place in the country and defeated communism (Lavín 1987). In this sense, the arrival of the mall has the embodying of an ideological victory.

For others, shopping malls were reviewed as the arrival of a material progress and modernisation landscape, characterised by consumption, cars, freeways, but more than anything, money, and freedom to spend it (Larrain 1996). For many conservative thinkers close to the Compendium of the Social Doctrine of the

Figure 7.1 Mall Florida Centre in Santiago.

Church (embodied in the figure of the Chilean Saint, Alberto Hurtado), the mall arrived to promote the 'splurged in what was still a poor country', as the first elected president after Pinochet, Patricio Aylwin, publically said in open television in 1993. The shopping mall constituted a moral and identitarian impact to the Chilean aristocratic asceticism, which promulgated the reserve against the turmoil of the popular masses for consumption (Tironi 1999, 2002). Again, intellectual leftist groups saw the arrival of massive consumption as the violent installation of Freidman's neoliberal society through deregulation, commodification, and privatisation of everydayness.

These groups were hypercritics of the first proto-malls of the seventies (small commercial buildings usually associated with architectural postmodernism in Chile) as well as with the enclosed shopping malls that were built in the eighties. The proliferation of extravagant commercial structures was seen as the installation of an Angelino or Miamense landscape, which shifted from a European aesthetic – like the Parisian-inspired passages in Santiago's downtown – to a "gringo" style of artificial palms and big boxes (Salcedo and De Simone 2013).

Nevertheless, the passionate critics gave the pass to a rapid normalisation of retail scenarios in popular culture. Shopping malls were spread all over the city and the rest of the country during the late nineties, and its campaigns were remodelled in other to place consumption as an integrative activity. Malls were published as the 'places for the encounter' between different people, sending the message that the reconstruction of a broken society after the dictatorship could also be happening 'inside' the mall. Malls started to be considered as natural pieces of urban landscape, and the critic's opinion suddenly banished. How this naturalisation of consumerist landscape took place? The spread of massive retail complex through the city of Santiago as, indeed, another dimension of the neoliberalised framework left by the Dictatorship. In 1975, two years after the military coup, Chilean economy was abruptly reformed by the introduction of neoliberal financial and taxation strategies, to open local economy to the global capital markets by eliminating any possible fiscal barrier. Changes in the land market did not wait, and from the central government was declared the land as a 'non-scarce resource' – Decree Law n° 420 (1979) stated the liberalisation of urban land through the creation of so-called "urban expansion area" around the city previously designated limit, with the abolition of localisation laws for social housing and equipment, summed with the cancellation of the restriction to urban sprawl. The consequences of this measures in Santiago's meant that the sprawling area doubled the former city limits, although new regulations restored again the city boundaries in the 'nineties. Nevertheless, the city expanded freely without any regulations, and other legal gap allowed developing suburban and detached projects in the middle nineties. Expansion corridors as the Autopista del Sol and Autopista Radial Northeast, freeways built under private concessions and foreign capitals, boosted the construction of gated communities and suburban typologies. In fact, the development of private and public road infrastructure is one of the boosting economical activities that dramatically increased GDP in Chile (Rufián 2002).

Supported by the private investment in roads, but far from being a suburban location, as it was in other countries, the installation of shopping malls in centric and pericentric areas changed Santiago's urban economy map (Imagen). The result, thirty years later of the arrival of the first enclosed mall, is a dense web of retail infrastructure that aims to provide a spatial organisation for privatised urban services (i.e. health, education, recreation), consolidating a privatised urban planning and a market-centred way of thinking citizenship.

The location of new shopping malls began to draw a metropolitan geography of retail that was dense and socioeconomically diverse, transforming the centralities that were previously planned in former planning instruments. The new retail

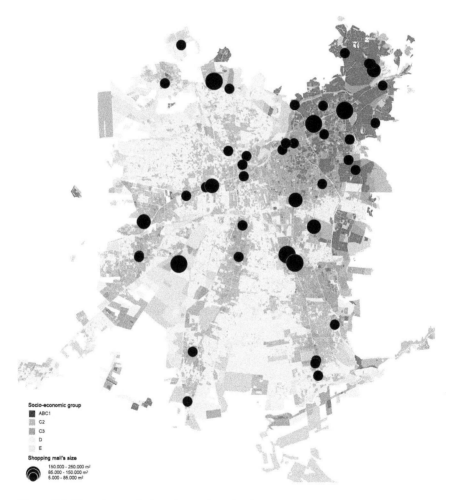

Figure 7.2 Shopping malls location and predominant socioeconomic groups (GSE) in Santiago.

urbanism became a force intervening in the real estate market of the surroundings, as in the perceptions of public space within citizen's imaginaries (Stillerman and Salcedo 2012; Salcedo and Stillerman 2010). Malls developers acted, in many cases, as private providers of traditional public amenities, in contexts of extreme socioeconomical urban segregation paired with greater lacks of public investment in peripheral areas of the city.

Retailers managed to profit of the gaps left by the poor urban legislation and convinced many mayors and authorities that their mall would be a catalyst for progress and development. As so they were. The shopping malls in Santiago's metropolitan area invaded every corner of middle-low to the highest classes, constructing a retail map of urban developments that changed the centralities pattern of the traditional city. This set of deregulations and developments promoted a strategic organisation of retail structures and retail real estate market in the city of Santiago during the last quarter of the twentieth century. Retail urbanism, in this case, refers to the sequential installation of retail infrastructure for consumption, but also reveals the coercion between the institutional governance – lacking territorial planning instruments – with real estate lobbyists – successfully convincing majors and bureaucrats of the 'extended roles' that retail infrastructure brings to the city by creating pseudo-public spaces for consumers. As the CEO of Mall Plaza framed, his corporation does not aim to build "shopping centres, we build urban centres for the community" (Mall Plaza Vespucio 2003).

In the case of Chilean retail urbanism, we can read the global patterns in which retail capitals and technical know-how develops cities and urban societies, by shifting investments from areas of primary or secondary production, to support new speculative real estate markets and financing the spatial structures of tertiary economies, characterised nowadays by the consumption of goods, services and experiences. In the lack of national resources aimed to develop public amenities, local governments recall on the participation of retail urbanism in order to renovate major strategic areas, bringing foreign capitals and reactivating economies by employing local workers – generally in informal or uneven conditions as part-time vendors or externalised services of the mall. For this, the legal framework is often altered, manipulated or erased in order to enable the installation of collective commercial equipment in the middle of the city. This is evident in the case of Chiloé, a cultural UNESCO protected area where an outlawed shopping mall was build, or in the case of Costanera Centre Shopping Mall by the CENCOSUD holding, in which retail lobbyist managed to subvert the legal framework in the Municipality of Providencia, the communal and metropolitan regulatory plans of Santiago city, and even managed to influence in the national budget for bridges and roads in order to enable the installation of a mega shopping centre in a very dense area.

The multiple roles that shopping malls perform in Chilean cities are, therefore, a spatial example of the global capitalist setting for the reproduction of capital at a local scale. As sub-centralities, malls include the provision and supply of globally valued commodities in a dispersion logic requested from demand. But in the Chilean retail urbanism configuration, they also ensure the access to recreation, interaction, and leisure spaces not provided by any other social actors. And moreover, after the unique privatisation of services undergone with the neoliberal reforms, malls also offer educational (universities and schools), cultural (museums, theatres, and galleries) and sanitary (hospital and clinics) services to a part of a widely deprived middle and low-income peripheral population. Furthermore, their construction activates a speculative market in the surroundings, with an increase of land value and rapidly growing real estate markets. Additionally, this Capitals gravitations impact in the state plans for infrastructure develops, as we can see in many cases where shopping malls have triggered significant changes in public transportations plans or public health policies. In some cases, main bus routes had to be modified to provide pedestrian access to a new mall, or roads and bridges being built by malls around their centric locations, or public hospital been built next to malls to ensure good connectivity).

This retail urbanism in the city is coupled with the democratisation of credit cards and personal loans for consumers – offered by banks owned by retail holdings. So the increasing in mortgages is also a financial sector of the retail business role in the city, affecting in a new dimension of financial instruments in the organisation of neoliberal urbanism (Labra Olivares 2012). As such, Chilean population became dependent of shopping malls in dimensions that can be addressed as spatial, financial, ideological and symbolic ways, in a configuration so extensive that can only be overlooked by the state.

Lefebvre early contributions on the role of the state in the in the management of urban space for industrial production, collective consumption and the circulation of capital, has been the base for Brenner's analysis of current globalised urbanisation (Brenner 2000, 2013; Peck and Tickell 2002). Lefebvre's analysis of the bureaucratic society of controlled consumption (Lefebvre 1991) was explicitly focused on the political-economic order of the fifties and sixties in Europe, but still enlighten the current articulation of capitalist production under the state control, in which the urban space became a mean for capitalist production, replacing industry's role in economic growth, as well as urban space, became a commodity, a consumption good, in which the urban consumes nature. By this, space is productive and producer at the same time, the city is consumable and consumer.

Conclusion

The neoliberal paradigm application in an economic, social and urban scale was a process launched around 1975 as a radical transformation of Chilean society. The re-planning of urban functions under consumption logics is a new engine for the production of space and the commodification of everyday life under the global neoliberalism constraints. In this process, the shopping mall was introduced in the middle of an accelerated structural change, without any assurance of success, but with enough political support to be representative of the new ideological shift.

In this co-produced city of consumption, built by private investors and everyday practices of appropriation, consumption-scapes were reformulated as the metropolitan dispersion of this hybrid phenomena reached new dimensions. This retail urbanism, by putting together main symbolic urban functions as socialisation, commerce, leisure and recreation, reshaped the meaning of public space in the context of the militarisation of traditional public places. In the following decades to nowadays, shopping malls became a natural part of the daily routines for thousands of Chileans. It gained a significant place in the life of citizens in a process that can only be understood as an assimilation of the global neoliberal patterns trough a violent cultural hegemony expressed in the urban life. By retracing the links between spatialised consumption and the production of space, neoliberalism becomes an embodied reality.

Retail urbanism denotes the performative character of neoliberalism in everyday life. It reflects on its power on articulating key spaces in the city through consumption infrastructure, as well as constructing iterative discourses around neoliberalism as the way of embodying urban experiences through consumerism of goods, services, and experiences (De Simone 2015). This performativity – intended as the capacity of the neoliberal urban project to construct an everyday way of being in the city – evidences the ideological dimension of neoliberal urban planning. As retail enables a framework to operate as a consumer in the formerly known as citizen arenas, shopping malls become the strategic hubs that connect the neoliberal project to everyday materiality, something that can be represented and enacted in daily life. The infrastructure for consumption can be seen as an instrument for re-enacting the everydayness of a political and economic project. More than ever, the production of the city can be addressed in an ideological manner, one that has profound significations in its political and ethical dimensions.

References

Agamben, G. (2006) *Che cos'è un dispositivo?*, Roma, Nottetempo.
Amendola, G. (2000) *La ciudad postmoderna: magia y miedo de la metrópolis contemporánea*, Madrid, Celeste Eds.
Augé, M. (1995) *Non-Lieux*, London-New York: Verso.
Baudrillard, J. (1978) *Le système des objets*, Paris, Gallimard.
Baudrillard, J. (1998) *The Consumer Society: Myths and Structures*, 1 edition. London; Thousand Oaks, CA, SAGE Publications Ltd.
Bauman, Z. (2000) *Trabajo, consumismo y nuevos pobres*, Mexico DF: Gedisa.
Bauman, Z. (2007) *Vida de consumo*, México, Fondo de Cultura Económica.
Birch, K. & Siemiatycki, M. (2016) 'Neoliberalism and the Geographies of Marketization the Entangling of State and Markets', *Progress in Human Geography*, vol. 40, no. 2, pp. 177–198.
Brenner, N. (2000) 'The Urban Question: Reflections on Henri Lefebvre, Urban Theory and the Politics of Scale', *International Journal of Urban and Regional Research*, vol. 24, no. 2, pp. 361–378.
Brenner, N. (2013) 'Tesis Sobre La Urbanizacion Planetaria', *Nueva Sociedad*, vol. 243, no. enero-febrero de 2013, pp. 39–66.
Brenner, N. & Theodore, N. (eds.) (2002) *Spaces of Neoliberalism: Urban Restructuring in North America and Western Europe*, Malden, MA; Oxford, Blackwell.
Cachinho, H. (2014) 'Consumerscapes and the Resilience Assessment of Urban Retail Systems', *Cities*, vol. 36, pp. 131–144.
Cushman, W. (2014) Latin America Shopping Centre Development Report. April 2014, [Online]. Available at: www.camaracentroscomerciales.cl/wp-content/uploads/fotos/ Latin_America_Shopping_Centre_Development_Report_April_2014.pdf.

De Mattos, C. (2001) *Crecimiento metropolitano en América Latina: ¿Los Ángeles como referente?*, Ouro Preto, Brasil, Centro de Desenvolvimento e Planejamento Regional de la Universidade Federal de Minas Gerais.

De Simone, L. (2015) *Metamall: espacio urbano y consumo en la ciudad neoliberal*, Santiago de Chile, Ediciones EURE UC y Ril Editores.

De Simone, R. L. (2016) *Consumption's Urbanism: Symbolic and Territorial Roles of Consumption Spaces in the Chilean City*, New York, LASA.

Foucault, M. (1977) ' "The Confession of the Flesh" ', In Gordon, C. (ed.), *Power/Knowledge Selected Interviews and Other Writings*.

Fuguet, A. (1990) *Sobredosis*, Santiago: Editorial Alfaguara.

Hackworth, J. R. (2007) *The Neoliberal City: Governance, Ideology, and Development in American Urbanism*, Ithaca, Cornell University Press.

Harvey, D. (2012) *Rebel Cities: From the Right to the City to the Urban Revolution*, London, Verso.

Iribarne, P. and Friedmann, S. (1984) 'Ayer Caracoles, hoy gasolineras', *AUCA*, vol. 48, pp. 21–23.

Kärrholm, P. D. M. (2013) *Retailising Space: Architecture, Retail and the Territorialisation of Public Space*, Farnham: Ashgate Publishing, Ltd.

Kearney, A. T. (2016) The 2016 Global Retail Development Index: Global Retail Expansion at a Crossroads, Global Retail Development Index, A. T. Kearney [Online]. Available at: www.atkearney.com/consumer-products-retail/global-retail-development-index/2015.

Labra Olivares, C. (2012) Financiamiento de la Vivienda en Chile: análisis del mercado de crédito hipotecario, Santiago: Ministerio de Vivienda y Urbanismo.

Larrain, C. (1996) 'El "Mall" y el Mal'., *El Mercurio, Santiago de Chile*, 4th September.

Lavín, J. (1987) *Chile, revolución silenciosa*, Zig-Zag.

Lefebvre, H. (1991) *A vida cotidiana no mundo moderno*, Sao Paulo: Editora Ática.

Lefebvre, H. (2003) *The Urban Revolution*, Minneapolis, University of Minnesota Press.

Lemebel, P. (2003) *Zanjon de la aguada*, Santiago: Seix Barral

Mall Plaza Vespucio. (2003) *Caso Mall Plaza: Creciendo en Tiempos de Crisis*. Santiago: Instituto Chileno de Administración y Racionalización de Empresas, Icare.

Massey, D. (1993) *Power-Geometry and a Progressive Sense of Place*. . pp. 59–69. In Bird, J., Curtis, B., Putman, T., Robertson, G., and Tickner, L. (eds.), *Mapping the Futures: Local Cultures, Global Change*, London, - New York: Routledge

Miller, J. C. (2016) *Consumption, Dispersed. Techno-Malls and Embodied Assemblages at Chiloé Island, Chile*, New York, LASA.

Moulian, T. (1999) *El Consumo Me Consume*, Libros del Ciudadano Chile.

*CentreCentre*Peck, J. & Tickell, A. (2002) 'Neoliberalizing Space', In Brenner, N. and Theodore, N. (eds.), *Spaces of Neoliberalism: Urban Restructuring in North America and Western Europe*, Malden, MA; Oxford, Blackwell, pp. 33–57.

Rufián, D. (2002) *Políticas de concesión vial: análisis de las experiencias de Chile, Colombia y Perú*. Naciones Unidas, CEPAL, Instituto Latinoamericano y del Caribe de Planificación Económica y Social, Proyecto ILPES/CAF.

Salcedo, R. & De Simone, L. (2013) Una crítica estática para un espacio en constante renovación: El caso del mall en Chile, *Atenea (Concepción)*, 1 (507), pp. 117–132.

Salcedo, R. & Stillerman, J. (2010) *Customers Spatial Practices in a Santiago*, Chile Mall: Control, agency and co-production.

Sassen, S. (1991) *The Global City*. New York, London, Tokyo, Princeton, Princeton University Press.

Soja, E. W. (1980) 'The Socio-Spatial Dialectic', *Annals of the Association of American Geographers*, vol. 70, no. 2, pp. 207–225.

Soja, E. W. (1989) *Postmodern Geographies: The Reassertion of Space in Critical Social Theory*, London, Verso.

Stillerman, J. & Salcedo, R. (2012) 'Transposing the Urban to the Mall Routes, Relationships, and Resistance in Two Santiago, Chile, Shopping Centres', *Journal of Contemporary Ethnography*, vol. 41, no. 3, pp. 309–336.

Tironi, E. (1999) *La irrupcion de las masas y el malestar de las elites: Chile en el cambio de siglo*, 1 edition. Santiago de Chile, Grijalbo, Grupo Grijalbo-Mondadori.

Tironi, E. (2002) *El Cambio Esta Aqui*, Santiago de Chile, La Tercera-Mondadori.

8 Under the politics of deactivation

Culture's social function in neoliberal Santiago

Francisco J. Díaz

Introduction

[Paris, 1971] Martin Pawley, Bernard Tschumi, Peter Cook, and a group of students from the Architectural Association (AA) in London are in Paris to know first-hand the experience of the UP6, the school of architecture that refused to follow the new educational structure André Malraux proposed to soften the tension of students after May '68. The difference between a school with a political discourse such as the AA and an actually politicised school like the UP6 becomes clear. In Pawley's and Tschumi's words:

> There is a strange and unnerving disparity between them, a disparity enhanced by the efforts of the AA leadership to draw close to the Beaux-Arts by comparing the seemingly imminent closure of the AA with the violent political engagement, which is evident from the militant posters, portrayed on the UP6 screen. 'We too are in a political situation [. . .]' begins Peter Cook – but he is wrong, we are all wrong; compared to those UP6 students who work on building sites, go to prison for spraying slogans on walls, build community centres for immigrant labourers, float newspapers demanding "everything" [sic], invade the offices of government ministers, hold lectures in the Louvre, department stores, or the street – we are not political. We do not know what the word means.
>
> (Pawley and Tschumi 1971: 576)

[Santiago, 2016] The city is back to normality. The days when the streets of Santiago were turned into a battlefield where people fought for education, participation, environmental protection, equality, rights and everything, are simply gone. I still remember the Chilean winter of 2011. I clearly remember the two-day national strike occurred on the 25th and 26th of August that year, and also the night of August 4th, when the city seemed to fall under a spontaneous orchestra of people hitting pots and pans from thousands of windows across Santiago, to protest against the repression of the students' demonstration that took place that day.

Five years later all those images seem a mirage. Now, four of the students who led these demonstrations are in the Congress while the fifth works for the Government. Following a well-known path in Chile, which Gabriel Salazar has called "the prodigal return" (Salazar and Pinto 2002), they have become part of the institutional system. Politics abandoned the streets to get back to institutions. The city has been depoliticised, again. And yet, Santiago is now full of activities. It's just that these activities have nothing to do with politics. Forty years after Chile hosted the first neoliberal experiment in the world, and when for the first time in history a generation born in neoliberal economy is taking positions of power, it seems we have forgotten what the word 'political' means.

Activating activation

About a decade ago, the word 'activation' suddenly appeared in Chilean architecture vocabulary. Buildings ceased to 'improve' their surroundings and began to 'activate' them. Urban interventions were expected to bring 'activity' to their neighbourhoods. Architecture students' projects began to aim at the 'activation' of the places in which they were located. Schools of architecture started to promote 'real interventions' capable of 'activating' cities and territories, and so on and so forth.

Such an amazing change in discourse, however, did not happen only in architecture. Instead of seeking a high-quality cultural programme, Museums and Cultural Centres began to be measured by the 'activity' generated inside their walls. State Cultural Funds for artists established the 'impact' – effect – of the work as a key factor to decide which project should be awarded. Municipalities started to develop 'outdoor activities' for their communities. And the most expensive, highly celebrated cultural project of the country, Teatro a Mil, not comfortable with presenting thousands of theatre plays in Santiago during the summer, began to develop a sort of 'theatre parades' to 'activate' the streets. In this way, a huge wave of 'activities' turned the city into a big, constant party, as if people were longing for the carnival that Chileans never had.

In a country afraid of laziness and inaction, activation became, then, the key word that opened the stream of funds to young professionals of arts and architecture. Whatever these young 'activists' said it could be activated achieved immediate funding, be it private or public. Authorities and private investors were eager for new events to put money on, and whose openings granted them the chance of being regarded as promoters of the activation of the city. This environment explains why, under the new discourse of activation, young architects and other cultural professionals quickly refurbished themselves as entrepreneurs dedicated to the production of – hopefully cultural – events.

In such context, Tschumi's idea of architecture as the programming of events (Tschumi 1994) was never so successful and yet misunderstood at the same time. Young architects were proud of presenting themselves as 'activators' or, even, as 'instigators' of activities. The charming word 'activation' found great support within a local cultural environment used to promote the idea of Chileans as *homini-faber* (Díaz 2011), as well as from a global post-critical discourse in architecture which, following the logics of management from the nineties, happily and unconsciously replaced 'thinking' by 'doing'. As pure thinking or deep reflection have never found fertile ground in Chile, a concept such as 'activation' achieved a quick success; turned into a mantra, it ended up becoming an ideology which – due to the lack of a better word to call it – has been known as 'activism'. Not by chance, in his recent book *Radical cities: across Latin America in the search of a new architect*, the English writer Justin McGuirk used the label 'activist architect' to define Alejandro Aravena, head of Elemental, an architecture 'do-tank' in the words of its founder (McGuirk 2014).

Therefore, and considering the cultural context described above, a question emerges: how did the discourse of activism find support in a country which, after the 1973 coup, had become very afraid of anything that could disturb the status quo?

Deactivation

As this book argues, Chile is not only the first country in the world where neoliberalism was tested but it is also a place where the neoliberal ethos percolated through the consciousness of people framing what is thinkable and what is not, up to the point that even fantasies and deliriums have neoliberal boundaries.

After Friedman's visit to Chile in 1975, the inception of neoliberalism started with the so-called 'shock therapy' that the regime conveniently renamed as "Program for Economic Recovery" (Délano and Traslaviña 1989: 46–47). This 'therapeutical' public policy – an economic recession led by the government in order to reduce its involvement in economy – had so many social consequences that it could not have been implemented without the systematic and inhuman repression of dissidence carried out by the regime.

However, and without the aim of minimising the role of the dictatorship, one of the most striking facts of Chilean recent history is that, right after the return of democracy in 1990, one of the first decisions taken by the democratic government was to maintain the economic system implemented fifteen years before by the dictatorship. Indeed, in July 1990, a consensus in the new congress between right and left-wing senators allowed the approval of the Tax Reform the new government was promoting; however, the price was not cheap, because, "in exchange for six hundred million dollars a year, coming from the higher revenues generated by new taxes and destined to social programmes, the economic model was legitimized, recording it on the hard drive of the new democratic government" (Otano 1995: 140).

But this was not the only capitulation made by the new authorities at that time. Right after winning the 1988 plebiscite – in which Chileans said 'NO' to Pinochet's continuity in power – the leaders of the opposition to Pinochet closed the '*Casas del NO*' [Houses for the NO], a network of campaign offices they have spread throughout the country to organise and mobilise voters, cutting at once and forever the channel of communication they had opened with the people. In this way, on Sunday October 5th, the same night of the victory, "opposition politicians squandered the most effective instrument of social dialogue they had designed. Then, was decreed a transition constructed for the people, but avoiding people" (Otano 1995: 69). And there's more. Two years later, when they arrived to power in 1990 and had to take care of a just recovered, still precarious democracy, the new authorities felt the need to show their capacity to rule and keep control the country, a strength test faced by just deactivating people's involvement in politics. As Otano sharply expresses:

> people's demobilisation was complete. The role of social leaders who sup-
> ported the transition process did not allow them to make trouble for the gov-
> ernment. They had to silence the demands and prevent any overflow. The goal
> was to project a sense that the country had not any threat from the civil power.
> Thus, control of macroeconomic variables was one of the keys and public
> tranquility the other. In an attitude of great political rationality, the leaders of
> unions, trade associations or universities rarely promoted any civil resistance
> that went beyond the symbolic. Therefore, there were hardly strikes, protests,
> land occupations, and nothing that could justify the use of force. The govern-
> ment was drove like an overprotective father, treating citizens like a child that
> cannot bear responsibilities. The success of this induced demobilisation went
> further than desired.
>
> (Otano 1995: 235)

Such process of deactivation – the original sin of Chilean democracy after 1990 – would percolate in people's minds along with the precepts of neoliberalism, up to the point that political nihilism was seen as a sign of maturity. If economy was going well there was no need to make demands: it was just a matter of time for the economy to 'trickle-down' its benefits across the population, so people were asked to have patience and wait. Therefore, in the two decades between 1990 and 2010, Chile's political stability was structured on two consensus barely challenged: on the one hand, that there was no world and no life outside neoliberalism and, on the other, that the lack of activism was a sign of political stability so it was ok that the streets of Santiago were boring.

The economic and political system feared the street up to the point that, during the nineties, for many political activists who fought dictatorship and then worked for the new democratic government, "the actual street only existed through the opalescent glasses" of their cars (Otano 1995: 236).

Activists

However, in 2011 Chilean cities were indeed 'activated' by political activists. In a lapse of six months Santiago saw at least twenty huge demonstrations by students, workers, environmentalists, and citizens in general, some of which gathered more than 100,000 people. The activation of the city by its citizens led many of us to think we were witnessing a historical change in Chilean society, an unexpected shift in the way people see their role in the city and society, which we expected it would finally bring a sense of empowerment and social responsibility.

People claimed for a new relation between themselves and the society. Neoliberalism was put into question and 'the system' was presented as the enemy. Profit,

abuse, and the actual impossibility of social mobility were the targets of a new class of young activists whom, like the Pied Piper of Hamelin, led thousands of people eager for a new social contract in Chile. Student's leaders in their twenties not only managed to get media attention but also to catch people's consciences with demands that, albeit quite logical and reasonable, had never been so strongly uttered since the return of democracy.

Sadly enough, however, five years after that widespread revolt almost nothing has been left. Today, the events of 2011 in Santiago are nothing else than a blurry memory. No traces of spontaneous activation can be found at the present, neither in the city nor in people's attitudes. Someone may reasonably argue that nowadays people quickly lose patience when they feel abused, or claim against the retirement funds and the pension system, for instance; however, the very idea of collective organisation to claim for something apparently non-urgent and abstract like a new social contract has been lost. People began to get used again to survive the life they already have instead of fighting for a better one – as we saw a few years ago.

But the vanishing of political activities in the streets – that is, outside the institutional system – goes in parallel with a sort of rebirth of 'urban life'. Not only does nightlife, cultural offers, foreign restaurants, and all these programmes that the 'creative class' begs for are flourishing in Santiago, but also the price of rents and apartments in 'active' urban areas have exponentially raised four years after the demonstrations of 2011 – and seven after the big economic crisis of 2008.

This is not to say that Santiago would have been full of urban life before 2011 so that the demonstrations would have imposed a pause on it. On the contrary, urban life and the activation of the city were nothing else than fantasies of architects, urbanists, and culture class promoters, without a fertile ground to flourish. Therefore, if the activity we currently see on the streets only happened once the city was activated by politics in 2011, would it be possible to trace a connection between these two moments in the city? Was there any seed planted in the city in 2011? How can we explain that the urban political activism of 2011 ended up becoming the ground for urban depoliticised activities to happen?

Double agents

In 2007, Elizabeth Currid noted, "many have argued that talented people are drawn to artistic and cultural amenities, but few have examined art and culture as a production system and drawn meaningful insights for urban planning and economic development based on understanding its inner workings" (Currid 2007: 454). Starting from this idea she found that "the mechanisms that structure and drive the cultural economy" not only had an impact on the development of urban life but they were also the seed to a broader urban economic development; in other words, "[cultural] industries depend on unique kinds of social interaction, from nightlife to gallery openings, to thrive. This is more than just fun and games, and is critical to the operation of this economic sector" (Currid 2007: 454).

If urban nightlife has the ability not only to bring 'activity' to a city but also to allow an economic sector to thrive around it, as Currid asserts, we could easily explain why the depoliticised activation of Santiago goes hand in glove with both the emergence of a new class of 'cultural promoters' and the exponential rise in the value of well-located urban land in the last years. However, things are not so simple, as Currid's findings only explain one half of the problem, while the other half needs deeper explanation.

For in the case of Santiago most of these cultural promoters who currently contribute to the depoliticisation of the city are the same who walked the city behind the students in 2011, backing their demonstrations and even acting as media consultants to aid the demonstrators to develop strategies to achieve public support. In a small metropolis like Santiago – where the elites are even smaller – the actual people who boosted the politics of the street and then crossed the sidewalk to be welcomed in the lobby of the institutional system are not hard to recognise. Close to reach forty, the first generation born in a neoliberal economy felt still young in 2011 – so as to take part in the demonstrations – but then realised they were becoming adults so they needed more stability or recognition.

Even those who didn't had the will or chance to take part in the traditional institutional system managed to create their own micro institutions, ranging from cultural centres to urban-activist entrepreneurships. They were the ones who took the baton of urban and street activation to refurbish it as an apolitical activity. At that moment the people – trained by the students to get out to the streets but already fed up of the violence of demonstrations – were eager for 'cool' urban activities with some taste of community participation, a new trend quickly detected and supported by sponsors – companies, universities, and real estate developers – ensuring a continuous stream of funds for these new cultural entrepreneurships.

The politics of the street, therefore, was not an end in itself. The promising idea of empowered people producing the commons, fighting for their right to the city and pushing its representatives to change whatever it needed to be changed, seems to have been just an initial step towards the final institutionalisation of the demands, so as the institutionalisation of the very people who promoted that way of doing politics.

Deactivators

Yet, once the 'politics of the street' faded out the adrenaline of demonstrations and the hype of collective gathering began to decrease. Therefore, under the need of a new 'activity' capable of producing the same levels of energy, two specific paths appeared: the political and the entrepreneurial.

The political path consisted of joining the new government – elected in January 2014 under the promise that the ideals of the street would be materialised – and implied a discursive continuity (under arguments like "I'm fighting for the same but on a different arena") while the stress of the political campaign ensured even higher levels of adrenaline.

On the other hand, the entrepreneurial path guaranteed the adrenaline of the economic risk while the cultural field provided the sense of collective gathering they previously discovered on the streets; and although this group seems more 'independent', their success actually depends on their ability to create micro institutions – studios, consulting agencies, event production offices, community centres and so on – which allow them to disguise the entrepreneurial aspect of their work in order to show it as 'collective', 'participative' and all those adjectives they learnt on the streets. Whereas both groups show different ways of reaching the shared goal of belonging to an institution, the deactivating function in the first group – the political path – is more evident while the second one – the entrepreneurial – needs further explanation.

As said before, the activation of the city by cultural activities was in the air but it lacked of a solid ground and local conditions to materialise. And the blowout of 2011 incepted the need for outdoor activities in a young generation otherwise addicted to virtual social networks. The coincidence of both logics in the same city after 2011 provided the fertile ground for new 'independent', 'outsider' cultural programmes to flourish. In a very short period, Santiago got full of artistic collectives, festivals, experimental cultural centres, exhibitions, theatre plays, performances and so on, which gave the impression that all the energies of the youth had been 'productively' channelled leaving as by-product the 'active' city that many people were aiming for. But a third unexpected consequence was brought by this new wave of activity. Because, as previously mentioned, both the audiences and the producers of these activities were the same people who had been in the streets in 2011. So, as individuals can't physically be in two places at the same time, the rise in the cultural offer in the city was paired with the drainage of political activity.

Although we are used to think that cultural activity creates political awareness – that an increase in the former should imply a further proliferation of the latter – this was hardly the case. Indeed, it was exactly the other way around: the politics of the street generated a need for activities which, once the streets were no longer 'cool', was satisfied by the new cultural offer. In this way, culture and politics were not connected by an increasing awareness but rather simply through 'activity'. That's the reason why a curious situation in which culture becomes the engine to deactivate the threat of politicisation of the city was finally reached. Cultural promoters became, then, the actual 'deactivators'.

Tactics

Although the discourse of the deactivator seems to go to the left, his/her first operation is to drain the subversive content from such discourse by defining new meanings for political concepts, showing that they can be harmless. The deactivator turns political ideas into 'cool' words so that audiences, sponsors, and authorities can accept them. In doing so, tactics are threefold.

The first is to create discourses and narratives using political concepts in such a way that its meaning remain ambiguous like, for instance, "[. . .] transforming the relationship between participation and culture through the temporal activation of communities and territories [. . .]", a sentence in which we do not know what participation and culture mean, and neither the political aim of transforming the relationship between them. In this way, a single sentence allows the deactivator to frame a double discourse: the strong, political interpretation for friends and well-informed audiences, and the depoliticised one for sponsors, authorities, and new audiences.

The second tactic is to mix political concepts with those coming from managerial discourses; words like 'innovation', 'management', 'data', or 'production' are freely combined with words like 'social' (as in 'social innovation'), 'culture' (as in 'cultural management'), 'gathering' (as in 'data gathering'), or 'collective' (as in 'collective production'). Thanks to this trick, the deactivator shows his/her ability to speak the same language than the sponsor, generating the necessary confidence to receive funds or commissions.

The third is to generate noise. Activation must be visible. Lights, devices, gatherings, and noise are the signs of activation, and they must be show off. But unlike the political activist, whose discourse generates collective movement by incepting awareness – and even anger – in people, the deactivator creates cool, cheerful, and friendly ambiances that are then photographed to be shown in the annual brochure they send to their networks. The deactivator has to show the ability to gather people but keeping them in a good mood; in this way he/she demonstrates – to sponsors and clients – that communities must not be feared but rather considered as 'allies', as their demands can be easily controlled through participatory games – often called 'tactics' – that make them think they are being heard when their opinions are actually being manipulated to match the needs of the client.

What these tactics produce is the sense of activation of the city paired with an actual softening of the urban conflicts. Collective gathering and participation do happen, but at a small scale and not tending to increase people's empowerment but rather to consolidate the role of the deactivator. Such an operation is made possible thanks to the institutionalisation of the deactivating function. Micro institutions such as studios, collectives, labs, NGO's, corporations, cultural centres, labs and others, are the alibi to make the deactivating function seem as a collective product. In this way the deactivator disappears within the collective (following the example from the politics of the street, and thus keeping a youthful component), while the institutional framework in which his/her work is developed ensures the recognition of adults, as institutions are seen as a demonstration of seriousness and responsibility.

In other words, while the deactivator is actually an individual, the deactivating function cannot be individually developed. For if an institution does not back the action, Chilean society considers it as infantile, non-serious, and potentially uncontrollable. Therefore, the institutionalisation of the deactivating function is the key for the deactivator could cross the bridge between youth's passion and adult's seriousness. That's what explains the anxiety to create micro institutions in Chile, as they guarantee that the former young-activist has finally become a trustable adult.

Entrepreneurship

The problem with the deactivator, however, is not only related to the replacement of the politics of the street with an apolitical one, but also to the vision of society that is embedded in these operations. We must remember, as this book does, that the Chilean context cannot be understood without considering the ground in which it unfolds: an extreme version of neoliberalism implemented through the "shock therapy" (Klein 2007) on a raw-materials production economy where capital is closely linked to landownership, where the production of immaterial goods is relatively weak, and where the welfare state has been completely erased. That is, a sort of North Korea of neoliberal economy.

In this scenario, and no matter what he/she says in his/her discourses, the deactivator is hardly independent. For instance, cultural promoters are forced to develop management skills to raise funds and to promote themselves as entrepreneurs within a free-market environment where resources for cultural programmes are always scarce. Instead of collaborating with other groups to generate cultural awareness or producing the commons – as Hardt and Negri (2000) would have expected – the deactivator has the need to do self-promotion. Boltanski and Chiapello have demonstrated that the new spirit of capitalism implies an increase of individual entrepreneurship, in which "people will not make a career, but will pass from one project to another, their success on a given project allowing them access to different, more interesting projects" (Boltanski and Chiapello 2005[1999]: 93); therefore self-promotion is the key, as "[t]he transition from one project to the next is the opportunity to increase one's employability. This is the personal capital that everyone must manage, comprising the total set of skills people can mobilize" (Boltanski and Chiapello 2005[1999]: 93).

In this context, collective work may appear but not in the form of collaboration or commoning but rather as outsourcing or, even worse, free labour. Therefore, the deactivator ends up becoming the vector that reproduces all those dirty practices of neoliberal labour markets. As resources for culture are always scarce and 'the product' has to have the best possible quality (to ensure further commissions), labour rights are the first item that is cut, relying on interns that are not paid but rather 'compensated' with a minor mention in the project's credits. In this way, on behalf of cultural production, the deactivator happily and unconsciously promotes precarious forms of labour.

To be clear in this point we must remember what the Chilean politics of the street was fighting for: a new social contract capable of overcoming the handicaps created by the implantation of neoliberalism in Chile. Such a goal cannot be achieved only by means of riots or street demonstrations; the intellectual and cultural class should also back it and demonstrate its support through fair practices. So cultural producers – mainly those initially connected to the politics of the street – not only have to promote certain discourses but they also have to put them into practice. Therefore, if they follow the same logics of neoliberalism both in the self-promoting tactics as well as the unfair labour practices, they end up doing exactly the opposite they supposedly strive for.

This phenomenon had already been noted by Pierre Bourdieu (1984[1979]) whom, in reference to the afterlife of some veteran revolutionaries of May 1968, realised of the inherent contradiction of their position, which forced them to "invent the skillfully ambiguous discourses and practices" (Bourdieu 1984[1979]: 366) as they, at the end, were aware of what they are working for. This reinforces the fact that they were not independent. Indeed, as Bourdieu clearly points out, narcissism seems to be the only way out of contradictions:

> these 'intellectual lackeys' are predisposed to experience with particular intensity the existential mood of a whole intellectual generation, which, weary of desperately hoping for a collective hope, seeks in a narcissistic self-absorption the substitute for the hope of changing the social world or even to understanding it.
>
> (Bourdieu 1984[1979]: 366)

However, the example from the seventies in Paris shows only the ethical side of the problem. In a way, what happened in Chile – and the world – after Friedman's visit to Santiago changes everything. From that moment onwards, the entrepreneurial ethics managed to erase the politics of the street, becoming the counterbalance to – or the partner of – the State, and excluding people from daily decision-making. Within neoliberalism, the jump from the street to the institutions was no longer just a political decision but also an economical one, since the lobby was crowded by representatives of the economic powers ready to purchase and reward any former revolutionary that could be 'turn' to neoliberalism.

In that context, within a country where the welfare state was dismantled in less than five years of dictatorship, and where the rules of neoliberalism were stated to favour the ones already in power – thus freezing the existing social classes – culture should not be 'turn'. Its first goal should be to counter the neoliberal ethos of Chilean society by prompting alternative discourses and practices. And although many cultural producers – writers, poets, musicians or filmmakers – have never forgotten that task, deactivators usually work within the system as if they had been turn. When those cultural promoters are also the same ones who backed the politics of the street, and when they institutionalise those neoliberal procedures – allowing the system to absorb and internalise critique by including the cultural producer as part of the 'elite' – the result is nothing else but the deactivation of any threat to the system.

Politics

However, this deactivating role of the young cultural elites is an old tale in Chilean history. In fact this is the usual path that every young, rebel generation follows in Chile:

> Chilean youth [. . .] has often broken into history by itself, generating 'historic blowouts' that have shaken the adult world. [. . .] Therefore, each of those generations has ended up acquiring a mythical, almost legendary historical profile, identifiable by the year or decade in which its 'incursion' occurred. But all of them, along with the mythical aura, have added long, flat, grey, and dark periods of aging – all ended up being adults, conformist, or patriarchal. They are better known by the former – their follies of youth – than by the

latter – the betrayals of their sensible aging. This shows that the so-called conflict between generations does not seem to be anything else than the internal conflict of the same generation.

(Salazar and Pinto 2002: 12)

In this sense, the only particularity of the contemporary generation would be its main by-product: the deactivation of the politics of the street paired with the activation of the city. That is, the transfer of the urban energy from a threatening activity to a harmless activation, so that both the status quo and the institutional system could be preserved.

And although the case of the progressive young who ends up becoming conservative as the time passes is not new, it gives us light to better understand the current social function of cultural activism. Because for a long time we have heard and read that Chile's case can be explained by its deep and premature – although forced – adoption of a neoliberal economic system, but things seem to be more complex than that.

It's true that Chile shows an extreme version of neoliberalism, but the political system seems to work with a different logic. For if neoliberalism survives through growth, flow, change, production, waste, and deterritorialisation, the Chilean political system strives exactly for the opposite: stillness, status quo, conservation, and localism. But as in Nietzsche's *Birth of Tragedy* (1886), these opposites need each other to ensure both economic growth and the conservation of political power. This could explain not only why most of Chile's wealth is only in a few hands, but also the strong ties economic power has established with the political system: in order for capital to flow and grow, it needs a stable ground to operate – a solid platform to take off as well as a safe place to land – which is ensured through political stability. Within such analogy, the role of the deactivator is akin to a stewardess: to keep passengers entertained, quiet, and happy, but also to quickly detect and deactivate any attempt to take control of the machine. In other words, the politics of deactivation is a neoliberal strategy, with urban activation being one of its tactics of mass deception.

For in Chile, forty years after Friedman had a meeting with Pinochet that changed history, the shock is no longer the therapy. Now we don't have to suffer. That's the social function of deactivation and the political role of culture: to provide entertainment in order to prevent disturbances.

What matters is to develop activity, but not any kind of it. There's no room for a violent political engagement like the one Tschumi saw in the UP6 in Paris in 1971. We are allowed to have fun but not to disturb. We are allowed to activate spaces but not consciousness. We can bring activity to the city but we can't bring activists to the streets. Neoliberal economy needs a soft political environment and the deactivator achieves this by draining the political content from urban activity. In this way, instead of political activism, we end up living under the politics of deactivation. This is not a lack of politics but rather a different way of doing it based on removing the political from the urban. At the end, it seems that Tschumi was wrong and Peter Cook was right: we too are in a political situation.

References

Boltanski, L., & Chiapello, E. (2005). *The New Spirit of Capitalism*. Translated by Gregory Elliot. London: Verso.

Bourdieu, P. (1984). *Distinction: A Social Critique of the Judgement of Taste*. Translated by Richard Nice. Cambridge, MA: Harvard University Press.

Currid, E. (2007). "How Art and Culture Happen in New York: Implications for Urban Economic Development", *Journal of the American Planning Association*, Vol. 73, No. 4, 454–467.

Délano, M., & Traslaviña, H. (1989). *La herencia de los Chicago Boys*. Santiago: Ornitorrinco.

Díaz, F. (2011). "El éxtasis de la práctica y la crisis de la crítica: notas sobre la arquitectura contemporánea en Chile". *Block*, Vol. 8 (March, 2011), 89–95.

Hardt, M., & Negri, A (2000). *Empire*. Cambridge, MA: Harvard University Press.

Klein, N. (2007). *The Shock Doctrine: The Rise of Disaster Capitalism*. New York: Metropolitan Books/Henry Holt.

McGuirk, J. (2014). *Radical Cities: Across Latin America in Search of a New Architecture*. London; Brooklyn, NY: Verso.

Nietzsche, F. (2005[1886]). *El origen de la tragedia*. Buenos Aires: Terramar Ediciones.

Otano, R. (1995). *Crónica de la transición*. Santiago: Planeta.

Pawley, M., & Tschumi, B. (1971) Beaux Arts since 68, *Architectural Design*, 9 (September) 534–555.

Salazar, G., & Pinto, J. (2002). *Historia Contemporánea de Chile V: Niñez y Juventud*. Santiago: LOM.

Tschumi, B. (1994). *Architecture and Disjunction*. Cambridge, MA: MIT Press.

9 Transparent processes of urban production in Chile

A case in Pedro Aguirre Cerda District

José Abásolo, Nicolás Verdejo,
Félix Reigada (ariztiaLAB)

Introduction

The transformation of the former Ochagavía Hospital in the district of Pedro Aguirre Cerda in Santiago, from being a hospital to become a Logistics and Business Hub, has put an end to a long and obscure process. The building passed on from being a public project – representing the physical manifestation of Salvador Allende's socialist government health policies (Amar 2008) – to become a private project. Managed by neoliberal market economic groups, the building represents a new symbol of the current relation between the city and the market. It operates across certain gaps left by regulatory plans and normative frameworks – in many cases modified by local political administrations pressured by business interests and lobbies developed by the private investors in order to ensure investment profits.

The initial project was violently interrupted by the arrival of Pinochet's dictatorship, which caused its abandonment and dilapidation for more than forty years since its current privatisation. This chapter considers the Ex-Hospital Ochagavia as emblematic and catalytic of social, political and economic processes of all Chile. For us, the Ex-Hospital Ochagavia is not as an isolated case. Moreover, its relevance is to be seen as part of extensive Neoliberal incidence, similar to the case of the Centro Cultural Gabriela Mistral (formerly UNCTAD) and, in general, to the perimeter highway concessions Santiago as well as the release and supply of land in the centre of the city in the mid-nineties.

How did the privatisation of a building that was part of an emblematic public project come about? Who were the actors and institutions involved in the building's historical process?

This chapter analyses the historical evolution of this building. Using the visualisation of data associated with the privatisation processes plus some other generated from participants' observations and fieldwork with the local community, the aim is to show the possibility of generating a tool of mediation and participation, through which the community is able to access information regarding the stakeholders, institutions and norms linked to the ex-Hospital's recycling. Furthermore, this tool developed in our design research should contribute to discuss and inform the territorial processes among the diverse organisations in the District, as well as encourage citizens to oversee and supervise the external agents that seek to intervene in the *Comuna*.

The shock economy in the Urbanism of Santiago

The coup d'etat of 11/9 in 1973 meant more than the breaking of Chilean democracy and the beginning of a period in which violations of human rights became a common practice. The overthrow of Allende also brought socioeconomical processes like the reduction of state powers and the complete dismantling of social welfare programmes, based on free-market paradigms imported from more open, competitive and barely regulated models of development. The dictatorship's adoption of the neoliberal model in Chile and the incorporation of Thatcherism and Reaganism (Theodore et al. 2009) brought severe transformations in the whole urban spectrum.

The limited capacity of the central government to control the multinational fluxes of money (Harvey 2007) and the adoption of a free-market approach in different areas of the city for attracting real estate businesses, consolidated the powers of local governments (municipalities) in the form of a law named Ley Orgánica de municipios (1994) approved just four years after the return to democracy.

The competences acquired by municipalities would guarantee to attract investments for urban renewal projects in central and pericentral areas of the city. These areas became an important part of investment capital targeted by speculators, to be seen as strips or "mitigation" zones supporting the development and growth of city centres.

This situation marked the beginning of a new phase of urban renewal strategies of recycling of damaged or underutilised areas, supported by the strengthening of local and external markets looking to capitalise on its proximity to the 'central' city (López 2008). On the other hand, the democratic governments of the nineties extended and perpetuated the neoliberal parameters established during the dictatorship, subsidising investments of capital in pericentral zones of Santiago through a *Subsidio de Renovación Urbana* (Urban Regeneration Subsidy) an instrument with fixed coverage of 200 UF per unit for dwellings that do not exceed the 2000 UF in market value (Arriagada et al. 2007).

Despite the increasing and favourable real estate offer in pericentral Santiago, Pedro Aguirre Cerda stands as an exception. Differently, from other pericentral districts, this one resisted several years against real estate speculations and urban renewal processes. However, there is a recent progression of neoliberal strategies characterised by an aggressive creative destruction (Weber 2002) executed by real estate developers and local governments. Using discursive practices, these actors aim to stigmatise areas and historical buildings in order to promote spaces for urban renewal, and the flexibility of local master plans. For example, the emblematic case of the ex-Hospital Ochagavia stands as a strategic enclave for triggering a significant urban renewal in Pedro Aguirre Cerda district.

Pedro Aguirre Cerda and the "White Elephants

Pedro Aguirre Cerda is a pericentral district of Santiago in the south of the capital. It has 90,565 inhabitants based on official data, and its quality of life is ranked

40th among all the forty-two districts of Greater Santiago (ICUV 2014). Although it has good connectivity with the rest of the city through Avenida La Marina and the Autopista Central, part of its area is defined as an urban renewal zone, and it remains one of the less developed pericentral areas – in both public and private investment – despite its relative centrality.

The history of the area known as such began in 1981, with the Decreto Fuerza Ley N°1–3260 9, which created new districts and set new limits for existing ones. The territory of Pedro Aguirre Cerda results from the fusion of urban pieces that constituted some areas of San Miguel, La Cisterna, and Santiago.

Within the historical evolution of the district, it is important to highlight two moments that mark the development of the area. The first is related to the *tomas de terreno* (land occupation), where emergent and self-managed social movements (Garcés 2002) localised a *terrain vague*, occupied it, and then built their houses. These processes started in 1957 with the takeover of Población La Victoria, a community with 1,200 families, and the occupation in 1961 of Población Santa Adriana, with 1,500 families. These communities were vital in the resistance against the harsh repressive measures taken by Pinochet's dictatorship (Cortez 2014). Besides being revolutionary community practices of production of urban space until 1973, these strategies allowed 90% of Pedro Aguirre Cerda's residents to become owners of the house in which they live in (2008), a fundamental condition to truly resist real estate threats on a highly fragmented territory.

Figure 9.1 Former Ochagavia Hospital view from a pedestrian bridge over General Velasquez highway.

Source: Cristian Kirby (2012).

The second historical landmark was the construction of the Ochagavia Hospital, which now is considered a fundamental part of the urban landscape in Pedro Aguirre Cerda. This building was planned by Eduardo Frei Montalva government (1969) and started its construction in the socialist government of Salvador Allende (1971). The future hospital would have approximately 84,000 m² and was destined to deliver services mainly to the working class. However, the construction process was halted and interrupted the coup-d'etat (1973). Thus, one of the flagship projects of Allende socialist government remained unfinished, and the building was abandoned. The big mass of concrete and tiling became known as 'The White Elephant'.

Over the years, this infrastructure in a state of permanent abandonment has become, on the one hand, a crime hotspot, which contributed greatly to the construction of a negative image in the collective memory of the people. Nevertheless, it also constituted an explorative platform where local alternative artists during the nineties started to develop multiple artistic performances. The video clip of the hip-hop band Rezonanzia in 1999, and performances by Lotty Rosenfeld and Pedro Lemebel are two interesting examples.

By 1999 the Chilean government, through the Ministry of Housing and Urbanism (MINVU), sold the building to the real estate company Mapocho S.A for UF 25,000 (US$ 750,000) for the development of a shopping mall project.

In parallel, a park project in the forecourt of the building was developed to celebrate the bicentenary of Chile, named Ochagavia Park. Currently, this large esplanade is converted into a large void, which accommodates various mass activities circus and manifestations. However, none of the mentioned projects were constructed, increasing the trend of unfinished initiatives in the district. During 2013, negotiations resumed around the property's future with Mapocho S.A. announcing the selling of the estate to Holding Red Megacentro, in order to transform the building into an office and warehouse logistics centre. This project was designed by the Architectural National Prize winner, Juan Sabbagh, and was named Nucleo Ochagavia while, immediately getting the support from the local government, who became guarantor and promoter of that new initiative.

However, some politically motivated local actors and cultural organisations, from inside and outside the area, recommended some critical observation to this new initiative, paying special attention to the architectural impact the intervention could generate, both in the historical building and in the quality of life of surrounding neighbourhoods and the rest of the community in the short term.

Devices: three different approaches with Pedro Aguirre Cerda's community

After the installation of certain multiple devices for interaction, such as dialogue roundtables, participatory consultations, drawings and maps; a fieldwork generated a method for mediating with the residents. These actions were set to incorporate new temporary, material and subjective dimensions (Risler and Ares 2013) to enable, enhance and strengthen the relationships between the different actors living in the district. This participatory approach was developed in three stages with close collaboration with local organisations such as Red Cultural PAC, Galería Metropolitana, Piñen, OOO Estudio, and Memoria PAC.

In the first stage, an exercise called Record Ochagavía (Figure 9.2) was developed. Therefore, taking advantage of the commemoration of the 40th anniversary of the military coup a participatory process addressed the collection of information, together with the introduction of a broadcast booth/stand for distributing information about the transformations that, at that moment, were being developed by Megacentro in the building.

A second phase was developed in Alhue park, through the implementation of two participatory devices: an Urna-Maqueta (Ballot-model) that consisted of an open ballot box, in which participants made suggestions and projected different modes of use for the esplanade in front of the former Hospital, then tracing their willingness and desires for this meaningful place. The second device, *El dibujo* (the drawing), served to channelise the wishes and histories of people for building narratives associated with the memory of the territory. In this activity, the main participants were children (Figure 9.3) and elderly people; who aimed to answer the question: What do you want for the Hospital's esplanade?

Finally, a third device in the form of urban action was developed called Operation Chalk (Figure 9.4) which consisted of a collective chalking over the forecourt

Figure 9.2 40-year commemoration of the coup d'etat, former Ochagavia Hospital frontcourt.
Source: Betania Álvarez (2013).

Figure 9.3 Community expressing their wishes through drawing.

Figure 9.4 "Operación Tiza", forecourt former Ochagavia Hospital.
Source: Betania Alvarez (2014).

in which the neighbours manifested and shared their wishes and dreams. The act of chalking the territory comes from a remembrance to the "Site operation", a process in which the State delivered housing solutions to families in the sixties, tracing plots in the ground in which they were to build their new houses.

These three moments of encounter and interaction were informative and helped to organise the community of the district, aiming to capture and share diverse perspectives and particular histories associated with the figure of the former Hospital.

Visualising the information: the diagram as power map and tool for participation

The construction of the territorial narrative related to the evolution of the former Ochagavia Hospital was then developed through a diagram (Fig 5) conceived as the retrospective visualisation of the actor's network involved around the building's process. This phase represents the second line of research, in which the whole collected information was ordered and represented.

The diagram as a tool presents the power of building relations and connections toward a topology of powers (Deleuze 1988:61 amongst the different actors that compose both the project and the territory. For Deleuze "the diagram is no longer an auditory or visual archive but a map, a cartography that is coextensive with the whole social field. It is an abstract machine". As an abstract machine, the diagram

Figure 9.5 Former Ochagavia Hospital Diagram: Time, events, actors and relations.

allows the incorporation of all data associated with the building: the starting play-ers who were historically involved in the different stages of building it, the social, political and economic factors, and the historical landmarks that represented sig-nificant inflexion points. A diagram also allows organising the information for building an effective narrative. Based on this, the diagram becomes a graphic exposition of a phenomenon's trajectory (Bijlma et. al. 1998).

Thus, the diagram serves as a potential double tool. First, it can open the data, mapping and order this information sequentially and, in a timeline, the actors linked at different stages of the evolution of the building. In this way, the informa-tion enters into a process of transparency and communicability. Despite the exis-tence of recent laws that help transparent information in Chile, even today, there is a great difficulty in consulting the data in municipal folders of large on-going architectural projects.

In the case of "Nucleo Ochagavia", the context is the same. We repeatedly vis-ited the municipality in order to gather information about the project. However, the documentation provided is incomplete. There are missing files and data that usually are commendatory for getting the permissions. For example, the absence of the Roads Impact Study which is fundamental for determining if big-scale projects have to implement urban transformations in the surroundings for avoiding a public space collapse. Due to the absence of a Town Planning Scheme in Pedro Aguirre Cerda, the confusion about the future of the commune depends on the capacity of stakeholders for influencing the authorities. In a city where neoliberalism has infil-trated all the structures of society, the stakeholders with the capital have become the most influential. Therefore, the lack of transparency on urban design processes is prejudicial for communities but highly profitable for speculating.

Therefore, the configuration and design of this diagram aimed to make visible the power relations between the stakeholders involved with these projects. By using graphical, conceptual and textual representations of Holding Megacentro connections with real estate developers such as Simonetti and Almagro, the power balance for the decision-making revealed itself as uneven. Indeed, these real estate companies are currently working in several districts around Pedro Aguirre Cerda, such as La Cisterna and San Miguel. The announcement of new Metro stations (Lo Valledor and Club Hípico), increased a 30% of the surplus value of land in zones for commercial developments. Consequently, the commune has become a key objective for entrepreneurialism.

As a conclusion of the initiative developed with the community, the diagram was put out in the exhibition named "¿Cual Sueño" (What dream?) (Figure 9.6), making it available to the whole community as a collective cartography. It pro-moted the production of multiple dialogue and exchange of experiences associ-ated with the image of the White Elephant.

Conclusion

The transformation of the former Ochagavia Hospital into a storage centre and offices not only represents the loss of meaning of a space that was born to become

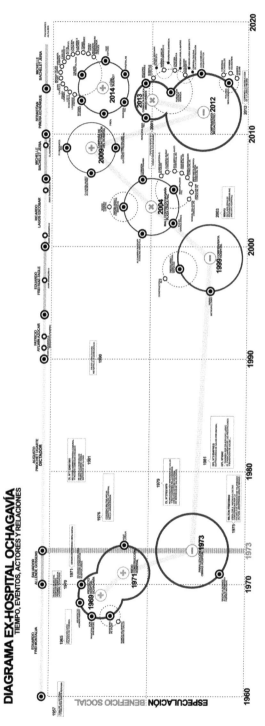

Figure 9.6 Mediation Exhibition ¿Cual Sueño? With students of the school Liceo Enrique Backausse, Pedro Aguirre Cerda.

Source: Félix Reigada (2014).

one of the bulwarks of public health infrastructure in Latin America. It also represents the arrival of influential capital investors to intervene in a district that resisted for years the aggressive campaigns of real estate companies. This space has become the key anchor for the potential development of pro-business proposals, taking advantage of the new construction of roads as well as the future Metro station in Avenida Carlos Valdovinos (North border of the district).

In this scenario, the displacement of residents and gentrification are imminent, anticipating conflict over the current traffic system (with scarce installed capacity) and service provision as a consequence of the eventual over-densification in the area. These problems may provoke a decayed quality in the social environmental as a result of the high-rise buildings near low-rise neighbourhoods.

Despite the existence of new media, indexed inventories on the Internet, as well as social networks, it remains complicated to get access to real and consistent information about public institutions and real estate companies in order to know their investments on going. However, the last years have seen the emergence of diverse groups involved in new practices of city making, advocating for cultural causes, struggling for changes on the production of the cities.

It should be noted that, as an emerging neoliberalism was cultured from the crisis of the Keynesian welfare state, it is now crucial the role of anti-hegemonic regional and local organisations. They have to commit in opening new fields of action and participation against the growing pro-business urban planning. Also, in turn, they would sustain local struggles for land access, the right to decent housing, and a just city with inclusive spaces and environments. For the future of this district, in particular, its rich history and roots have to prevail. The origins of a common built on solidary organisations and collaboration between communities must survive to the onslaughts of neoliberalism.

References

Amar, M. (2008) *Salvador Allende: Vida política y parlamentaria 1908–1973*. Ediciones Biblioteca del Congreso Nacional Chile: Santiago.

Arriagada, C., Moreno, J. C., & Cartier, E. (2007) *Evaluación de Impacto del Subsidio de Renovación Urbana (Estudio del Área Metropolitana del Gran Santiago 1991–2006)*. Edit. Departamento de Estudios, DITEC: Santiago.

Bijlma, L., Garritzmann, U., & Deen, W. (1998) Editorial. *OASE Journal of Architecture*, (48), p. 1.

Cortez, A. (2014) El movimiento de pobladores chilenos y la población La Victoria: ejemplaridad, movimientos sociales y el derecho a la ciudad. *Revista EURE*, Vol. 40(119), pp. 239–260.

Deleuze, G. (1988) *Foucault*. University of Minnesota Press: Minneapolis.

Garcés, M. (2002) *Tomando su Sitio. El Movimiento de pobladores de Santiago, 1957–1970. Ed.* LOM: Santiago.

Harvey, D. (2007). *A brief history of neoliberalism*. Oxford: Oxford University Press.

Indicador de Calidad de Vida Ciudades Chilenas (ICVU). (2014) *Indicador de Calidad de Vida Ciudades Chilenas*. Editado por el Instituto de Estudios Urbanos de la Pontificia Universidad Católica de Chile y la Cámara Chilena de la Construcción: Santiago.

López, E. (2008) Destrucción creativa y explotación de brecha de renta: discutiendo la renovación urbana del peri-centro sur poniente de Santiago de Chile entre 1990 y 2005. *Scripta Nova Revista Electrónica de Geografía y Ciencias Sociales*, Vol. 270, Universidad de Barcelona, p. 96.

Risler, J., & Ares, P. (2013). *Manual de mapeo colectivo. Recursos cartográficos críticos para procesos territoriales de creación colaborativa*. Buenos Aires: Tinta Limón.

Theodore, N., Peck, J., & Brenner, N. (2009) Urbanismo neoliberal: la Ciudad y el Imperio de los Mercados. *Revista Temas Sociales 1 (66). Ediciones SUR*, pp. 1–11.

Weber, R. (2002) Extracting value from the city: Neoliberalism and urban development. *Antipode*, Vol. 34(3), pp. 519–540.

10 Artists' self-organisation on the context of unregulated transformations in territories and communities

Fernando Portal

Introduction: practicing in unregulated spaces

Over the last ten years, a slow paced process of gentrification has transformed the identity, land value and dwellers of Barrio Italia, a light-manufacture and residential sector in midtown Santiago. This working-class residential neighbourhood – filled with old furniture shops and car services ¬ has received over the last years different waves of economic investment coining its new identity as a design firms and food district. Indeed, these changes in the uses of the spaces represent an evident sign of gentrification in the area, a common pattern with other districts in the downtown of this metropolis.

In the context of Santiago's real estate ecology, gentrification has not been addressed as a specific process to be planned or even regulated by political institutions. This lack of a regulatory framework – proper to the neoliberal context of urban development in Santiago – has allowed for real estate speculation to ignite processes of urban transformation with severe social consequences. In the case of Barrio Italia's development, the displacement of historical dwellers by gentrification adds up with the lack of public policies focused on the recognition and management of industrial heritage buildings and on the fostering and regulation of creative labour.

The intersection of these unregulated fields has created a social space where not just land use and value are volatile, but where notions of material and immaterial heritage, community and labour are constantly changing. Within this context, a self-organised cultural project emerged in Barrio Italia in January 2013. Through the collective effort of a numerous group of neighbours and artists, this independent cultural platform has allowed for the practical exploration of a new approach towards neighbourhood transformations, cultivating citizen participation and creative labour.

The topics of gentrification, deregulations, and heritage preservation, has been addressed by this cultural project through the development and testing – first locally and later nationwide – of diverse prototypes for new cultural institutions and participatory devices, aimed to test new methods for the collective generation of content and knowledge (Gielen 2011).

By reviewing the experience of this project may illustrate the relation between obsolete industrial infrastructure, gentrification, cultural production and cultural policies within a neoliberal context, characterised mainly by the lack of regulatory tools to manage real estate operations and citizen participation.

The sustained effort of operating in the unregulated spaces of gentrification, industrial heritage and creative economies, had allowed for the practice-based definition of general concepts. These concepts had informed the designing process of the main strategies for the group's actions.

The first one relates with the temporary use of infrastructure. A common practice associated with real estate speculation is the seizing of opportunities provided by the unregulated flow of land value, using the eviction notice as a tool for taking advantage of several unused spaces in the city. In the project, temporary use strategy allows the development of both site-specific projects and methodological outputs. This strategy aims to activate communities whose causes render visible the necessity for further policy development to defend their cultural identities. This experience is reviewed in the following section.

A second strategy considers the design of methods for the collective generation of content and knowledge. These methods mean to produce encounters and engagement between members of the Santiago's urban society that suffered spatial segregation, using design, architecture and art to catalyse spontaneous participation. The second section exposes the experience of this strategy.

Finally, this chapter identifies public and private testing grounds wherein third parties have recently deployed these prototypes.

Prototyping institutions in vacant spaces

Barrio Italia is a neighbourhood that takes his name from the historical presence of Italian migrants in the area. They constructed a series of industrial estates in the last years of the nineteenth century, defining the development of the neighbourhood as a working middle-class settlement. Among these factories was Girardi's Hat Factory, one of the main hat producers of the country. Both the factory and the adjoining residential buildings flourished in the late twenties and – after a fire destroyed part of the administration building – in the late thirties a flamboyant cinema was built for the amusement of the factory managers and workers.

The gradual decrease of industrial activity and the crisis of cinemas after television's introduction in the early sixties marked the factory decay. Consequently, all industrial activities were concentrated in the east part of the lot, subdividing the west building into smaller units to be rented as office space, and exploiting the theatre, like a discotheque.

This rent based process of subdivision, got an unprecedented capital injection in 2010, with the purchase of the whole original Girardi family lot, by the real estate developer Factoría Italia SA. The plan of this company involves the construction of a commercial district aimed to round off the new identity of the neighbourhood as a design and food district.

In this context, a specific opportunity arose closely related to the unstable logic of real estate speculation. As the developers ran out of financial liquidity just after closing all lease contracts, they had to postpone the demolition of the factory and to deal with the maintenance of a 20,000 m2 empty urban lot in the midtown of Santiago. This forced them to become more receptive to potential tenants interested in renting the vacated factory buildings for a short period.

One of these tenants was a group of neighbours and artists who – supported by one employee of the real estate developer – proposed to open one of the main buildings in the site as a temporary space for public meetings. The resulting activation of 1,000 square meters of industrial space, gave rise to the precarious development of a self-organised community centre, named Mil M2 (One thousand square meters).

Centre for citizen participation and innovation

Mil M2 started in January 2013 under a 136 days consensual agreement for using the factory's main industrial shed. The first action proposed by the recently formed group of artists, architects, and art administrators – all closely bound to the neighbourhood – was an open call upon all the neighbours asking "What would you do with one thousand square meters, during 136 days?" The content generated by this activity – ranging from texts to drawings – formed the first collective work enabled by Mil M2. The social and cultural expectations of the community that answered the group's call became a background for measuring the collective goals of Mil M2's initiatives.

Figure 10.1 Opening of Mil M2 Centre for Citizen Participation and Innovation.

As the real estate developer lacked the necessary funds to break ground, the demolition date was constantly delayed, allowing for a series of short-term extensions of the rent agreement. These monthly or bimonthly extensions generated a constant feeling of creative anxiety for maximising the use of this space. This "now or never" condition, invigorated all participants to contribute as much as possible, enabling for numerous projects and collaborations to take place during each of these extensions. Finally, these extensions added up a whole year.

Over the course of this first year, Mil M2 hosted more than 190 events, ranging from performances and seminars to political meetings, fairs and workshops, bringing together different types of agents and communities. Hosting these events required the definition of a foundational working group, which later became Mil M2 board. The work of this foundational group, in conjunction with a large number of volunteers who embodied the communal growth of this space, was able to explore the design and implementation of widely assorted formats to convene and engage with fellow citizens.

By these means, the self-denominated "Centre for Citizen Participation and Innovation Mil M2", consisted not only of a collective space, but also of a shared experience of self-organizing a community centre. In order to enhance this shared experience, the centre operated through open curatorial criteria, making the space and production work available for collective programming, granting space and productive back-up to initiatives coming from groups with such diverse interests as the arts, politics, communal development, education, crafts, and communication technologies.

Thus, Mil M2 project became a platform for the development of numerous emergent practices and cultural communities, acting as an enabler for different neighbours, artists and other professionals to develop community-oriented projects. Within these projects, it's worth to mention the "Mil M2 Radio"; an online radio community developed by a number of enthusiastic neighbours. The radio quickly became the radio with more shows on schedule in Chile, and "La Ocupación" (The occupation); a one-week-long performance, co-curated by Mil M2 and Grupo TOMA, in which participated more than twenty artists from Chile and Argentina. Both experiences, in conjunction with the shared activation of Mil M2's shed, may be interpreted as an initiation rite for a new generation of artists, architects and cultural managers.

In addition to this open curatorial approach, the Mil M2 team developed two artistic programmes; one devoted the visual arts and the second to performance arts. These programmes were focused on the relational aspects of both artistic frameworks, as an effort for fostering otherwise improbable encounters, engagements and participation. Regarding visual arts, a non-commercial gallery was organised, for one-week exhibitions that managed with all efforts to produce the maximum amount of openings, to foster spaces for the social interaction between the different communities that Mil M2 was activating. About the latter performance arts, a series of dance and performance pieces were hosted which had a strong participatory focus.

Finally, the shed's unavoidable demolition became imminent by the end of 2013, demanding for a definition from the board. For some of the members, the project was intimately related to the building's body. For other members of the board, the project made sense beyond the building itself. They understood the project as a process defined by a series of methods – and the design of its enabling devices – toward foster particular types of collectivising activities, through the temporary using a vacant infrastructure. With this conviction, the second group continued with the Mil M2 project, looking for new spaces to intervene in the old factory site.

Site-specific gallery

January 2014 marked a new beginning, as the lease of the old hat factory was terminated due to its demolition in April 2014. From this point, a diaspora of agents took the experience gained over this year and aimed to identify new opportunities, establishing a precarious network of self-organised and autonomous projects based on temporary use. Over time this diasporas has allowed for the forming of new cultural institutions, both public and private, that seek to echo the collectivising approach of Mil M2. Among them worth to mentioning "Infante 1415", a creation centre aimed to fostering innovation and creativity through collaborative work and participation, opened recently by Providencia Municipality, the same commune in which Mil M2 operates. Another example is "Estudio Panal", an artist-run space that promotes interdisciplinary artistic creation.

For the board members who decided to stay, a new space to intervene became available in the upper plateau of the old factory cinema, a space that was foreclosed and inaccessible for more than 40 years. For ensuring the access to this venue, Mil M2 developed a remodelling project for the old cinema – after years of being used as a discotheque – in exchange for a 3 years loan for use (bailment) agreement with a real estate development firm that sublets the cinema form Factoría Italia SA.

The demolition of the main industrial shed and most of the buildings in the west side of the lot also affected the cinema, destroying a monumental staircase that gave access to the upper plateau. This unavoidable gesture of market driven architectural design from Factoría Italia SA's architects, compelled to install a 10 meters high scaffolding staircase for accessing to the upper plateau, from the old cinema's main space.

Under these constrictions and after a self-financed recovery project that lasted six months, Mil M2 inaugurated the upper plateau of the cinema as a site-specific gallery called Proyecto Pendiente ("Pendiente" means both "slope" and "pending" in Spanish). Its inaccessibility seemed reinforced by its architecture, defined by a slope of 90 square meters area and 29 degrees inclination that makes for almost the 60% of the gallery's area.

These unique spatial conditions had restricted the space from being used by a wider community, distancing the project from its previous communal ethos. Instead, Proyecto Pendiente might be understood as a creative arts centre rather than a community centre, focusing more on providing artistic residencies. The goal of these residencies is to create site-specific works, capable of problematizing

Figure 10.2 Valor! (Value!) a series of site-specific performances on heritage and value, including the auction of debris from the gallery slope.

and disseminating the critical aspects of urban transformation that the space symptomatises.

Through a series of self-organised palimpsest, Proyecto Pendiente has become a platform for a series of performers, artist, architects, choreographers, poets and designers to explore the instability of space, proper to an industrial ruins. Currently, this creative platform upholds a wide range of projects. While some of this projects have been widely disseminated and re-enacted on major cultural venues in Chile – opening the opportunity to share a critical view of community and urban transformation – others remain critical, gathering small communities around issues of real estate speculation and the documenting of immaterial heritage.

Prototyping devices for the collective generation of knowledge

The communal ethos derived from prototyping these site-specific cultural institutions has led Mil M2 to develop a series of devices able to spread the type of public sharing and to inquire reached at this institutions, furthering communal engagement and participation. These devices had been developed both for artistic events and for advocating projects; becoming the basis of the economic sustainability of the group.

Designing and producing more than 190 events in a self-organised cultural centre, allowed for the conceptualisation of a specific approach towards community engagement using artistic tools. This approach involves aiming for projects to work against communal expectations, and to develop methodologies that can be assimilated by its users, taking their ownership as collectivising assets.

This aim has led to the design and activation of a series of participatory devices, conceived as tools for the collective generation of knowledge. Each of these devices seeks to stress the relationship between participatory politics and performance arts. Moreover, these devices had allowed Mil M2's project to go beyond its walls and into public spaces, engaging with specific communities in each instalment. These devices are thought of as both places and methods, using public space as input for collectivising performances.

An art critique of participatory politics

The deployment of these devices takes place in a social context where participatory politics represents a way out of the neoliberal conundrum. However, its development has not been able to overcome the erosion of sociability and collectivism proper of market driven policymaking, and even less, to re-establish confidence in public institutions.

An uncritical reproduction of participation methodologies by public officers have smoothed the rough edges of the demands of communities, taking apart their causes and neutralising its transformative power. In other words, community participation methods have become a way to deactivate social demands, replacing the protests motto with checklists of quite controlled activities.

Within this context, Mil M2's devices aim to inquiry the complexity of citizen participation, by using art as a tool to explore new tools and new rules for the recovering of direct citizen engagement, its manifestation in public spaces and the documentation of such explorations.

Asking questions

Proyecto Pregunta (Question Project) is a tool for community engagement and participation designed to foster the collective generation, visualisation and viralisation of debates on the public space. Proyecto Pregunta is a critical device, aimed to intervene with civic participation methodologies in order to question and open new types of community awareness and civic engagement.

Since its first installation in Valparaiso between February 2014 and May 2015, it has been performed more than thirty times, touring the country as a tool to ignite civic engagement. Over this first round of nationwide activations, the project has gathered more than 2,000 questions. A second series of international activations of the project has allowed to transfer this methodology to discuss the crisis of democracy in Brazil (Rio de Janeiro, January, 2015), the development of cultural institutions in the context of cultural policies calling for austerity in Europe (Barcelona, March, 2016), and the refuge crisis in Germany (Dresden, May, 2016).

The project works as a temporary performance with documentary outcomes. It starts from a set of original questions that always lead to a new question, opening

Figure 10.3 First deployment of Proyecto Pregunta, featuring a question from the
participants: –What would you ask your city? –Why do you keep covering
your squares with concrete?

debate through the collective act of questioning – instead of posing statements.
Over an established period of time, an ad hoc editorial committee selects a question to be displayed in public spaces, composed of a hand-made typographic set.
Each one of these activations develops its own archive, based on the templates
used to gather questions, and the photographic record of each displayed question.

The project relies on a set of objects, activated by a precise sequence of interactions with the community. These objects are: a typographic set made out of wood
tablets with one hand-painted letter in each of them, a set of printed templates
for audiences to posit a question, and a metallic portable billboard to display the
tables in the public space.

The sequence, establishes the definition of a daily original query, constructed
as a question that ignites more questions (i.e. "What would you ask your government?"). This original query is mounted as the community is engaged in order to
gather new questions through interaction. Over a defined period of time, an editorial committee formed with members of the community, selects one question out
of all received questions to be mounted on the billboard.

The project develops both a textual and a visual archive, by means of both
printed documents filled by participants and photographic record of each mounted
question.

During its first year, the project also became a toolkit, currently used nationwide by communities and non-profit organisations to visualise their demands as

part of advocacy campaigns. As an open toolkit, a digital version of the typographic set and a manual are available for free download. On the other hand, as a material device, FAVA Foundation, a non-profit organisation that focuses on art education as a tool for social inclusion in Latin America, has acquired one copy of the project. This dual development – as a deployed open toolkit for civic engagement, and as an educational work of relational aesthetics – fosters new questions about the types of tools being developed to address social issues through the arts.

The original concept for Proyecto Pregunta asked for the development of an enabling device for the immediate publication of dialogues in the public space. This original inquiry has later been developed in other devices, such as Imprenta Ciudadana (Citizen's Press), an itinerant publishing office and press to be deployed in communal public centres to strengthen grassroots organisations efforts in documenting projects, and Construir una Biblioteca (To build a Library), a relational performance staged in the National Museum of Fine Arts, as a citizen's critique of the crisis of public libraries in Chile.

Conclusions: testing grounds

Working in the unregulated fields of urban and social transformation has meant to embody and to criticise the pivotal role that artists play in gentrification processes (Rosler 2013). In order to tackle this agency, we have chosen to directly engage in conversations with those who own the means to define the material, economic and social future of the cultural contexts in which we operate, offering a "neutral" ground for both private and public initiatives to gather strategies, programmes and prototypes (Dodd 2012).

From the vantage point of a self-organised cultural organisation, it is clear that cultural production (Moore 2015) serves as a contrast medium to signal blind spots in public policy, and that new sets of regulations have yet to be commonly envisioned and publicly defined in order to achieve socially sustainable processes of transformation. In order to socially activate these agendas, we understand our role as catalysers of communal visions that ask for further regulation.

In our relationships with private agents, who work with neoliberal tools, we seek to maintain a critical stance, offering our clients the developing of participatory projects and programmes that allow for the free exchange of information and opinions. This standing has allowed for some of our projects to unveil publicly urban and social conflicts related to private projects, signalling a request from communities for further regulation.

Regarding the public sector, after granting Mil M2 with the National Innovation Award as Cultural Innovators, different governmental departments at both local and central levels, have gather some of our prototypes. The implementation of these initiatives is part of major cultural policies related to community and local economic development, such as Providencia's Creation Centre Infante 1415, and the national plan for Creative Centres (CeCrea).

Finally, the self-organised character of Mil M2 has contested the common understanding of what a cultural institution should be. Neither a public cultural

Figure 10.4 Proyecto Pregunta in the window of the old factory teather inviting passer-by and neighbours to engage asking, "What would you ask to this building?"

institution, nor a commercial gallery, the civic and independent approach of Mil M2 has allowed assessing our current understanding of cultural development, as expressed by public cultural policies. We seek for our practice and prototypes to influence further the emergence of communal political visions and public policies directed to tackle problems that went unseen for a long time.

References

Dodd, M. (2012) The Double Agent, in R. Hyde, ed., Future Practice. *Conversations from the Edge of Architecture*. New York: Routledge, pp. 72–84.

Gielen, P. (2011) Mapping Community Art, in P. De Bruyne, P. Gielen, eds. *Community Art: The Politics of Trespassing*. Amsterdam: Valiz, pp. 15–34.

Moore, A. (2015) *Making Room: Cultural Production in Occupied Spaces*. Barcelona: Other Forms: *The Journal of Aesthetics and Protest*.

Rosler, M. (2013) *Culture Class*. Berlin: Sternberg Press.

11 Building the democratic city

A challenge for social movements

Fundación Decide (Valentina Saavedra,
Karen Pradenas, Patricia Kelly, Pascal Volker)

Introduction: a regulatory framework for real estate development

During the seventies, a new cycle of economic crises struck the world in the context of capitalism. This crisis, as the previous ones, demanded a deep reclassification of the accumulation patterns and implied the modification of institutional frameworks of both the public and private apparatus (Méndez 2014). These transformations affected not only the economic and social aspects of our countries but also and the urban and territorial elements. In delivering this restructuration, financial mechanisms for capital accumulation played a key role. Broadly, these territorial and economic dynamics work by spatial operations with the assets of real estate companies that, through the purchase-retention-selling of land, ensure the creation of wealth via property price speculation. The constant growth of land values, with the following revalorisation of assets, demands the creation of capital and getting liquidity aiming at maintaining a virtuous growth cycle. Such dynamics constitute an urban landscape stimulating the reproduction of capital, and segmenting the urban fabric by using zones according to the necessities of these enterprises (Lopez and Rodríguez 2010). Some authors (Remy 2002; De Mattos 2006) interpret this phenomenon as an interaction between the invisible city – that of capital – and the visible – the materials – where the latter is in a metamorphosis caused by the invisible city. In this context, the subsidiary state is not a passive spectator of this type of land development: it articulates institutions that not only allow, but also encourage, real estate activity. This evidence is derived from an analysis of the elaboration of the instruments of territorial planning and of the General Law of Urbanism and Constructions. Regarding the first, several authors note the strong presence, in several stages of the elaboration of these instruments, of organisms, officials or authorities that do not have autonomy or independence from central government (Hidalgo et al. 2014; Hidalgo and Zunino, 2011; López et al. 2012; Zunino 2002, 2006). Likewise, the technical nature of the instances of elaboration of these instruments precludes the emergence of political considerations or the existence of any sign of civil society's participation, expressing the exclusionary nature of these instruments (Hidalgo et al. 2014). In the second case, the National Law of Urbanism and Construction requires the existence of a building permit that must be granted by the Municipal Works Department.

In this way, the LGUC limits urban development through political or discretionary criteria. This limitation extends from civil society to Municipal Works Directorates who are required by law to approve these permits regardless of the magnitude or impact of the project, expressing the antidemocratic nature of urban development in Chile (Zunino 2006), since the implementation of neoliberal reforms.

In this way, growth, determined principally by the real estate market and the restrictive tools for the incorporation of society in the configuration of urban development, have achieved a city form that develops unequally, with excluded areas and even deprived, segregated and deprived by their location territorial. On neoliberal foundations, this exclusionary and antidemocratic structure of the city is generated.

In the same manner, the Chilean Chamber of Construction (CChC), a hegemonic actor of urban development in the country, is consolidated as the largest business union in Chile. According to its own words, "the object of the Company will be the investment in all kinds of real estate and in shares, rights, bonds and other transferable securities, particularly those issued by social security, insurance, clinical or hospital, educational institutions and electronic services" (ILC Inversiones 2014: 20). Consequently, to date, the CChC controls important companies in the pension sector (AFP Habitat), health (Isapre Consalud, RedSalud and several private clinics), insurance (CORPVIDA, CORPSEGUROS, VidaCámara, among others) and educational (CFT ProAndes and several schools) (ILC Inversiones 2014).

Under this logic, CChC has woven numerous networks within the public apparatus, both nationally and regionally (Hidalgo et al. 2014; CChC,2013). The CChC is linked to and participates in almost all the activities that must be carried out in the development of planning instruments, be they communal or inter-communal (metropolitan) scale. It also participates in an important way in other endeavours, such as the elaboration of the National Urban Development Policy (Hidalgo et al. 2014; CChC 2013; CNDU 2014).

In this sense, the role of progressive governments – according to the nomenclature of the region – is outlined in the conservation and deepening of this pro-business urbanism (Lopez et al. 2012). In the debate that can be made of these governments and their participation in the institutional problem of urban development as already mentioned, exists the key issue of social housing, which in the same way is done through subsidies. Although the New Housing Policy (1978) was implemented during the military dictatorship, it was retained by the subsequent governments of the Concertación and their successive mandates (1990–2010). Through various types of housing subsidy (subsidies to demand), large resources are transferred from the State or financial entities to real estate companies (CChC), which define where future housing projects will be located according to profitability criteria (Ducci 2000; Rodríguez and Sugranyes 2004; Sugranyes 2005). The consequences of this policy are not the reduction of the most extreme conditions of urban poverty, but the generation of new pockets of inequality and segregation in the periphery of the city, where the cheapest land is located (Stiglitz 1997; Rugerio 1998). Moreover, these social housing estates demand the construction of other services – such as public transport, streets, commerce, and education – to supply these new neighbourhoods.

The engagement of politicians in urban development

For this reason, important leaders of the Concertación – now New Majority – and the Right have assumed as their political banner the importance of integration in urban planning as a way to overcome spatial segregation. But what is meant by integration? Given the policies proposed in the last five years, integration has been assumed to be the co-existence of housing estates of different economic segments in the same *comuna* (local administrative scale), assimilating integration – or segregation – to a scale problem. To achieve this goal, the public policies proposed include public investments, incentives, subsidies and specific urban interventions that can 'achieve an exemplary effect' and 'detonate processes of urban improvement'.

Although policies of this type contribute to increasing the value of land change in the affected areas, they trigger processes of displacement of vulnerable populations that end up in other devalued and/or peripheral areas (CNDU 2014). By the same logic, they promote the installation of homes of higher value in areas with high concentrations of social housing, in addition to mixed projects with different housing. This kind of urban politics has become common in cities in Europe and North America, under the assumption that it increases opportunities for interaction between diverse social groups, in addition to activating local and interpersonal networks. However, there is little evidence in these regions that such policies effectively contribute to promoting social integration among diverse groups. On the contrary, it can be observed that exclusively sectoral policies – rural – are not sufficient to achieve the objectives proposed when institutions and organisations reproduce the mechanisms of exclusion and social segregation that are sought to prevent, and in comparative experiences it has been seen that the phenomenon of gentrification is massive when it comes to establishing a forced and superficial integration (Fine 2001; Kearnes 2003; Doherty et al. 2006; Cheshire 2007; Lees 2008).

In this context, it becomes necessary that social actors emerge that contest the production of the urban form that the State and real estate agents, in close relation, have promoted until now. The context in which the city's development and urban development are being managed today has generated discontent amongst the population, which has fostered the emergence in Santiago and in other cities, of various urban social movements that have revolved around the unleashing various conflicts over the territory.

Urban social movements and space

In Chile, urban social movements up until the sixties were related to the proletariat, as a workers' movement organised in *central*, such as the Central Unitaria de

Trabajadores (CUT), as well as groups of people fighting for the right to houses. These movements in a certain way conceived the State as an entity that could be instrumental for its own transformation. Since the seventies – after the coup – urban social movements have been mainly made up of popular movements, marginal sectors and peripheries of cities, with an important role assigned to young people and women, but which lack an organisation such as the labour movement. It is important to emphasise that popular and social forces against Pinochet's regime did not aim for the formation of a centralised political and military structure, but rather conceived social mobilisation (protest) as a means to destabilise and overthrow the regime.

After the definitive introduction of the neoliberal project in the nineties, the new urban social movements took a leading role that has gained more force since the twenty first century (Renna Gallano 2010). These collective actors today cohabit in the political and social arena, with an increasing importance of the student movement. These urban social movements are unfolding against the old and new practices of exploitation, crossing the whole city, and involving important parts of the social classes.

Although these movements do not always have a properly confrontational character, they have the capacity to organise socially by building a political struggle contrary to established power relations and the institutions that sustain them. Consequently, the State ceases to be conceived "as a possible entity to be used against the logics it defends, but as a political force with its own corporate interests and acting in their own right" (Gallano 2010).

These new social movements – defined as urban – are characterised by having a multiple territorialisation, to maintain a certain condition of autonomy and internal plurality (Ducci 2004; Gallano 2008, 2010). In some cases, as Gallano suggest, they express themselves as "vital forces that arise from the borders (geographical, cultural, age, racial, economic, ethnic and sexual) of the hegemonic order" (Gallano 2010: np).

For others, they are the result of contradictions in the socioeconomic model established as the student movement, settlers and environmental movements, among others.

The autonomy (of the traditional political parties) manifests itself as the axis of the current urban social movements, and is expressed in the innovation of the strategies and actions to make public its demands, which in turn, are in constant redefinition. Its central character lies in its capacity for self-management of territories. Some exemplary cases from the last decade include the *Movimiento de Pobladores en Lucha*, Ukamau and *organisaciones de reivindicación patrimonial* (Gúzman et al. 2009).

The plurality of these, in turn, is expressed by their demands that extend beyond "the housing rights claims and point to broader sociopolitical projects, expanding the struggles" (Renna Gallano 2010: np). Many of them are associated with citizen movements, linked to the middle or upper classes, as opposed to densification in height, or to changes in the character of neighbourhoods from residential to commercial. On the other hand, there are also movements based in the popular sectors, in disputes over housing or the quality of life, based in conflicts that orbit around the urban periphery (such as landfills, industry, highways and transport infrastructures) (Ducci 2004; Lopez et al. 2014).

Recently there has also been oppositions to the concessioned Central Highway, where neighbours and organisations of the *comuna* La Florida, Macul and Puente Alto have converged, as well as the Vespucio Oriente highway, where people from La Reina and Peñalolén have organised a response.

Spaces of political empowerment

From the map of urban conflicts in Santiago between 2006 and 2009 (Corporación SUR), it can be observed that 48% of these correspond to conflicts that emerged from urban growth (expropriations, construction in height, impact of road or commercial projects), 23% of conflicts related to housing (relatives, debtors, takings, etc.), 19% due to environmental impacts, and 10% around neighbourhood deterioration, traversing practically all the *comunas* of Greater Santiago (Gallano 2010). All of them involve some form of struggle for the right to the city; to reclaim control over how it is produced and inhabited.

Somehow this multiple territorialisation of struggles indicates that conflicts cross and encompass the city in its totality, from the centre to the periphery. Such is the case of movements against urban growth: expropriation, densification and displacement by market forces, construction in height, depredation of green cloths and agricultural areas by expansion or impacted by the location of roads and/or commercial projects; Housing conflicts, such as relatives, deterioration of housing and landholdings; those produced by environmental impacts and by neighbourhood deterioration, whether through the destruction of historic heritage or recovery and occupation of public spaces, amongst others.

Understanding that the territory generates feelings of belonging and community, it is possible to identify common elements in these struggles. It is not conservative nor reactionary motivations that motivate the defence of neighbourhoods, but instead, they constitute spaces that are "generating – and sometimes generalising – solidarity and collaborative attitudes among different groups and different social classes, which are learning rapidly the value of collaboration and mutual support to advance a common goal: a better quality of life in the city we live in" (Ducci 2004: 164).

However, as was elaborated previously, these urban social movements have taken a leading role recently and have expressed their discontent through visible manifestations in streets, squares, towns and vacant properties, representing, simultaneously, struggles for public space and the city conceived as a public good.

Within this context there are a series of political manifestations that have happened in the last few years in Santiago that call attention to the massive appropriation of the public space. Such demonstrations began with the opposition to the Hidro Aysén electric project, where more than forty thousand people gathered. In relation to the student conflict, more than 75 marches have been authorised in Santiago, a figure that does not consider unauthorised marches and other forms of artistic-cultural mobilisation carried out by students. Also, 48 of the 75 authorised marches were developed in the city centre (Fernández 2013).

Despite the particular challenges confronted in each manifestation in all of these it is possible to determine a high degree of heterogeneity. As Zibechi (2003) indicates, the city has become a scenario for conflicts that exceed the educational claim to include what is properly concerned with 'the urban'. In this space "there have also been massive demonstrations with environmentalist, regionalist, feminist claims, and against the exclusion of historically excluded groups such as gays and indigenous Mapuche" (Fernández 2013: 93).

This massive occupation of the city has come to rebut the thesis regarding the decay and disappearance of public space, a problem that has dominated the urban debates of the last decades, evidenced by growing privatisation, homogenisation and hyper-vigilance of urban public spaces, reducing encounters, social inclusion and the diversity of uses (Borja 2012).

In turn these manifestations have shown a transformation of citizenship from a passive and controlled nature to a more active and critical character with respect to the political and economic model imposed since the military dictatorship. This citizenship reflects a re-appropriation of voices and political manifestations, which was institutionally silenced in the post-dictatorship era. Thus, it was argued that to ensure a return to democracy and the departure of the military rule, moderation and centralisation of decision-making was required, limiting the appearance of demonstrations and social mobilisations, seen as threatening to the social order (Moulian quoted in Fernández 2013: 94).

Thus, social mobilisation was managed and promoted from the majority political parties through the "construction of a new type of citizenship, away from the conflicts of the dictatorship and oriented to the normalisation of democratic life under the imposition of important restrictions on the exercise of the right to demonstrate" (Del Campo quoted in Fernández 2013: 94).

Among the main territories of these manifestations are the Alameda or General Bernardo O'Higgins Avenue, one of the main arteries of the city, which crosses the centre and contains a concentration of important public buildings such as universities, and the majority of Government structures and various ministries as well as other urban landmarks such as the National Library and the State Bank.

The reasons to go for the Alameda are different. Because of its size, history and relevance, this road is recognised as the most symbolic one in the country. At the same time, it allows the concentration and circulation of a large number of demonstrators. This urban aesthetic and symbolical relevance is complemented by its historical importance. All the great political manifestations of Chile's recent history have developed in this avenue, in addition to having been the scene of the 1973 coup d'état, when La Moneda was bombarded by the Air Force. The density and the scale of these manifestations have come from the hand of a series of restrictions, developed under the argument of the maintenance of public order. This prerogative has been applied on several occasions, which has had the effect of raising tensions and causing clashes between demonstrators and police forces, mandated by political power (Fernández 2013).

It is possible to make visible the dispute for space in the occupation of the streets, which alters the normality of traffic and life in the city. Under this perspective, citizens can achieve sufficient power to critically transform the uses and meanings of space proposed by producers (Salcedo 2002), that is to say by those who have the power to define those uses and meanings.

Conclusions

The ideal notion of public space as a "political space, of creation and expression of collective wills, the space of representation" (Borja 2003: 29), is the very dimension where citizens appear and become visible before constituting its political subjects. The existence of public space becomes a condition and requirement for the development of movements that seek to overcome existing social relations and that aim to shape new social and political orders. It is in turn a space in constant dispute for the democratisation of societies and the reconfiguration of the citizen's place in the system of political decision-making, since "the segregating, exclusive dynamics exist and are renewed permanently" (Borja 2003: 27).

The last decade has been shaped by a particular period of manifestation of discontent and a resurgence of social movements. Citizenship has questioned the legitimacy of state power, as evidenced by its relationship with large economic groups and the low incidence of majorities present in decision-making. Citizens are less and less interested in traditional partisan politics, which seems incapable of "capturing and solving the new problems of society, turning into a serious deficit of representation and interlocution" (Mirza 2006).

Public space has been equated in contemporary times with the concept of streets. Insofar as the political manifestations of society have not occurred in the fields that are institutionally designated for this, discontent has been expressed in the occupation of the paradigmatic space of the public and in open ones of the city. This occupation of the streets has not taken the form of an exercise of harmonious dialogue between equals, from the classic and ideal vision of public space (Arendt 1958 [1958]), but on the contrary the manifestation of social conflict, which underlies the contradictions and inequalities of the neoliberal system. "Poverty, marginalisation, discontent, not infrequently rage continue to be part of the public, but understood now as what is there, in the sight of all, refusing to obey the slogans that condemned them underground" (Delgado and Malet 2007: 11), has explicitly turned the street into a space in dispute and an expression of the forces that exist between powers that stress different projects and visions of society.

Faced with such a situation, political institutions have been unable to respond to citizen discontent that have taken on greater force since the student demonstrations of 2011, enabling and supporting the neoliberal capitalist accumulation regime to continue to reproduce inequality and segregation, with evident impacts on the quality of life of the population.

This scenario has generated favourable conditions for these demands to be channelled through citizen action in the streets. It is not by chance that urban social movements are not a passing and irrelevant phenomenon; instead, their weight in the play of powers that moves the urban assemblages is far from disappearing and rather tends to increase (Ducci 2004: 164).

While urban areas in Chile comprise more than 86% of the whole population (based on Census of 2002), cities become inescapable arenas of confrontation of political projects, oriented towards the dispute for the construction of society, rights to territory and the form and character of the State.

As an integral part of these movements, we believe that the beginning of any power dispute begins with the articulation of agendas based on common (structural) elements that unfold in these processes; the identification and sharing of criticisms and projects that articulate and generate social mobilisation. It becomes an important task to direct the discussion and reflection of these movements towards a horizon that reconstructs a vision of an urban totality. In this, the possibility of proposing a project formed of an alternative society is played and is the main challenge that we face confronted by a State that is characterised by impelling the fragmentation of social actors; limiting the constitution and scope of collective organisations, and promoting the proliferation of individual identities, characteristic of postmodern discourses.

In this sense, social movements are developing in a context that has been characterised in the last decades by the absence of common cultures of struggle, but which today show a transversal link; a demand for greater participation, democracy and equality, in a context of diversity and conflict. The relations of power can be contested only if the social actors are politically active. The emergence of subaltern social actors in the realm of politics depends on the alternative transformation of society, the State and territory.

References

Arendt, H. (1958). *La condición humana*. Barcelona: Paidós.

Borja, J. (2003). La ciudad es el espacio público. Espacio público y reconstrucción de ciudadanía. Mexico DF: Facultad Latinoamericana de Ciencias Sociales (FLACSO)/ Editorial Porrúa.

Borja, J. (2012). *Espacio Público y Derecho a la Ciudad*. Barcelona.

Cámara Chilena de la Construcción (CChC). (2013). Seremi Minvu explicó detalles de la aprobación del premval a comité inmobiliario. Artículo de prensa. Disponible en internet: www. cchc.cl/2013/07/seremi-minvu-explico-detalles-de-la-aprobacion-delpremval-a-comite-inmobiliario/www.cchc.cl/2013/07/seremi-minvu-explico-detalles-de-la-aprobacion-delpremval-a-comite-inmobiliario/

Cheshire, P. (2007). *Segregated Neighbourhoods and Mixed Communities: A Critical Analysis*. York: Joseph Rowntree Foundation.

Consejo Nacional de Desarrollo Urbano. (2014). Política Nacional de Desarrollo Urbano. Disponible en internet: http://cndu.gob.cl/wp-content/uploads/2014/10/L4-Politica-Nacional-Urbana.pdfhttp://cndu.gob.cl/wp-content/uploads/2014/10/L4-Politica-Nacional-Urbana.pdf

Delgado, M. & Malet, D. (2007). El espacio público como ideología. Jornadas Marx siglo XXI, Universidad de la Rioja, Logroño, diciembre. 1–11. Disponible en www.sistema mid.com/panel/uploads/biblioteca/7097/7128/7129/83414.pdf

De Mattos, C. (2006). Modernización capitalista y transformación metropolitana en América Latina: cinco tendencias constitutivas. En publicación: América Latina: cidade, campo e turismo. Amalia Inés Geraiges de Lemos, Mónica Arroyo, María Laura Silveira. CLACSO, Consejo Latinoamericano de Ciencias Sociales, San Pablo.

Doherty, J.; Manley, D., & Graham, E. (2006). *Is Mixed Tenure Good for Social Well-Being?* York: Report for the Joseph Rowntree Foundation.

Ducci, M. E. (2000). Chile: The dark side of a successful housing policy. Social development in Latin America. *The Politics of Reform*, 12: 149–174.

Ducci, M. E. (2004). Las batallas urbanas de principios del tercer milenio. Santiago en la globalización: ¿Una nueva ciudad? De Mattos et al. (eds.). Santiago de Chile: Ediciones SUR: 137–166.

Fernández, R. (2013). Espacio público y manifestaciones políticas en Santiago de Chile: ¿el regreso del ciudadano? URBS. *Revista de Estudios Urbanos y Ciencias Sociales*, 3 (2): 93–109. Disponible en internet: http://nevada.ual.es:81/urbs/index.php/urbs/article/view/fernandez_droguett

Fine, B. (2001). *Social Capital versus Social Theory*. London: Routledge.

Gallano, H. R. (2008). (Vi)viendo la lucha por la ciudad. Actores y conflictos urbanos en América Latina. Documento de trabajo Corporación SUR de estudios sociales y educación, Santiago de Chile. Disponible en www.sitiosur.cl/documentosdetrabajodetalle.php?id=77&seccion=9

Gallano, H. R. (2010). La situación actual de los movimientos sociales urbanos. Autonomía, pluralidad y territorialización múltiple. *Diseño Urbano y Paisaje*, 7 (20): s/p.

Gúzman, R., H. Renna, A. Sandoval, & C. Silva. (2009). *Movimiento de Pobladores en Lucha. A tomarse Peñalolén para conquistar la Ciudad*. Ediciones SUR. Santiago de Chile.

Hidalgo, R., Volker, P. & Ramírez, N. (2014). La ciudad inmobiliaria: Mecanismos institucionales y relaciones de poder. El caso del Área Metropolitana de Valparaíso. Scripta Nova. *Revista electrónica de Geografía y Ciencias Sociales*, 493 (34): s/p.

Hidalgo, R. & Zunino, H. (2011). La urbanización de las áreas periféricas en Santiago y Valparaíso: el papel de las relaciones de poder en el dibujo de la geografía socioresidencial. *Eure*, 37 (111): 79–105.

ILC INVERSIONES. (2014). Memoria Anual 2014. Disponible en internet: www.ilcinversiones.cl/pdf/Memoria_Anual_ILC_2014.pdfwww.ilcinversiones.cl/pdf/Memoria_Anual_ILC_2014.pdf

Kearnes, A. (2003). Social capital, regeneration and urban policy. In: Imrie, R. & Raco, M. (eds.). *Urban Renaissance? New Labour, Community and Urban Policy*. Bristol: Policy Press: 37–60.

Lees, L. (2008). Gentrification and social mixing: Towards an inclusive urban renaissance? *Urban Studies*, 45: 2449–2470.

López, E., I. Gasic, & D. Meza. (2014). Actores sociales y políticos contestando un modelo de urbanismo pro-empresarial: el lado B de la renovación urbana de Santiago de Chile. XIII Coloquio Internacional de Geocrítica. El control del espacio y los espacios de control. Barcelona.

López, I. & Rodríguez, E. (2010). *Fin de Ciclo. Financiarización, territorio y sociedad de propietarios en la onda larga del capitalismo hispano (1959–2010)*. Madrid: Traficantes de Sueños.

Méndez, R. (2014). Expansión y crisis del modelo neoliberal en Madrid. En: Hidalgo, R. y Janoschka, M. (eds.). *La Ciudad Neoliberal*. Santiago de Chile: Serie GEOlibros: 217–232.

Mirza, C. A. (2006). Movimientos sociales y sistemas políticos en América Latina: la construcción de nuevas democracias. Buenos Aires: CLACSO.

Remy, J. (2002). Ville visible, ville invisible: un réseau aréolaire. L'accès à la ville, les mobilités spatiales en question, 299-328.

Rodríguez, A. & Sugranyes, A. (2004). El problema de los con techo. *Eure*, 91 (30): 53–65.

Rugerio, A. (1998). Experiencia chilena en vivienda social. 1980–1995. *Boletín INVI*, 35 (13): 3–87.

Salcedo Hansen, R. (2002). El espacio público en el debate actual: Una reflexión crítica sobre el urbanismo post-moderno. Eure (Santiago), 28(84), 5-19.

Stiglitz, J. (1997). *La economía del sector público*. Barcelona: Antoni Bosch Editor.

Sugranyes, A. (2005). La política habitacional en Chile, 1980–2000: un éxito liberal para dar techo a los pobres. En: Rodríguez, A. y Sugranyes, A. (eds.). *Los con techo. Un desafío para la política de vivienda social*. Santiago de Chile: Ediciones Sur: 23–58.

Zibechi, R. (2003). *Los movimientos sociales latinoamericanos: tendencias y desafíos*. OSAL: Observatorio Social de América Latina: 185–188.

Zunino, H. (2002). Formación institucional y poder: Investigando la construcción social de la ciudad. *Eure*, 28: 103–116.

Zunino, H. (2006). Power relations in urban decision making: Neoliberalism, techno-politicians, and authoritarian redevelopment in Santiago. *Urban Studies*, 43: 1825–1846.

12 Especulopolis

A play in seven acts. A history of celebrations, displacements, schizophrenia, utopias, colonisation and hangover

Grupo TOMA (Eduardo Pérez, Ignacio Saavedra, Ignacio Rivas, Mathias Klenner, Leandro Cappetto)

Introduction

This chapter is presented in the form of a theatre play, as an attempt to build a continuous history through the different territories we have worked at during the last years in Santiago de Chile. We believe that the deficiencies of those trying to put up this collective reflection can be compensated by certain dramatism, together with a fictional narrative continuity. With the first person plural, we refer to us, TOMA. A group of friends and a *collective* of five architects. For this writing experience, we summarise nearly for years of work we experienced in different sites of engagement.

As architects, we have had the chance to witness some urban transformation processes, and we have observed and experienced some of the mechanisms under which the contemporary city develops in the current neoliberal context.

In this chapter, we propose to reflect on those places where we have settled in during our journey of exploring contesting territories of engagements hoping to highlight the different logics and machinations of our times. As we retire from the scenes, their particular script, scenography, costumes and cast reveal new information.

A constant atmosphere of lack of control, the multiple characters that have temporarily had a certain impact in our practices, and the diverse territories on which the scenes have been mounted and soon dismounted, have all increased the levels of the contradiction of our work and our contexts. Consequently, this paradox goes all through the script of this chapter.

This journey we summarise here has been guided mostly by our intuition. As such it is full of mistakes and ingenuity. However, there are also some moments of lucidity, endurance and collaborative motivation, which have led to the development of an early stage of 'collective architectural intelligence'. For this reason, the chapter insists more in the description of scenes rather than offering conclusive reflections. Each section has been introduced with quotes and excerpts to nurture the reflections and to suggest alternatives lines of disputes.

The acts are organised chronologically, according to the locations where we have lived and worked. Although probably many of the readers have never heard the names of these places, we believe that they embody some of the global behavioural patterns that shape the neoliberal city; therefore, these names can be replaced by similar and more familiar ones coming from another global context.

Our aspiration goes far beyond our capacities, but we trust our motivations and that of our colleagues contributing in this book as well as the active intelligence of the readers. Our ambition is to mend the architecture behind our work, so that we can see the architectures that lie behind our society, and ultimately, of our times. Making Especulopolis visible we aim to contribute to making visible the paradoxes of neoliberalism in shaping city spaces and the complicit nature of architecture in its silent dimension.

Prelude: out of control

The curtain is still down. Hastily, the narrator moves to the centre of the stage. Looking ahead, he announces: "This driving, dynamic city has been made possible by the free market. Indeed, the freest market in the world. The free market enables people to buy in the cheapest market around the world, to sell in the dearest market all around the world. If they fail, they pay the cost. If they succeed, they get the benefits. And is that atmosphere of incentive, that has seduced him to work, to adjust, to sale, to produce a miracle" (Friedman 1980)

The scene is not yet set. At the back, the city of Santiago can be seen, vast and boundless.

Voice-over.

This is the history of a collective experiment over an already experimental social and urban reality. This is the history of the contradictions we have been immersed ourselves to try to understand the social delirium we are into. The complexity of the world we live in may seem infinite, even paralysing. But on our hands, we have powerful tools for its transformation.

Neoliberalism has permitted that certain sectors of our society attain very high degrees of wealth. While, thousands have been left at the side of the road and mired in underdevelopment, and the human survival on this planet has been put at serious risk.

Silence.

Act 1, scene 1: Nothing to celebrate – Mapocho station (December 2013)

The curtain rises. There is a luminous stage. The racket fades while the narrator rises his voice: "The aesthetic strategies of the counter-culture: the search for authenticity, the ideal of self-management, the anti-hierarchical exigency, are now used to promote the conditions required by the current mode of capitalist regulation, replacing the disciplinary framework characteristic of the Fordist period. Nowadays artistic and cultural production play a central role in the process of capital valorisation and, through 'neo-management', artistic critique has become an important element of capitalist productivity" (Mouffe 2007).

Scene: An old train station, a massive vegetable market and shady places not far from the very centre of the city. Street vendors, homeless, tourists and immigrants swarm about. A tangled circuit of public transport tracks and streets hamper the circulation of the pedestrians. We chose this site in the context of an urban interventions festival, pretty much a trend in many cities of the world. The regional government with the support of several private companies sponsors the festival. Colourful signs announce the event.

Actors enter the stage.

The interventions, with a very limited budget, are formulated during one month, built in fifteen days, mounted in two, and functioned for three days. Some interventions from the festival achieve their objectives. All in all, nothing seems very relevant.

The actors leave the stage.

No trace is left at the place. After the festival, our follies is gone, just as all other interventions. The smoke of the cars and the noise of the buses remain just the same, and the crowd moves here and there as if nothing ever happened.

The light gradually goes off; the scene gets dark.

Voice-over.

The festival happened to be one of those events that seem to be comfortable with a conception of culture as a mechanism of entertainment, more like a public marketing strategy than an occasion to experiment or to bring into question the capacities of art in public space. It is more a simulation than a celebration because there is nothing to celebrate. A State that pretends to care of territories deliberately abandoned it by political and economic purposes. Distract, simulate, confuse and fake: all reasons to celebrate without reason.

The stage darkens.

Act 1, scene 2: The gentrification factory – factoría italia – (January 2014)

Slowly, the lights go on. From one side, the Narrator raises his voice: "The yuppie, the hipster, the *flaneur*, the gentrifier, the urban explorer who modifies the environment with his presence and pursues an authenticity that disappears beneath his feet. . . . Different models guided by the same pattern of consumption, the same that during the last decades has pushed this new creative class to return to the abandoned city centre. However, the creative class is only the scapegoats of new urban development policies, a series of global strategies that build a model of the hyper-economized and exclusionary city" (Left Hand Rotation 2012: 6).

Scene: Still in Santiago but four kilometres away to the east. In a wealthy neighbourhood, an old hats factory, almost abandoned, invite us to enter. The rent of spaces for offices to young and emerging collectives has been the chosen strategy to begin an area based recovery process. Many cafes, bike shops, art galleries and design shops sprout up in the area during the last five years. They will be not more than the icing on the cake. In the corner of a vast property formerly part of the *Girardi* hat factory, a warehouse hosts a community centre for cultural innovation. It is an experiment for a limited duration that seeks to expand the margins of the local cultural scene. There are only a few days left before its final demolition.

The actors enter the stage.

The action is concentrated in a very short period. Different artistic and architectural collectives are organised to establish a small *ephemeral* city. To make it functioning, space is occupied with temporary institutions that promote collective actions and reflections on the current society of our present.

Critical actions, lectures and debates, photographic performances, meditation spaces, night parties and community meals are made available to reflect on possible forms of socialisation, which are based on mechanisms of cooperation and exchange, opposed to conventional market mechanisms.

The actors leave the stage.

It was an attempt to demonstrate the political contents of an experiment before its death. But, also, it was just one of the many contributions that the humble agendas of various groups operating in the place, made in the process of placing the *Factoría Italia* as the icon of a new urban culture. A new culture that did not take long to smell bad and agonise.

A number of emerging practices were the last guests of a real estate group that renovated almost the entire neighbourhood. Today, when half of the building complex -and of the temporal activities in it- is demolished, the owner is crowning this process with the construction of an exclusive and huge commercial/cultural centre.

Slowly the lights go off, the stage darkens.

Voice-over.

The gradual arrival of political parties, corporations and charitable foundations has turned the scene into a happy and beautiful, innovative and enterprising sight.

Two dynamics overlap: on the one hand, there is the ability of large companies and institutions to co-opt contents produced by small-scale actors, for the sake of nourishing their own agenda. For that, they use a less politicised face of those actions, emptying the substance of the work of many to strengthen a few.

On the other hand, real estate inflation process of land value, with the radical transformation of the social landscape that it implies. As a result, the beneficiaries are only a few, once again.

The curtains go down.

Act 2, scene 1: The schizophrenic convent – Diana Cultural Centre (March – October 2014)

The curtain rises.

The narrator claims: ". . . in order to blast a specific era out of the homogeneous course of history – blasting a specific life out of the era or a specific work out of the lifework" (Benjamin 1968)

Scene: The scene goes back nearby the city centre. A small and decaying amusement park contributes to the frantic activity in San Diego Street. A mixture of Chinese knick-knacks, auto parts, bicycles, schools and bars make this neighbourhood one of the most metropolitan sceneries of the city. A few blocks away there is the government palace and the civic-administrative axis: this is the arena for demonstrations and struggles between citizens and police forces.

Actors enter the stage.

The action takes part on the second floor of the ex-convent, where more than a hundred guests sit on improvised tables. Huge amounts of homemade *gnocchi* and music bands are the excuse to invite people to collaborate in funding the works for opening the rooftop of the convent to be used by cultural actors, students and vicinity groups in the area. Several months of work were needed for a preliminary set up.

Unexpectedly, the actors leave the stage.

The collective and collaborative funding agenda was truncated. The business model of cultural enterprises demands financial efficiency too, and the balance is negative as the economical development of the project was not enough for the expectations of the owner. A TV producer will be in charge of the new management of the space. In this way, a space that was emerging with combined efforts and energy subdues to the prevailing conditions and all of a sudden takes a new course.

Voice-over.

The requirements of profitability over the use of space for cultural activities are harassing. The commoditisation of actions that are not productive of goods and services for exchange hinder the viability of any other alternative practices. Some isolated activities could do little against the synchronised and pervasive actions of the market.

Concurrently, gentrification processes usually triggered when an agenda of capitalisation support such cultural actions through land value increase, in certain cases resistance to the social and cultural inertia of a neighbourhood that still fights back on disputes for identities. San Diego has endured what Barrio Italia couldn't. Virgin territories, weak social ties and fragile collective identity are the Promised Land for the market. It is establishing new colonies, and culture is at the forefront.

Act 2, scene 2: Utopia remix – Villa San Luis – (May – July 2014)

The lights come back and the narrator, looking straight ahead, says: "The changes in this ideological skyline will be rapid and continuous: a rich spectacle of ethical joy, moral fever or intellectual masturbation. The collapse of one of the towers can mean two things: failure, giving up, or a visual Eureka, a speculative ejaculation: A theory of works. A mania that sticks. A lie that has become a truth. A dream from which there is no waking up" (Koolhaas 1978: 294).

Scene: Our gaze shifts now towards a new destination. Now a wealthy district and far away from the tragedies of the centre of the city, over the past forty years this site has been populated by residential buildings, amusement parks, consumption hubs, golf clubs, temples and monuments. In this continuous expansion, a group of modern glass towers comprise a new financial district, renaming it as Nueva Las Condes. Meanwhile, closer to the ground level, the remains of modest social housing blocks silently bring the distant memories of another time and another idea of society.

Actors enter the stage.

The Young Architect Program PS1 MOMA, a well-known architecture contest, abruptly lands in Santiago. After some editions, it's finally settled in the centre of this scene: in this beautiful park surrounded by impressive buildings in one of the richest municipality in the country. Supported by most of the local architectural scene, the contest is presented as an interesting opportunity to anticipate architectural futures, and the emerging studios are all eager to take part. And so, in this context, the contest is a silent witness of the dispute between the real estate market and the last residents of the socialist housing block, who slowly are surrendering, one by one. It should be clarified: that place was the site of the most radical urban experiment in the history of this city: Villa San Luis, a social housing project – for homeless families – in the middle of the most expensive neighbourhood in the city. These residential blocks were the last survivors of a huge residential complex. There was an invaluable opportunity for architecture to look at such a precise time and space, and to give it a chance to tell the history of the most important utopia of our urban history. Invaluable, but unfeasible.

The actors leave the stage.

A set of rest areas is chosen to decorate the place, to continue the show of a discipline always committed with the same discourses . . . progress, entertainment, depoliticisation. Tell me what you do not see, and I will tell you who you are.

The lights go out suddenly.

Voice-over.

Among the last contest and the realisation of the winning project, the real estate developer bought the last apartment of 47 m2 for 1 million US$.[1] The acquisition of more than 200 apartments was completed. Everything is ready for the definitive demolition, and the establishment of the new order of things will be absolute. The complicity of our discipline -which chose not to pay attention for more than three years – is painful, but it is the most faithful manifesto of our times. In this case, the juvenile hope to emerge with a different voice was a naive and fragile ally. The memory of an almost unprecedented event in the city will disappear under the glare of urban progress.

Act 2, Scene 3: The plaque of history – GAM Cultural Centre – (July – October 2014)

The curtain rises, and the narrator does not waste a second:

> "Ordinary people know what's happening now,
> the gods know future things
> because they alone are totally enlightened.
> Of what's to come the wise perceive
> the thing about to happen.
> Sometimes during moments of intense study
> their hearing's troubled: the hidden sound
> of things approaching reaches them,
> and they listen reverently, while in the street outside
> the people hear nothing whatsoever"
>
> (Quetglas 2001)

Scene: We move to the historic centre of the city. We find ourselves over the Alameda, the avenue where all the big manifestations have walked along throughout the last 50 years. Here, a huge metallic roof stands over concrete columns. From its privileged position, the building has observed stoically the conflictive events of Chilean history.

Built in only 275 days during the socialist revolutionary government of Allende, this collective work between architects, engineers, workers and artists was erected to house the 3rd United Nations Conference on Trade and Development. After that, it became the biggest cultural centre of Chile, and its rooms were the venue for the new identities of a forging country. In this context, the facilities of the casino played a crucial role in putting artists, workers, intellectuals, students all behind the same roof, around the same fire. As in other occasions in these latitudes, the history takes a dramatic turn. A powerful dictatorship replaces a stumbling democracy, and the building turns into the headquarters of a new oppressive regime. The plaque gets obscured, its pieces of art disappear, its windows covered up, machine guns and helmets decorate its access. It rises like a fortress that contained the anger of a militarised country for seventeen years.

Once democracy was back, the building is left alone. It only receives occasional visitors, until one day, almost like expiation, the building immolates itself. People celebrate in the streets. A symbol of the military dictatorship has burned.

The democratic government at that moment decides to recover the original vocation of the building as the most important cultural centre. A corten steel cladding hides the wounds and, incidentally, its memory. But now it is an international culture centre with design stores and elite audience. It ceased to be a place for popular culture. Some profound changes have occurred.

The actors enter the stage.

Spring is coming. September is a month of celebration and sorrow for the country. Independence Day, the coup and the arrival of the Spaniards in America are just a few days apart in the calendar. A temporary cafeteria is installed at the central plaza. A kitchen in a corner serves Chilean food at affordable prices, while red dining tables occupy the plaza. Trays with phrases that refer to the political history of the building compel the guests to remember. This intervention meant to accommodate in the current conditions, a programme that used to be the very core of the building during its first years.

To bring back a smashed, massacred and burned piece of history was an opportunity to gather people under its roof and inquire about an apolitical cultural agenda of the cultural centre, too committed to audience measuring.

The actors leave the stage, the scenography remains.

The tables are in the central plaza of the building. The kitchen and the trays left the place. This place of modernity was equipped for informal conversation. Was there to wait until the next show begins. The memories of grieves and cramps are back again deep inside the cellar.

Lights dim, a subtle light remains on the stage.

Voice-over.

No other building in Chile has held so many opposed and extreme episodes like this. The constant will to suppress its own past contradicts its historic multiplicity.

This is the scene of the symbolic dispute. Though overlooked at times, it becomes relevant when we want to see how infrastructures can stay up while they house such antagonistic programmes and ideologies. With the resignation of the last administration, and the employee's fragility denounced by the workers it is possible to expect a definitive awakening. Maybe, the main sign of vitality comes from the various informal agendas that make use of the semi-public spaces of the building. Like the huge number of teenagers that use of the reflections of the façade to practice their choreographies. For them, the building is a ruin, and they sneak into the cracks of its structure and its programme.

Act 2, Scene 4: Speculative colonisation – Tupac Amaru and the glass factory – (July – October 2014)

The lights go on too soon. The scenography is installed, and the narrator rushes: "Capitalist urbanisation plays a particularly active absorbing the surplus product that capitalists are perpetually producing in their search for surplus value" (Harvey 2012: 6).

Scene: In spite of the hurry, the setting seems very appealing. We are at the thin piece of flat land joins San Cristobal and Blanco Hills, at the north of Mapocho River and La Chimba. This land, originally occupied by indigenous settlements, later became the place for the poor of the city, those who were left at the other side of the river. Immigrants from the Middle East, Korea and China joined them throughout the last century. During the last years, Peruvians and Colombians have made this social mixture even more complex. This cultural diversity is deployed across a territory that manages to integrate its humble past, some old urban institutions – as the General Cemetery, Recoleta Dominica Church, the psychiatric hospital, the main market.

In this context, a social housing complex – part of the same socialist agenda of the seventies previously described- accompanies an old factory, abandoned when the industries left the centre of the city. Their location, distant from the main avenues, allowed them – neighbourhood and factory-, to stay away from the development agendas, both from private and public sectors. But lately, an emerging real estate pressure has begun to move forwards without caring much about its context. At the same time, one of the heirs of the factory got a partner and credit and bought the rest of the building. With so much oblivion, it is important to bear in mind that – even when hid somewhere across the river- we are still about a mile away from downtown.

However, some movements can be perceived, and new inhabitants can be seen. Without being too aware of what is going on, the neighbourhood witnesses the presence of luxury cars and fancy people starting to swarm about.

The actors enter the stage.

Groups of youngest start making use of the factory. A photographer, a studio related to cultural production and a collective of are among the first ones. Quickly, the agenda starts to prosper. Design fairs mixed with start-up, innovation, entrepreneurship, all concepts brought from contexts very unfamiliar to this site and its dwellers. In parallel, under the roof of one of the warehouses of the factory, multiple groups and collectives expose and discuss their agendas, to align their objectives and share their mechanisms. The conversation explores the collective self-management, linked to matters on city and territory. Temporarily, this space is open to coordinate the actions of these groups against the complex and unequal distribution of power in the city. A neighbourhood movement talks about their struggle against the local government to preserve a cultural space they had recovered, while a young couple of architects expose their editorial project based on the work of Henri Lefebvre.

The actors leave the stage.

As we knew from the beginning, this act, even if a bit longer than the rest, was still brief. The process of inflation of the land value was too fast. Only lucrative contents would survive, such as design fairs and 'innovation' hubs. Conversations about community organisation would have to be held somewhere else next time.

A few months later, the process intensified. A successful solidarity foundation took over the factory, standing firm in the wicked plan of turning any good idea into another product of the market.

The lights dim.

Voice-over.

The process of commoditisation on our territories was associated in this case with the illusion of entrepreneurial success: an ideological bomb. Neoliberalism 2.0 is avid of virgin territories, and it finds a fertile soil when the work of young people can be co-opted. Big entrepreneurs disguised as philanthropists take control of these new dynamics, at the same time as they multiply the value of the land and displace communities.

The curtain goes down.

Act 3, Scene 1: The state and the art in architecture – Chicago architectural bienniale – (October – December 2015)

The curtain rises. The narrator, disconcerted by the last movements, stands on a very different ground. Admired, he recites: "Only a crisis -actual o perceived- produces real change. When that crisis occurs, the actions that are taken depend on the ideas that are lying around. That, I believe, is our basic function: to develop alternatives to existing policies, to keep them alive and available until the politically impossible becomes the politically inevitable" (Friedman 1962: 7).

Scene: We are in the United States: Chicago, a global metropolis very far from home. There are many reasons why this city and a long list of its citizen have been relevant throughout history. But looking from Santiago de Chile, it is inevitable to pay attention to an exceptional figure: Milton Friedman. Chicago was the laboratory where free market was devised, and where many of its followers attended, many of them from Latin America: the so-called Chicago Boys. Santiago, the protagonist of this history, was their first field test. This makes of Chicago some motherland for us.

Precisely here is where many architects around the world, us among them, are convened. A luxurious building by the Millennium Park is the place. The occasion:

Chicago joins the global *biennalisation*, aroused by the local government to position the city into the global cultural events agenda.

The actors enter the stage.

The opening of the First Chicago Architecture Biennale includes some parties and events. It is hard to concentrate, and the participants and visitors spread around the many stimuli. The idea of confronting stances and points of view became diluted in alcohol and blurred with flashes. Architecture seems more attracted by getting dressed in fancy clothes than by questioning itself. Political interrogations seem like an attack to the disciplinary joy. Some conversations do occur, but only in the margins of the great event.

The actors leave the stage.

With the financial support of British Petroleum, the – Chicago Biennale was able to project a global image. Still, most of the interventions related to the Biennial took place at the downtown. The true Chicago was out of the map during those days, and just a few blocks away, the consequences of the segregating model of the Burnham Plan could be seen A few days after the Biennial opening days, the 'Black Christmas' brought big trouble to the local government, and then another case of racist police brutality during the Democratic primaries. Among all that glitter, the exposition focused on the wide spectrum of the discipline but forgot to bring up some less comfortable issues of our society.

The lights go off; the flashes vanish in the dark.

Voice-over.

A Biennale, or architecture-turned-into-spectacle, is a space of exposition for a disciplinary market offer to consumption. Architecture usually works on irrelevant areas of urban contemporary development. The most transcendent may be ornamenting this development from its formal and symbolic characterisation. . . a pretty secondary role in the play, comparable with the *maquillage* and the decorating of the scene. But if, as many argue, the urban development – along with military expenditure – is one of the columns of growth of neoliberalism, architects should attempt to acquire a leading role, acting on a script that initiates the action. By this, there's a chance to cast doubts on the prevailing model.

Act 3, scene 2 and last: architectural hangover – and the danger of official participation – (November 2015 – January 2016)

The curtain rises for the last time. The narrator looks exhausted and has no words to say.

Scene: Back in Santiago, the scene unfolds in two places, not far from each other and not too far either from most of the previous acts. Without much order, actors take their places and resume their tasks. On the one hand, another abandoned factory supposed to become a centre for innovation, creativity and social innovation, but a local government leads the whole project this time. On the other hand the rooftop of a building, part of a private university with students mostly from an emerging middle class. Both places require infrastructure to be open to the community, to the outside. In one case, the administration needs to reinforce its political programme: elections are coming, while the university needs to satisfy the need for an open space to be consumed by the students. Both seem interested to make use of the hackneyed 'participation'.

The actors enter the stage.

The process normally develops, too normally. The collective organisation for decision-making and the work carried out brings some hope of the possibility to consolidate entities that can transcend the design and the execution of a built intervention, to face future challenges and stand as political forces in an appropriated territory. The hope is nourished by the materialisation of both projects, conceived as 'headquarters' for local assemblies. The interventions are built: urban gardens, community kitchens, stages and an open meeting space.

The actors leave the stage.

When committed to lead a collaborative work and participative design, there's a risk of doing what you are asked for, what you are hired for, a place for what people wants. The headquarters are barely used. Questions crop up: Is it a space for politics what is needed? What the possibility of creating the scenario for questioning reality?

The problem becomes political; architecture is a physical medium as it is of representation. People are happy, the local government is happy, the university is happy. But architecture has the capability to agitate, to make people ask themselves how they live.

The curtains come down for the last time.

Voice-over.

Neoliberal structure articulates a concrete network of actors, some of them very powerful. Urban festivals, cultural management, innovations and start-up, real estate development, art market, millionaire inheritance, reclaimed buildings, audience measurement, big companies, mortgage credit, foundations, centres of studies, government labs, technology, DIY installations, inaugurations, massive events, colourful logos and branding, profiting education, political campaigns, urban development and architecture collectives.

In all cases, depoliticised discourses and contents – or at least maintaining the politicisation restricted to technical areas as urban agriculture, DIY or bike fixing – is a general condition. The most relevant actors of the neoliberal structure writhe when the action comes politicised when its political content becomes evident. By offering precise mechanisms of decision-making to the technical areas, Neoliberalism has found a way to make invisible a powerful political content.

The interest to understand the complex relationship/space into which our practice and critique unfold pushed us to incorporate to our repertory of actions, a constant research on those immaterial constructions that affect our work. Neoliberalism has erected as one of the strongest, most reckless and aggressive constructions. Politicising our work to unveil these structures became inevitable.

It may sound repetitive, but we do live in a world of brutal and increasing inequity, where those dead or displaced by war are counted by thousands, where every single sphere of our life is being turned into a consumer good, while the habitability of our planet is in a serious crisis. Collaborating with the embellishment of the scene and the continuity of the show seems very similar to denying the horrible acts behind the scenes.

From now on, the play will be political or will not be at all.

Blackout.

Postscript

By making these territories 'speak', we intend to considerate the political role of architecture as quotidian activism. It is an attempt to understand the different means through which architecture is able to politicise spaces and reflections and to identify disputes and conflicts. In this retrospective reflection, biographical, we have used our own experiences, but the discussion remains open to be redefined as new aspects and elements of urban transformations in the Neoliberal context will continue to appear.

The complex organism of the contemporary city often imposes the vision of a seemingly unchangeable state of affairs. The size and amount of wicked issues that ultimately affect our practice is overwhelming. How can we confront big issues such as imbalanced distribution of power, content co-opting, business disguised as cultural programmes, illicit private/public activities, the concentration of economic and political power and the dominion of the market over territorial development? We believe that our work has not only the capability but also the obligation to encourage the opposition to points of view, the faculty to render visible the contradictions and the power to envisage new possible scenarios.

The construction/setting up of new programmes, structures and spaces can be taken as an opportunity not only to establish standing points for collective analysis and debate but even more, they must become bastions of resistance and give way to the production of conflict. Those acting and reflecting over the environment – built or not – must assume their role as critical agents to unveil the complexity of territorial, understand it and affect it, which means that open conflict and political confrontation is crucial. Only then it will be possible to become as agents of transformation.

Note

1 http://diario.elmercurio.com/detalle/index.asp?id={cd299846-eb69-4e37-8f7e-19f0a7d98d8a}

References

Benjamin, W., (1968) *Theses on the philosophy of history*, Illuminations Schocken Books, New York. Translated by Harcourt Brace Jovanovich, Inc.

Friedman, M., (1962, 1982), *Capitalism and freedom*, Chicago, United States: University of Chicago Press.

Friedman, M., Friedman, R. (1980) Free to Choose: A personal statement. New York: Harcourt Brace Jovanovich.

Harvey, D., (2012), *Rebel cities: From the urban right to the urban revolution*, London, United Kingdom: Verso Books.

Koolhaas, R., (1978) *Delirious New York: A retroactive manifesto for Manhattan*, Oxford, United Kingdom: Oxford University Press.

Left Hand Rotation, (2012) Gentrificación no es un nombre de señora, Madrid, Spain: Universidad Complutense de Madrid. www.lefthandrotation.com/museodesplazados/publicaciones/Ext08_gentrificacion.pdf

Mouffe, C., (2007) Artistic activism and agonistic spaces. *Art & Research*, Volume 1, No. 2. www.artandresearch.org.uk/v1n2/mouffe.html

Quetglas, J., (2001), *El horror cristalizado: Imágenes del Pabellón de Barcelona de Mies van der Rohe*, Barcelona, Spain: Actar.

Afterword

A conversation with Miguel Lawner

The implementation of neoliberalism in Santiago's urban development dismantled a significant number of planning instruments and institutions for delivering all decision-making power in the hands of the private sector. In doing so, several practitioners witnessed with frustration how after decades of struggling for making the city a human right was wipe out for transforming it into a commodity. Also, because of the violent installation of neoliberalism, many of these practitioners – architects and urbanists- were victims of the fierce repression of Pinochet's dictatorship, in order to eradicate critical thinking and ease the way for the Chicago Boys. Neoliberal urban development nowadays is in crises which have brought renewed attention to the past, to those institutions and urbanists that the dictatorship attempted to wipe out, but that remained as examples of a humanistic approach to what Henri Lefebvre would name the right to the city.

Among the most representative voices of this past is Miguel Lawner, who since his return to Chile from the exile has been a claim for a better future for cities. Lawner was the Director of Urban Improvement Corporation (CORMU)[1] during the administration of Salvador Allende. Since his early years as an architect, he worked close to communities by guiding the process of designing informal settlements in the very core of Santiago (for example in Toma de La Victoria), a radical practice of a discipline sometimes forced to go beyond the limits of the norms in order to achieve spatial justice. A committed architect with a strong political position was a key actor in the implementation of diverse social projects for enhancing the everyday experience of urban life. After 64 years of practice, he is an eminence in tracing the possibilities of defining a post-neoliberal urban development in Chile.

This interview meant to provide the reflections of Lawner's critiques on the neoliberal city and will help to understand the ethical transformations experienced by urban specialists that allowed the persistent prevalence of the commodification of space.

CAMILLO BOANO, FRANCISCO VERGARA PERUCICH: Miguel, you had the privilege of witnessing in first line all the process of neoliberalising the urban disciplines, but also you occupied a leading role in the previous stage of Chilean urbanism. What are your primary reflections when somebody asks you about the neoliberalisation of Santiago?

MIGUEL LAWNER: Santiago is the first city in the world where neoliberalism was implemented and where it has been applied fanatically since then. The dictatorship devastated with all the structures of urban development that were developed by years. These structures aimed to put in the hands of the State strong attributions for ensuring an urban development for the common good and not only for the private interests. All that long process of building these urban institutions started in 1939, after the earthquake of Chillan. This earthquake marked the creation of the Corporation for Reconstruction and Aid (Corporación de Reconstrucción y el Auxilio) and Caja de la Habitación (Housing Public Bank), created previously, both institutions of the state responsible for producing better cities for everyone. These institutions were populated by new Chilean urbanists, which was a new discipline developed mainly in the Architecture Department of Universidad de Chile under the guidance of Karl Brunner[2] and Rodulfo Oyarzún. This disciplinary development brought a consistent advance in urban development with the state as main actor and the common good as the principle. Without regard to the political ideology of the government (Centre, Liberal, Socialist), the state was the driving force of urban policy and development, prioritising the social housing before the high rates of the deficit. The private sector's role was mainly of building these public initiatives, but the whole design process was in entitled to state institutions, even with architecture studios embedded in the state structure as public institutions.

CB, FVP: There are diverse perspectives on neoliberal hegemony: the organisation of an entrepreneurial class for defending their own class interests, the state seduced and co-opted by a political project based on monetarist theories, a passive civil society fragmented and without reaction to abuses, a group of intellectuals incapable of developing feasible alternatives to neoliberalism, for mentioning a few common arguments. What types of urban practices were eradicated after the implementation of neoliberal urban development in Santiago?

ML: When looking back at the projects before neoliberalism, we could say that it was a golden age of urban development and public policies for housing in Chile. Not only because the number of projects built but mainly because of their quality. Now, these projects are being studied by several specialists for receiving the protection as urban heritage, and in general, Chilean architects are proud of these achievements. I wonder if you can name one single social housing project built in the last 40 years better than the projects of those developed before the dictatorship. For instance, in Santiago, we can see Villa Olímpica, Villa Frei, Unidad Vecinal Portales, Unidad Vecinal de Providencia, Remodelación San Borja, and so many others that I could recall that even today remain as referential spaces of the city. This entire ethos in the production of social housing ended with the dictatorship and excuse that the state has to play only a subsidiary role in the provision of goods and services. Consequently, all the attributions of the Housing Ministry passed to the private sector and since then real estate companies and builders control the whole cycle of social housing production. Also, with this change, the urban development, not only as housing but also as the comprehensive production of the urban space, disappeared. The neoliberalisation was not only in housing, but also in the construction of health facilities, educational buildings, and so on. These transformations occurred after the almost complete elimination of regulations that used to ensure the design and construction of good spaces, and also the control over these activities in order to facilitate the participation of private investors in public affairs such as social housing.

CB, FVP: Following your words, we could say that there is nothing left from those modes of spatial production. Nowadays everything seems to have fallen into an abyss of free-market oriented urban development. What effects were the most obvious urban consequences of the implementation of neoliberalism in Santiago?

ML: If we made a balance of the results after these years, the outcome is unquestionable. Our cities exhibit outstanding levels of social segregation, thus reproducing in the urban space the shameful social inequality that characterises the country. You can see how wealthy condominiums are built few blocks away from pockets of poverty. For Example, in 2014 the Housing Ministry generated a database of social housing in Chile since 1906 concluding that between 1984 and 2000 were built 200.000 housing units that are disposable. Mostly composed by housing blocks that I call these buildings as penitentiary housing blocks because of their horrible configuration. Many of them have been demolished. For example, in Bajos de Mena, in Quilicura, in Cerro Navia, etc. Never before, while the state was in charge of designing and building social housing, was needed to demolish units constructed with public funds. I defy to someone to mention one single project built before of 1973 whose spatial qualities are worse than those developed during or after the dictatorship. Do you realise of the price that we all had to pay? It is impressive. The excuse that usually is used for defending these waste-housing projects is that there was a huge deficit of housing and it was urgent to provide shelter for many people. Nevertheless, the deficit still remains. What I am sure, is that without the state there are no possibilities to develop an urban development policy for pursuing the common good, period. For me, these are the most radical transformations made under the implementation of the neoliberal model. All this was possible only because the terror, violence and fear infringed by the dictatorship and its consequence is there, in reality.

CB, FVP: While you were in the exile in Denmark, you were acutely aware of what was happing regarding these neoliberal transformations. What were your reflections on that time about the future of Chilean cities considering the imminent transformations that they would experience by this neoliberal agenda?

ML: My wife, Anamaría Barrenechea, and I were lecturing a course for postgraduate students about housing policies in the developing world, a matter that we well knew in which people from diverse countries came to study this subject. So, as soon as we realised of the transformations that the dictatorship was implementing in urban development policies we included this transformation in our classes for building a critical perspective about these changes. Everyone there could not believe these changes, how could not be the state who leads the social housing policies? It was just inconceivable. For exposing an accurate version of the facts, we presented the ideas of Arnold Harberguer – the mastermind of the liberalisation of urban development, and close friend of Milton Friedman – the lectures that Friedrich von Hayek gave in Viña del Mar in 1977 about restricting democracy, and of course the public statements made by the urban authorities of the dictatorship. I still remember the words of Marco Antonio Lopez, chief of urban development by those years: En el crecimiento de las ciudades opera la economía y no los sentimientos (In urban development rules economics not feelings). These guys were all fanatics of their ideology.

CB, FVP: What about the return to democracy, are there any changes after the end of the dictatorship?

ML: That is the worse part for me because the democratic governments after 1990 did not change anything at all. You know that Michelle (Bachelet, current Chilean President) asked me to be part of the National Commission of Urban Development, and we have made a tremendous effort – specially due to the opposition of the Builders Chamber[3]-, for changing many of the inherits of the dictatorship's urban development model. Two years ago we presented a robust proposal for transforming the land policies and rebuild some urban planning institutions that we considered as key for improving cities. For instance, we proposed the creation of a Regional Service of Urban Development (SRDU) with broad powers for defining local urban policies and with authority for partnering with other public institutions such as municipalities and other public institutions, and private institutions. The aim of this SRDU was to empowering the state in the coordination and management of urban development in order to recover the spirit and capabilities of the CORMU.[4] However, what have changed since we delivered the proposal, Michelle put it in a drawer and failed to address an issue when it was obviously urgent. For example, in last March the entire town of Santa Olga was burned in a fire, and its reconstruction is in charge of one single man, Sergio Galilea, who was assigned to be the Presidential Coordinator for the Reconstruction. A delegate, just an individual. Instead of an empowered institution capable of response to catastrophic events such as what happened in Santa Olga the government decided to trust in a person. What can do the inhabitants of Santa Olga if they have any problem, to knock the door of Sergio Galilea? What if they have a health issue or if they need water, which institutional response may offer the state to their citizens? Not many. In my opinion, this is dramatic.

CB, FVP: We would like to know your opinion in an awkward issue: the role of your colleagues in the implementation of neoliberalism. We cannot deny that urbanists and architects have been principal characters in shaping the neoliberal city of Santiago, even when most of them remain absent from discussions about the common good, they have designed projects that actually affect the whole society. What can we reflect on the ethics of urbanists and architects under the rule of neoliberalism?

ML: I have a theory. After so many years that architecture schools have educated their students for entering the labour market that the way of teaching has adopted the market rules, producing practitioners that already in the undergraduate school are alienated. So, architects and urbanists are educated for fitting in a given reality, instead to aim to change that reality. Then, they learn to deal within the margins of what private companies allow. For illustrating this point, I would like to mention the art of designing mitigations. The existence of mitigations as a standard practice implies that the private companies will do something wrong in developing some areas of the city. I wonder why. Instead, I believe, we should stop doing things wrong at the beginning for then mitigate; and start to do things well from the outset. Many of our colleagues were conquered by the rule of the free market losing the sense of the spirit of urban development. So then you can hear urbanists using formulas and justify aberrations by a supposed effectiveness, explaining urban transformations with borrowed arguments from the neoliberal economists. It does not make any sense.

CB, FVP: So, do you believe that the neoliberal ideology succeeded in conquering the urban disciplines for the sake of the profit?

ML: I, for one, have no doubt about it. A colleague of us has designed and signed the blueprints of the vertical conventillos[5] in Estación Central, there is an architect that designed Bajos de Mena without one single plaza or facilities. There are architects and urbanists that organised for months these projects, that planned to deliver this kind of spaces for people.

CB, FVP: It seems like a very complicated scenario. What you think we could do in order to start changing things?

ML: There is hope in the grassroots, but I am not sure if urban practitioners are aware of their role in the society. People organised and protested for demanding changes in education, and they actually achieved to produce a political agenda, transforming several things in short time. Insufficient changes if you want, but changes that otherwise would never happen. It was because of mobilisations. Nowadays in Chile people is marching for changing the unfair pension system inherited from the dictatorship. How is it possible that we, the urban practitioners, are not marching in protest against the neoliberal city? It seems like citizenship is not aware of the importance of the city in their lives. When I try to explain the absence of the city in the main concerns of people I end blaming the use of subsidies for financing individual requirements for housing. The subsidy is a perverse mechanism of alienation. A single piece of paper makes think people that they have resolved their housing questions, weakening the organisation of collective forces. In the urban history of Chile, the organisation of slum dwellers was fundamental for transforming the urban policy and for fostering the design of more just cities. Part of the main strategies of the neoliberal urban development is preventing the organisation of collective forces by promoting individual responses to housing problems.

CB, FVP: Indeed, along with Chilean history, most significant changes in urban policy have emerged from the demand of collective forces claiming for shifts in the way cities were produced. It happened in 1925 with the League of tenants; also it happened in 1965 with the Agrarian, and with the diverse Tomas[6] between 1957 and 1973. How can social movements pass from protesting and demanding to an actual transformation of the political?

ML: It is vital the way these social movements are oriented by their leaders. For example, the organisation behind the movement NO+AFP[7] is not only thinking in protest but they actually have a new pension scheme, ensuring good incomes for retired people. Indeed, the movement managed to design this system for the next 100 years, demonstrating its feasibility. I participate in the design of this proposal, and we demonstrated that if we eliminate the AFP system right now, we immediately could double the pensions of people. This is an excellent example of how a social movement is supported by serious arguments, based on evidence and proposals for the common good. The slum dwellers of the mid-twentieth century were actively organised for improving their build environment. Certainly, I saw myself with other many architects participating in the design of La Victoria, defining patterns based on the ideal cities of the modern movement in a settlement for 3.000 families. Many things changed since then, but the project that we developed was a comprehensive attempt for build spaces of dignity for people. Sadly, we couldn't build the park that we designed at the beginning because of the aggressive expansion of the population in this Toma. Nevertheless, even today you can see how that urbanisation that started by an informal settlement has become an emblematic neighbourhood of Santiago.

CB, FVP: Let's recall the other spatial practices of the past, those referred to real estate development. Nowadays the private companies of real estate are considered as money lovers lacking of concern for developing good cities. Nevertheless, before 1975 even real estate developers had a different approach to business.

ML: Well, there was a significant change in this realm as well as well. In projects developed with private companies was also a concern for building good cities not ruled by mercantile rules only. Even in the most conservative areas of the city of the past, you would see the presence of great plazas, with public facilities and generous public spaces. I believe that before 1973 the country was not prepared for the levels of commodification that we see today, there were basic principles about the common good. A great example on how a real estate company behaved within the minimum frames of an ethic architectural development was the studio of Schapira Eskenazi. I witnessed how Raquel Eskenazi, one of the leading architects of the studio, was explaining step by step the process of building a residential complex for all their clients, from the design to the after-sales service. Nowadays it is very rare to see the architect meeting the client of real estate buildings. Schapira Eskenazi was not only ethical in the behaviour with their customers, but also with the architectural projects that they built, all of them great contributions in configuring the urban space, for example in Viña del Mar. You can also find the same level of commitment to the city in the real estate developments of Avalos y Gonzalez, Môller Perez-Cotapos, Neut Latour, at least in their early projects.

CB, FVP: How do you explain these changes in the real estate development of spaces?

ML: For me, one of the significant changes was produced by the intromission of financial institutions in the business of real estate development. The financial capital eliminated every kind of sensibility with the architecture, design, public space, or the city. The financial capital is only interested in profitability and renting from investments. Even they have preferred to implement marketing strategies for selling apartments than good architecture that sells itself. Mostly, because, they are not experts in the space or in cities but in investments and in making money. While the early real estate companies pursued quality and also were regulated by the state with strict control measures and regulations; now the only aim is the money. For example, nowadays the material tests of construction in real estate projects are made by the same builder.

CB, FVP: What is the future of this model of urban development is there a deeper neoliberalism waiting for us in the future?

ML: I do not believe it. This model is collapsing by both sides. For one hand, the left is reorganising and learning from its failures, and on the contrary side, the right-wing is radicalising its fascism and neoliberalism may collapse by that side as well.

CB, FVP: Neoliberalism has been ruling the urban development decisions for more than 40 years. After all this time, some spatial products in our cities tell the history of these times. For you, what are the representations of this neoliberal urban development in Santiago?

ML: For me, there are two primary representations, one public and one private, both developed in different times. The first is Bajos de Mena, in the south of Santiago: 120.000 people living without services, connectivity, commerce, and public spaces. All of them forced to move in there because the irrational decision of privileging quantity rather than quality in the early nineties with a government pressured by the impressive housing deficit inherited by the dictatorship. The second representation is what has been named as vertical ghettos in Estación Central commune, which represents the unleashed way to do of real estate companies in Santiago. No ethics, no design, only profit and exploiting the irrational ambition of people for having their own private property 24 flats per floor completing towers of 528 apartments per plot of land, and I have information that there are 70 more municipal permissions are granted in Estación Central for constructing more of these buildings. Outrageous. Both spatial outcomes share the same cause: a deregulated urban development. The authorities in Chile have been wholly responsible for the urban crises provoked by this neoliberal urban development.

CB, FVP: How can we interpret the role of private property in the consolidation of the neoliberal urban development model?

ML: The right to private property has been a great obstacle, if not the bigger, for overthrowing the neoliberal urban development. All that we were capable of doing in CORMU was thanks to the creation of the Housing Ministry and the modification to the Political Constitution introduced by Eduardo Frei Montalva in the sixties that assigned a social function to private property. This means that the land was always subjugated to the common good. This was fundamental because it did not eliminate the right to own land but changed the priorities putting first the people needs and then the private interest. This was extinct, and without changing the current Political Constitution of Pinochet, we are doomed. Nowadays the right to private property seems more important even than the right to live, and for sure it is much more important that most of the civil rights. The social function of land was promulgated in the Law 16.615. This legal instrument established how plots of land may be acquired, what are its possible uses, and its limitations and obligations in order to make it accessible for everyone. Therefore, the social function assigned the state the role of controlling its use to (or "intending to") ensuring that the specific plots of land were used for balancing the private interest with the common good. This would have changed everything; the private property is a keystone for progressing.

This model offers us any possibility of significant transformations, we need a profound change from this urban catastrophe.

Notes

1 CORMU was a public institution entitled to define, develop and coordinate urban planning and housing projects for cities in Chile.
2 Karl Brunner was an Austrian urbanist who in 1932 founded the Urbanism Department in Universidad de Chile (First in the country) and then developed the first urban planning comprehensive plan for the future of Santiago.
3 CCHC, or Cámara Chilena de la Construcción (Chilean Builders Chamber) is a union of building and real estate companies.
4 Urban Improvement Corporation
5 Conventillos was the name given to the primary types of housing in Santiago's Slums, at the beginnings of twentieth century.
6 "Toma" is the name in Chile for slum, although it may differ in outcomes. The Toma is the occupation of private plots of land by organised people in order to urbanise this plots without permission and settle in particular areas of the city, near the urban centre. The organisation is strong, and they may even work with its own governance system, hierarchy and politics. Lawner was commonly assisting the organisation of these Tomas since the mid-twentieth century.
7 NO+AFP is a social movement organised for removing the pension system designed by Jose Piñera during Pinochet's dictatorship based on individual capitalization during work years that promised people that after retired they would receive a 70% of their last salary but in reality it barely reaches the 30% in average. NO+AFP has emerged for wipe out this system and develop a new one.

Index